# Documents in Contemporary History

*General editor*
Kevin Jefferys
Faculty of Arts and Education, University of Plymouth

## The Vietnam wars

*Documents in Contemporary History* is a series designed for sixth-formers and undergraduates in higher education. It aims to provide both an overview of specialist research on topics in post-1939 British history and a wide-ranging selection of primary source material.

*Already published in the series*

Richard J. Aldrich  *Espionage, security and intelligence in Britain, 1945–1970*

Stuart Ball  *The Conservative Party since 1945*

John Baylis  *Anglo-American relations since 1939: the enduring alliance*

Alan Booth  *British economic development since 1945*

Stephen Brooke  *Reform and reconstruction: Britain after the war, 1945–1951*

Steven Fielding  *The Labour Party: 'socialism' and society since 1951*

Sean Greenwood  *Britain and European integration since the Second World War*

Kevin Jefferys  *War and reform: British politics during the Second World War*

Scott Lucas  *Britain and Suez: the lion's last roar*

Ralph Negrine  *Television and the press since 1945*

Ritchie Ovendale  *British defence policy since 1945*

Panikos Panayi  *The impact of immigration*

Harold L. Smith  *Britain in the Second World War: a social history*

Chris Wrigley  *British trade unions, 1945–1995*


*Forthcoming*

Rodney Lowe  *Britain's postwar welfare state*

Documents in Contemporary History

# The Vietnam wars

Edited by
## Kevin Ruane

*Department of History,*
*Christ Church University College, Canterbury*

Manchester University Press
Manchester and New York
*distributed exclusively in the USA by St. Martin's Press*

The right of Kevin Ruane to be identified as the editor of this work has been asserted by him in accordance with the Copyright, Designs and Patents Act 1988.

*Published by* Manchester University Press
Oxford Road, Manchester M13 9NR, UK
*and* Room 400, 175 Fifth Avenue, New York, NY 10010, USA
http://www.man.ac.uk/mup

*Distributed exclusively in the USA by*
St. Martin's Press, Inc., 175 Fifth Avenue, New York, NY 10010, USA

*Distributed exclusively in Canada by*
UBC Press, University of British Columbia, 2029 West Mall, Vancouver, BC, Canada V6T 1Z2

*British Library Cataloguing-in-Publication Data*
A catalogue record for this book is available from the British Library

*Library of Congress Cataloging-in-Publication Data applied for*

ISBN    0 7190 5489 3    *hardback*
        0 7190 5490 7    *paperback*

First published 2000

07  06  05  04  03  02  01  00          10  9  8  7  6  5  4  3  2  1

Printed in Great Britain by
Bell & Bain Ltd, Glasgow

# Contents

| | | |
|---|---|---|
| *Acknowledgements* | *page* vi |
| *Abbreviations* | viii |
| *Chronology of events* | ix |
| *Map* | xvii |
| | Introduction | 1 |
| 1 | War and revolution, 1930–1946 | 9 |
| 2 | The Franco-Vietminh war, 1946–1954 | 33 |
| 3 | War renewed, 1954–1960 | 56 |
| 4 | The struggle for South Vietnam, 1960–1965 | 81 |
| 5 | The American war, 1965–1968 | 103 |
| 6 | Wars of peace, 1968–1975 | 127 |
| 7 | Assessments and reflections | 149 |
| | *Notes* | 172 |
| | *Guide to further reading* | 181 |
| | *Index* | 183 |

# Acknowledgements

I am grateful to my colleagues in the Department of History at Canterbury Christ Church University College for creating and maintaining a wonderfully convivial and sympathetic scholarly environment. My particular thanks go to Sean Greenwood, whose own fine research and leadership have done so much to establish that environment; to Jackie Eales, an early-modernist by trade but superbly supportive of her 'twentieth century' colleagues; and to Alison Finch for contributing, in her own distinct and valuable fashion, to a most positive working atmosphere. James Ellison of Queen Mary and Westfield College, University of London, temporarily suspended his research into the many fascinations of the European Free Trade Area to offer a dispassionate and penetrating critique of the penultimate draft of this work, an act of denial for which I am greatly appreciative.

My Year 3 Vietnam group at Canterbury Christ Church University College (1999–2000) 'road-tested' the material in this book, thus thanks are due to Gavin Barling, Phil Baxter, David Birmingham, Charles Bown, Paul Dennis, Douglas Ede, Douglas 'Ken' Fisher, James Garrett, Steven Geiss, Gareth Greer, Roger Hazelden, Maria Jeffery, Helen Malone, Abigail Peters, Nutan Saran, Richard Searle, Mark Sedge, Robert Tipper and Mark Woolf.

I wish also to thank Lady Avon for permission to use material from the private papers of Lord Avon (Anthony Eden) at the University of Birmingham (extract 2.11). For permission to publish copyright material, I would like to thank the following: the Controller of Her Majesty's Stationary Office for Crown Copyright material from the Public Record Office, London, and from Command Papers (extracts 2.4, 2.7–8, 2.10, 2.13); Beacon Press for material from *The Pentagon Papers: The Defense Department History of United States Decision-making on Vietnam*, Senator Gravel edn, © 1971, several volumes

## Acknowledgements

(extracts 1.12–13, 2.2–3, 2.5, 3.9); the estate and family of Bernard B. Fall for material in Bernard B. Fall (ed.), *Ho Chi Minh on Revolution: Selected Writing, 1920–66*, © Praegar/Signet Books, 1967 (extracts 1.1–2, 1.4, 1.6–7, 1.9, 1.14–15, 2.3, 2.14, 3.4, 3.6); the Gioi Publishers, Hanoi, Socialist Republic of Vietnam, for material in *Ho Chi Minh: Selected Writings, 1920–1969*, © 1973 (extracts 2.12, 7.4); Harcourt Inc. for extracts from Truong Nhu Tang, with David Chanoff and Doan Van Toai, *A Vietcong Memoir*, © 1985 (extracts 3.10, 5.9, 6.3, 7.6); Harper Collins Publishers for the use of a passage from Marilyn B. Young, *The Vietnam Wars 1945–1990*, © 1991 (extract 7.9); Harper Collins Publishers and André Deutsch Ltd for the use of material from Doris Kearns, *Lyndon Johnson and the American Dream*, © 1976 (extract 4.15); C. Hurst & Co. (Publishers) Ltd for selections from Bui Tin, *Following Ho Chi Minh: The Memoirs of a North Vietnamese Colonel*, © 1995 (extracts 1.10, 3.7, 5.1, 6.13, 7.7); the McGraw-Hill Companies for passages from William J. Duiker, *Sacred War: Nationalism and Revolution in a Divided Vietnam*, © 1995 (extracts 6.9, 6.14, 7.3); the Office of the Historian, US Department of State, for extracts from *The Foreign Relations of the United States* series, various volumes, and from *Department of State Bulletins* (extracts 2.3, 2.6, 4.3, 4.5–10, 4.13, 4.16, 5.5); Random House Inc./Doubleday Books for the use of a passage from Le Ly Hayslip, with Jay Wurts, *When Heaven and Earth Changed Places: A Vietnamese Woman's Journey from War to Peace*, © 1989 (extract 4.1); Random House Inc./Times Books for selections from Robert S. McNamara, *In Retrospect: The Tragedy and Lessons of the Vietnam War*, © 1995 (extracts 4.4, 7.1); M. E. Sharpe Inc. for an extract from Jayne S. Werner and Luu Doan Huynh (eds), *The Vietnam War: Vietnamese and American Perspectives*, © 1992 (extract 5.11); the US Government Printing Office, Washington DC, for selections from *The Public Papers of the Presidents* series, various volumes (extracts 2.9, 3.1, 4.2, 5.2, 5.6, 5.14, 6.2, 6.4–5, 7.10). Every attempt has been made to seek the permission of copyright holders. If any proper acknowledgement has not been made, copyright holders are invited to contact the publisher.

Finally, my thanks go to Catherine and Niamh for bringing a healthy non-historical perspective to my work; to my father, Tom, and my aunt, Kathleen, for years of love and support without measure; and to my mother – Mary Elizabeth Ruane of Aughnagallop, Drumshanbo, County Leitrim, Ireland – who passed away just as this book was completed and to whose memory it is lovingly dedicated.

# Abbreviations

| | |
|---|---|
| ARVN | Army of the Republic of Vietnam |
| CCP | Chinese Communist Party |
| CIA | Central Intelligence Agency |
| CMAG | Chinese Military Advisory Group |
| COSVN | Central Office for South Vietnam |
| DMZ | Demilitarised Zone |
| DRV | Democratic Republic of Vietnam |
| EDC | European Defence Community |
| FBI | Federal Bureau of Investigation |
| ICP | Indochinese Communist Party |
| MAAG | Military Assistance Advisory Group |
| MACV | Military Assistance Command, Vietnam |
| NATO | North Atlantic Treaty Organisation |
| NCRC | National Council of Reconciliation and Concord |
| NLF | National Liberation Front (South Vietnam) |
| NSAM | National Security Action Memorandum |
| NSC | National Security Council |
| OSS | Office of Strategic Services |
| PAVN | People's Army of Vietnam (North Vietnam) |
| PLA | People's Liberation Army (Communist China) |
| PLAF | People's Liberation Armed Forces (Vietcong) |
| POW | Prisoner/s of War |
| PRC | People's Republic of China |
| PRG | Provisional Revolutionary Government |
| PRP | People's Revolutionary Party |
| RVN | Republic of Vietnam |
| SEATO | South East Asia Treaty Organisation |
| VC | Vietcong |
| VWP | Vietnam Workers' Party (Lao Dong) |

# Chronology of events

| | |
|---|---|
| *1887* | Establishment of the Indochinese Union, solemnising French colonial control over Vietnam, Cambodia and Laos. |
| *1890* | Birth in central Vietnam of Nguyen Sinh Cung, better known as Ho Chi Minh. |
| *1914*<br>August | Outbreak of the First World War in Europe. |
| *1917*<br>October | Bolshevik revolution in Russia. |
| *1918* | Ho Chi Minh settles in Paris. |
| *1919* | Ho Chi Minh joins French Socialist Party. |
| *1920*<br>December | Ho Chi Minh becomes founder member of French Communist Party. |
| *1930*<br>February | Founding of the Vietnamese Communist Party in Hong Kong. |
| October | On Comintern instructions, Party's name changed to the Indochinese Communist Party (ICP). |
| *1939*<br>September | Outbreak of the Second World War in Europe. Severe French repression of ICP in Vietnam. |
| *1940*<br>June | Fall of France to Germany. |

**1941**

| | |
|---|---|
| May | Formation of Vietnamese Liberation League, or Vietminh. |
| July | Japanese control of Indochina formalised in collaboration with French colonial authorities. |
| December | Japanese attack on Pearl Harbor triggers start of Second World War in Asia and the Pacific. |

**1945**

| | |
|---|---|
| March | Japanese intern French colonial administration in Vietnam. |
| | Vietnam declared independent under Emperor Bao Dai. |
| July | Potsdam agreement on Indochina. |
| August | Japan surrenders, end of Second World War in Asia and the Pacific. |
| | Vietminh take power in Vietnam in the 'August Revolution'. |
| September | Ho Chi Minh declares Vietnam independent and announces birth of a Democratic Republic of Vietnam (DRV). |
| | Arrival of British forces in Saigon to take formal Japanese surrender. |
| October | Arrival of Nationalist Chinese forces in northern Vietnam. |
| | French control over southern Vietnam consolidated. |
| November | Dissolution of the ICP. |

**1946**

| | |
|---|---|
| March | Ho–Sainteny agreement permitting return of French to northern Vietnam. |
| July–August | Fontainebleau conference fails to agree basis for Vietnamese independence. |
| September | Franco-Vietminh *modus vivendi*. |
| November | French shelling of Haiphong. |
| December | Outbreak of full-scale Franco-Vietminh war. |

**1949**

| | |
|---|---|
| March | Signing of Elysée agreement making Vietnam an 'associated state' within the French Union under leadership of Bao Dai. |
| October | Birth of the People's Republic of China (PRC). |

**1950**

January     The Soviet Union and the PRC extend formal diplo-
            matic recognition to the Vietminh (DRV).

February    French parliamentary ratification of the Elysée agree-
            ment.
            Formal United States recognition of Bao Dai govern-
            ment in Vietnam.

April       Communist China establishes Chinese Military Advi-
            sory Group (CMAG) to Vietminh army.

May         Start of major American military aid programme to
            French, followed by establishment of US Military
            Assistance Advisory Group (MAAG) in Saigon.

June        Outbreak of Korean war; American aid to France
            stepped up.

December    Vietminh 'borders' campaign secures mountain route
            from north Vietnam to China and delivers major
            defeat to French forces.

**1951**

February    Creation of the Lao Dong, or Vietnam Workers' Party
            (VWP), the successor to the ICP (dissolved 1945).

**1953**

July        Armistice in Korea.

November    Ho Chi Minh declares readiness to negotiate settle-
            ment with the French; French public and political
            opinion increasingly war weary.
            French forces occupy Dien Bien Phu.

**1954**

February    Berlin foreign ministers' conference agrees to call
            further conference in Geneva in April on the Korean
            and Indochinese problems.

March       Vietminh attack French at Dien Bien Phu.
            US government calls for 'united action' to save French
            in Vietnam.

April       Geneva conference opens.

May         French defeated at Dien Bien Phu.

June        Ngo Dinh Diem made Prime Minister of Associated
            State of Vietnam.
            Pierre Mendès-France becomes French Prime Minister;

|  | sets 20 July as deadline for peace in Indochina. |
| July | Geneva conference ends in agreement; Franco-Vietminh war ends; Vietnam temporarily partitioned pending countrywide elections in 1956. |
| September | Manila pact signed – birth of the South East Asia Treaty Organisation (SEATO). |
| October | US government agrees to provide aid direct to Diem government in southern Vietnam. |

**1955**

| April | Diem finally overcomes non-communist opposition in southern Vietnam and consolidates power. |
| July | Diem regime makes clear its opposition to 1956 national elections. |
| October | Diem's control of southern Vietnam completed with victory over Bao Dai in referendum for Head of State; birth of the Republic of Vietnam (RVN – South Vietnam). |

**1956**

| July | Scheduled date for all-Vietnam elections passes. |
| August | Ho Chi Minh publicly apologises for excesses of North Vietnam's land reform. |

**1957**

| January | Moscow proposes admission of both Vietnams to United Nations. |
| May | Diem state visit to the United States. |

**1959**

| January | Fifteenth plenum of VWP Central Committee decides to take greater and more direct interest in the situation in South Vietnam. |
| May | Diem regime promulgates Law 10/59. |

**1960**

| April | Caravelle manifesto issued by political opposition in South Vietnam. |
| September | Third VWP National Congress in Hanoi adopts policy of armed struggle as complement to political action in liberating South Vietnam. |
| November | Unsuccessful army coup against Diem. |

## Chronology of events

| | |
|---|---|
| | John F. Kennedy elected President of the United States. |
| December | Establishment of National Liberation Front for South Vietnam (NLF). |

**1961**

| | |
|---|---|
| January | VWP Politburo votes to increase level of military effort in the south; decision gives rise to the People's Liberation Armed Forces (PLAF or Vietcong). Soviet leader Khrushchev gives public support to wars of national liberation. |

**1962**

| | |
|---|---|
| February | Formation of US Military Assistance Command in Vietnam (MACV). |
| March | Onset of Strategic Hamlet programme in South Vietnam. |
| July | Geneva accords on Laos signed. |

**1963**

| | |
|---|---|
| May | Beginning of Buddhist crisis in South Vietnam. |
| August | Diem regime attacks Buddhist temples. |
| November | Overthrow of Diem regime by dissident army officers; formation of Military Revolutionary Council in South Vietnam under leadership of General Duong Van Minh. Assassination of President Kennedy. |
| December | VWP Central Committee in Hanoi opts to escalate North Vietnam's military commitment to the struggle in South Vietnam. Approximately 16,000 US military advisers in South Vietnam at end of 1963. |

**1964**

| | |
|---|---|
| January | General Nguyen Khanh seizes power in Saigon. |
| June | General William Westmoreland appointed head of MACV. |
| 2/4 August | Gulf of Tonkin incident(s). |
| 7 August | Passage of Gulf of Tonkin resolution. |
| November | Lyndon B. Johnson elected US President in his own right. |

**1965**

| | |
|---|---|
| 7 February | Vietcong attack on US base at Pleiku near Saigon; |

|            | Johnson authorises Operation Flaming Dart in retaliation – US Air Force raids against North Vietnamese targets. |
|------------|---|
| 2 March    | Operation Rolling Thunder – sustained US bombing of North Vietnam – commences. |
| 8 March    | First US combat troops arrive in South Vietnam. |
| June       | Air Vice Marshal Nguyen Cao Ky takes power in Saigon. |
| July       | US government agrees to despatch large numbers of ground troops to South Vietnam. |
|            | Approximately 200,000 US troops in South Vietnam at end of 1965; first major anti-war demonstrations in US cities (October–November). |

**1966**

| March–May  | Major Buddhist-led unrest in South Vietnam. |
|------------|---|
|            | Approximately 400,000 US troops in South Vietnam at end of 1966. |

**1967**

| April      | Large-scale anti-war demonstrations in America. |
|------------|---|
| September  | Nguyen Van Thieu elected President of South Vietnam. |
| October    | Anti-war protesters lay siege to the Pentagon in Washington. |
| November   | Westmoreland, in United States, gives optimistic account of war and prospects for victory. |
|            | Approximately 500,000 US troops in South Vietnam at end of 1967. |

**1968**

| 31 January | Launch of communist Tet offensive in South Vietnam. |
|------------|---|
| February   | Westmoreland requests 206,000 additional troops. |
| March      | Johnson advised by 'wise men' against further escalation. |
|            | Johnson announces an end to escalation, a near-total halt in the bombing of North Vietnam, and a commitment to a peaceful solution. |
|            | My Lai massacre. |
| May        | Preliminary US–North Vietnamese talks in Paris. |
| August     | Violent anti-war protests mar Democratic National Convention in Chicago. |

| | |
|---|---|
| October | Johnson orders total bombing halt against North Vietnam. |
| November | Richard M. Nixon elected President of the United States. |
| | Approximately 540,000 US troops in South Vietnam at end of 1968. |

**1969**

| | |
|---|---|
| January | Four-party (US, North Vietnam, NLF and Saigon regime) talks get under way in Paris. |
| March | Nixon administration begins 'secret' bombing of Cambodia. |
| June | Nixon announces withdrawal of 25,000 US troops from South Vietnam. |
| | NLF now officially styled the Provisional Revolutionary Government (PRG) of South Vietnam. |
| September | Death of Ho Chi Minh. |
| October | Massive anti-war demonstration in Washington. |
| November | Major anti-war demonstrations continue in US cities. |
| | Nixon announces continuing troop withdrawals from South Vietnam in context of 'Vietnamisation' of the war. |
| | My Lai massacre of 1968 made public. |
| | US troop strength in South Vietnam down to approximately 475,000. |

**1970**

| | |
|---|---|
| February | Secret US–North Vietnamese peace talks commence parallel to public peace process, both located in Paris. |
| April | Joint US–South Vietnamese ground invasion of Cambodia. |
| May | Major demonstrations in US against Cambodian adventure. |
| December | US Congress legislates against use of US combat troops in Laos or Cambodia. |
| | US troop strength in South Vietnam down to approximately 330,000. |

**1971**

| | |
|---|---|
| February | US-backed South Vietnamese ground invasion of Laos. |
| June | *New York Times* begins publishing *The Pentagon Papers*. |

| | |
|---|---|
| October | Thieu re-elected President of South Vietnam. |
| | US troop strength in South Vietnam down to approximately 155,000. |

**1972**

| | |
|---|---|
| February | Nixon visits Communist China. |
| March | North Vietnam launches spring (or Easter) offensive against South Vietnam. |
| May | US resumes major bombing of North Vietnam. |
| | Nixon visits Soviet Union. |
| October | US and North Vietnam reach provisional peace agreement; peace deal subsequently rejected by Thieu. |
| November | Nixon re-elected as President. |
| December | US (Christmas) bombing of North Vietnam. |
| | US troop strength in South Vietnam down to approximately 25,000. |

**1973**

| | |
|---|---|
| 27 January | US, North Vietnam, Saigon government and PRG (NLF) sign Paris peace agreement. |
| March | Last US soldier leaves South Vietnam. |
| July | US Congress bans further US air action against Cambodia. |
| November | US Congress approves War Powers Act over Nixon's veto; Congress legislates against further US military action in Indochina area. |

**1974**

| | |
|---|---|
| January | Thieu declares that war has started again in South Vietnam. |
| April | US Congress rejects Nixon administration request for increased military aid to South Vietnam. |
| August | Nixon resigns in disgrace over Watergate scandal. |
| December | VWP Politburo decides to launch all-out push for victory in south. |

**1975**

| | |
|---|---|
| March | Hanoi authorises final offensive against Saigon – the Ho Chi Minh campaign. |
| 21 April | Thieu resigns and flees Saigon. |
| 30 April | Saigon government surrenders to North Vietnamese army. |

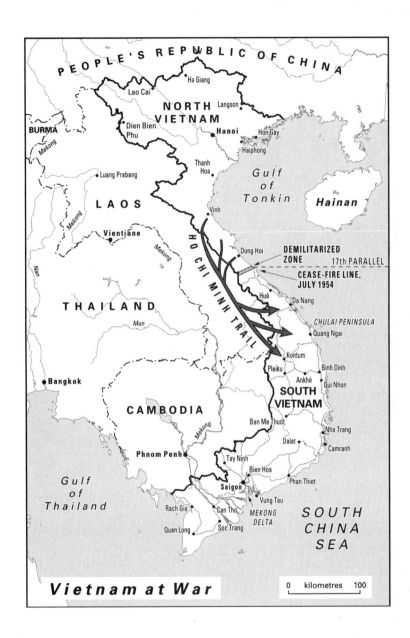

Vietnam at War

0  kilometres  100

# Introduction

## Historians and the Vietnam wars

The conflict that engulfed Vietnam in the middle years of the twentieth century continues to exert a firm grip on the attention of historians
and students of history alike, with its causes, course and consequences
the subject of endless debate. This high level of interest testifies in turn
to a generally held conviction that the conflict was important,
although *why* it was important is a question that produces many differing answers. For some, the war's significance derives from the sheer
scale of the death and destruction it unleashed. Of the principal participants, an estimated 500,000 Vietnamese died during the French
war of 1946–54, and anywhere between two and three million native
combatants and non-combatants died during the later American war;
French and French Union losses amounted to 75,000; and by 1975
American war dead had added a further 59,000 to the grim reckoning.
Alongside this human cost, note should be made of the tremendous
devastation wreaked upon Vietnam's urban and rural landscape, its
eco-system and its traditional societal structures. Yet the importance
of the conflict cannot and should not be measured simply in levels of
violence. Writing in 1986, James Cable argued that an ostensibly
localised conflict owed its abiding significance to its international
character:

> Americans, Australians, British, Chinese, French, Japanese,
> Koreans may each single out certain months or years as the
> period of their involvement in actual combat; most of the indig-
> enous inhabitants now alive have never known a time when
> there was no fighting in Indochina. Many of them never will.
> These Cambodian, Laotians, Vietnamese, to name only a few of

the indigenous peoples, suffered most, but the turbulence in Indochina spread more than ripples through the world. Distant governments fell from power, remote peoples were agitated, the quivering kaleidoscope of international relations early acquired and still in part retains a distinctively Indochinese rhythm to complicate its shifting patterns. Of the world's continents South America has so far been the least affected, but Africa not merely furnished many soldiers, but felt on its own soil – in Algeria and Angola and Ethiopia – the repercussions of those distant shocks.[1]

Until relatively recently, however, this international dimension was not fully reflected in a Western historiography on the war that was dominated by American historians in search of the roots of American involvement and the causes of American defeat in Vietnam. With regard to the former question, most scholars agreed that the US Cold War strategy of containment was the principal determinant. As George C. Herring has argued:

> The United States' involvement in Vietnam was not primarily a result of error of judgment or of the personality quirks of the policymakers, although these things existed in abundance. It was a logical, if not inevitable, outgrowth of a world view and a policy, the policy of containment, which Americans in and out of government accepted without serious question for more than two decades. The commitment in Vietnam expanded as the containment policy itself grew. In time, it outlived the conditions that had given rise to that policy. More than anything else, America's failure in Vietnam calls into question the basic premises of that policy ...[2]

Containment might explain why the United States was sucked into the Vietnam vortex, but it offers no answer to the related question: why, once fully committed from 1964–65, did America fail to achieve its key objective of preserving a separate non-communist state in southern Vietnam? The answers offered by historians are various and complex, ranging from deficiencies in American military tactics and strategy to the deleterious impact of domestic anti-war protest on the will of the US government – particularly the Johnson administration – to prosecute the war with full vigour.[3] However, from the mass of competing interpretations, two broad schools of thought emerged.

According to the 'quagmire' thesis, the war was always unwinnable, but US policy-makers only realised this *after* American power was fully committed in 1964–65. With considerations of national pride and prestige preventing withdrawal, the American government thereafter could only wage an inconclusive war until, eventually, US public opinion tired of the whole costly enterprise and 'peace with honor' rather than victory became Washington's declared objective. 'American leaders from Truman to Johnson had undertaken a series of incremental steps in Indochina which ended in disastrous U.S. involvement', writes Robert A. Divine of the 'quagmire' thesis. 'This came about by chance, not design, and if any of the presidents had known where his policies were leading the nation, he never would have approved them.'[4]

A more critical explanation of American failure can be found in the 'stalemate' theory, which gained prominence in the wake of the publication of *The Pentagon Papers*, the top-secret US government analysis of Vietnam decision-making which was made public in 1971.[5] At the heart of 'stalemate' is a searing indictment of presidential leadership: concerned about the domestic political impact of a large and costly war in Vietnam, successive US presidents refused to sanction the kind of military effort required to bring victory and settled instead for the lower-level objective of simply not losing. 'American presidents had taken a series of steps with full knowledge that none was likely to achieve the desired result', concludes Divine. Although the White House was given sound advice by political and military experts, presidents, notably Kennedy and Johnson, 'decided on dubious actions for political reasons'. These 'reasons' included concern to preserve favourable public opinion ratings and electoral prospects by avoiding the increases in taxation that might be required to finance a major war; the prioritisation of domestic legislative programmes over vital foreign policy objectives; and the related need to shepherd finite budgetary resources for voter-pleasing initiatives at home. The result was 'a stalemate in Vietnam', not through inadvertence – as the 'quagmire' theory suggests – 'but one deliberately achieved as a foreseeable consequence of American policy'.[6]

Although American-centred studies continue to form the largest single element in Vietnam historiography, a growing number of scholars now argue that the US military intervention in the 1960s, though massive in its scale and implications, did not in itself make Vietnam an *American* war. The first scholarly work to stress fully the importance of the conflict as an international phenomenon was R. B. Smith's multi-volume *International History of the Vietnam War*.[7] This same international approach has informed more recent studies on the Soviet, Chinese and British roles in the war, to name but a few of the perspectives now available.[8] This is not to say that there is nowhere for American scholarship on American involvement to go. On the contrary, the 1990s have witnessed the publication of volumes of documents in the *Foreign Relations of the United States* series for much of the Kennedy and Johnson years, with the prospect of the Nixon years to come, while transcripts of secretly taped White House telephone conversations during the Johnson presidency have been published, initially for 1963–64 but with the whole 1963–69 period as the ultimate objective.[9] Armed with these and other newly released sources of evidence, historians will doubtless produce even more de-tailed, subtle and nuanced accounts of US decision-making.[10] Yet even American scholars are increasingly disposed to integrate US policy into an internationalist analytical framework. Frederik Logevall's stimulating and provocative book *Choosing War* is a good example of this approach, emphasising as it does the interdependence of Ameri-can, British and French diplomacy during the crucial 1963–65 period.[11] However, this recent expansion of an already large corpus of scholarship has led, not to consensus on the key issues relating to the conflict, but to a proliferation of rival interpretations. The greater the body of primary source material, its seems, the greater the potential for competing and conflicting viewpoints.[12]

Although the internationalisation of Vietnam historiography is an important development, the danger exists that arguably the most important perspective, that of the Vietnamese, may be overshadowed. For many years, those historians in the West who sought to give the Vietnamese – and in particular the communists – a voice had to rely on a narrow primary source base. As Jean Lacouture observed in his 1968 biography of Ho Chi Minh, this dearth of evidence meant that any account of Ho's life, particularly his early years, must be 'frag-mentary, open to dispute, a mere approximation of the truth'.[13] How-ever, a number of Western historians, whilst acknowledging this difficulty and the associated methodological problems, still sought to use what evidence there was to provide a Vietnamese view of the con-flict. In R. B. Smith's *International History of the Vietnam War*, for example, a detailed exposition of communist policy is the axis around which his international analysis revolves; William J. Duiker and

Gabriel Kolko, whilst also acknowledging the international dimensions of the conflict, have as their principal focus the source, shape and consequences of communist decision-making within Vietnam itself; and Carlyle Thayer, William Trullinger and Eric Bergerud have filled the gaps in the documentary record by fieldwork in Vietnam and judicious utilisation of oral testimony in producing studies of the war at the village level.[14] Recently, however, the Vietnamese source base has expanded – although methodological problems remain. Writing in 1996, William Duiker observed that

> [m]onographic studies, memoirs and documentary collections published in Vietnam and elsewhere are beginning to fill the gaps in our knowledge of the Vietnamese side of the conflict. These materials provide the researcher with a clearer picture of what decisions were made, who made them, and why. Although a number of crucial questions have not yet been resolved, we are today much closer to obtaining a balanced picture of the war as viewed from all sides, not just from Washington and Saigon but also from Hanoi, Moscow and Beijing.[15]

Memoirs in particular have introduced the 'human factor' into Vietnam historiography, especially in regard to communist decision-making, although like all post-facto recollections, they operate best as an accompaniment to, rather than substitute for, more solid, contemporary, primary source evidence.[16] In the latter connection, recent research based on newly available Chinese communist sources, and on documents housed in the hitherto closed archives of the former Soviet Union, have contributed to a greater understanding of Sino-Soviet policy and decision-making on Vietnam, and to a more acute appreciation of the troubled relationship between the Vietnamese communists and their major allies.[17] Moreover, in one of the most important advances in Cold War studies in recent years, the Cold War International History Project (CWIHP), based at the Woodrow Wilson International Center for Scholars in Washington DC, has located, transcribed, translated, and made available a large amount of primary source material on the Vietnamese, Soviet and Chinese side of the war. But the CWIHP is more than an archive; the Project's annual bulletins contain the more significant documentary discoveries alongside analysis and contextualisation by historians. Those same historians offer more detailed treatment of the documents in working papers, available free on request from the Project directorate in Washington DC.[18]

Inevitably, Vietnam features prominently both in the CWIHP's published output and on its World Wide Web site – an excellent demonstration of the growing value of the Internet to the scholarly community.[19] The Vietnamese source base, therefore, is broader than it was ten years ago – a recent study of Sino-Vietnamese relations by Ang Cheng Guan has made excellent use of currently available documentation, as does Robert K. Brigham in a new study of the National Liberation Front of South Vietnam, his documentary research augmented by extensive interviews with surviving participants from the war years.[20] All things being relative, however, the Vietnamese source base perforce remains narrow. The key sources continue to be those captured from the Vietcong or North Vietnamese during the conflict, or materials officially sanctioned and published by the Hanoi government (and thereby the object of some suspicion). It is true, as already noted, that much new evidence has been unearthed in Moscow and (especially) Beijing, but this tends to deal with the triangular Hanoi–Beijing–Moscow relationship rather than Vietnamese communist decision-making on the war in and of itself. Despite the Socialist Republic of Vietnam's professed commitment to greater archival openness, new insights in this connection are dependent, Robert Brigham argues, upon 'a dramatic change in Hanoi's access practices'.[21] But to repeat: all things are relative, for compared to writing on the communist side of the war, the non-communist perspective is a virtual historiographical black hole. In the absence of evidence upon which to construct an alternative interpretation, the Saigon government and armed forces will continue to be the victims of blanket characterisations portraying them as wholly corrupt, inefficient and devoid of martial ardour. This may well have been the case, but it is worth pointing out that generalisations – especially the cruder type – usually fragment into more complex and nuanced constituent parts upon close analysis, except that in the case of the Republic of Vietnam there is little to analyse, closely or otherwise.

## The documents

The documents in this volume tell the story of the Vietnam conflict in chronological order, beginning with the birth of the Vietnamese Communist Party in 1930 and ending with the triumph of the Vietnamese revolution in 1975. Although the documents cannot impart this tale in a comprehensive or detailed manner, they do illuminate and illustrate important aspects of the conflict and so act as a valuable accompaniment to other narrative-based studies of the war. In particular, the collection seeks to acknowledge both the international and the Vietnamese dimensions of the conflict, thereby dovetailing with current historiographical trends. The American role in Vietnam will obviously feature strongly in the following pages, and at times it will dominate, but the overall intention is to place it in its true perspective: Vietnam knew war before the massive escalation in the US military presence between 1965 and 1968, and it would know war after this escalation was reversed and the Americans finally departed in 1973. Indeed, the overarching theme of this book is that Vietnam witnessed not one but several interlocking, overlapping and interdependent wars. The American war of 1965–73, for example, was preceded by a failed French war of colonial reconquest, ran parallel with a southern Vietnamese civil war, and would be followed by a war of national reunification waged by North Vietnam and its southern supporters. Vietnam was also a theatre in, or at the very centre of, some of the wider international conflicts that have scarred the twentieth century – the Second World War (during which Indochina was occupied by Japan), the Cold War (arguably the most important external influence on Vietnam's post-1945 history), and the Sino-Soviet dispute (with Vietnam an ideological battleground for the two communist giants in their own bitterly contested Cold War). Therefore, as both Marilyn B. Young and Justin Wintle have argued, Vietnam *wars* in the plural is a far more apt description of what took place than the traditional Vietnam *war* in the singular.[22]

The selection and editing of material for this book has been a matter of personal authorial preference. While there are certain key documents that a reader would expect to find in any collection, the remainder – the majority – reflect the author's view of the conflict. The documents themselves range from official US government analyses and directives, to internal Vietnamese communist communications; from memoirs of politicians and soldiers to oral testimony from non-combatants; from the work of historians to that of journalists. Inevitably, given the constraints imposed by the relatively limited scale of this volume, there are gaps and omissions in the coverage of the conflict: events in Laos and Cambodia, for example, are located at the periphery of this study when, some historians would argue, they ought to be more central, or at least more fully integrated into the

Vietnam picture; similarly the American anti-war movement is given limited documentary treatment, not because it is unimportant, but because it is so well served in other document-based studies. In this last connection, it should be stressed that the present volume has benefited greatly from the existence of other published collections, and should be seen not as the final word on source and evidence but as an entrée to these larger and more wide-ranging compilations.[23]

# 1

# War and revolution, 1930–1946

In 1930, an Indochinese Communist Party (ICP) was formed under the leadership of Nguyen Ai Quoc, better known as Ho Chi Minh. In its founding programme, the Party dedicated itself to the creation of an independent and communist Vietnam, hence to two revolutions: a national revolution that would end fifty years of French colonial dominion, and a social revolution to provide the basis for Vietnam's post-colonial future (1.4). Initially, the question of which revolution should take priority caused a split in the ranks of the ICP leadership, with Ho and a minority faction urging the primacy of the nationalist cause, and a majority – mostly Moscow-trained ideologues – arguing for simultaneous national *and* social revolution. Matters were aggravated by disagreements over the revolutionary role to be allotted to the peasantry, with the Communist International (Comintern) coming out strongly in support of the Moscow wing of the Party and against Ho and the nationalist wing (1.3, 1.5). A combination of internecine warfare and harsh French colonial repression thus ensured that the ICP's revolutionary progress was limited during the 1930s.

However, the end of the decade witnessed the virtual demise of the Stalinist ideologues and, as a corollary, the domination of Party decision-making by those who, like Ho Chi Minh, believed in adapting Comintern instructions to suit the particular needs of the Vietnamese revolution. The outbreak of the Second World War led to a severe French crack-down on the ICP, with the Stalinists evidently bearing the brunt of the repression. Then, in June 1940, the fall of France encouraged predatory moves by an expansionist Japan that culminated in an agreement whereby the French, in collaboration with occupying Japanese forces, ran Indochina for the benefit of Tokyo. It was against this backdrop that Ho Chi Minh, sensing a revolutionary opportunity, presided over the formation in May 1941 of a

9

Vietnamese Independence League – the Vietminh. The Vietminh was an umbrella grouping of anti-French and anti-Japanese nationalists, but with the handle of the umbrella – hence control – held firmly in hidden communist hands. To Ho and the ICP, the success of the national revolution would require mass support, but if the Vietminh was seen as a communist-front organisation, it would deter non-communists from participating. Hence, the Vietminh's manifesto emphasised simple patriotic themes and was designed to appeal to a wide spectrum of Vietnamese nationalist opinion (1.6). Later, when the national revolution had been completed, the ICP could abandon its bourgeois and progressive 'allies' in the Vietminh and move to implement its Marxist-Leninist agenda (1.6).

Between 1941 and 1945, the Vietminh grew steadily in size and popularity as it prepared (necessarily clandestinely) for a seizure of power. That prospect was brought closer in March 1945 when the Japanese, anticipating an Allied invasion of Indochina and fearing that their French 'collaborators' would turn on them, imprisoned much of the colonial administration. Finally, in August 1945, the sudden surrender of Japan in the wake of the atomic bombing of Hiroshima and Nagasaki left a power vacuum in Vietnam that the Vietminh – in the so-called August Revolution – were quick to fill (1.7, 1.8). On 2 September, Ho Chi Minh declared his country independent and announced the birth of the Democratic Republic of Vietnam (DRV) (1.9). However, as a result of decisions taken at the last Big Three wartime conference at Potsdam, this independence would be short-lived. In mid-September, British-Indian forces, acting in accordance with the Potsdam directive, arrived in southern Vietnam to take the formal Japanese surrender; ignoring the *de facto* Vietminh authorities, the British released the imprisoned French colonial forces and thereafter assisted in the full restoration of French authority in the south (1.11). In the north, Chinese Nationalist forces, also present under the Potsdam agreement, not only took the Japanese surrender, but appeared intent on fully annexing the area. Ho looked for support from the United States – the supposed champion of freedom for colonial peoples – but Washington, mindful of a possible future confrontation with Soviet power in Europe, was increasingly reluctant to do anything to undermine good relations with France (1.12).

In an act of desperation, Ho Chi Minh – who clearly looked on China as a greater long-term threat than France – agreed to French re-entry to the north on the understanding that the Chinese would withdraw (1.13). At this stage – early 1946 – with the French in control of the south, and in a power-sharing arrangement with the Vietminh in the north, the DRV's independence was clearly limited. However, the Vietminh remained cautiously optimistic that a timetable for French withdrawal could yet be agreed at a scheduled conference in Paris in the summer of 1946. In the event, with the French determined to maintain their overseas empire as a means of speeding France's postwar rehabilitation, the negotiations collapsed (1.14). Although Ho retained some hopes of a peaceful transition to independence, extremists in the Vietminh were now ready to eschew diplomacy in favour of war. At the same time, the French colonial regime in Vietnam, worried that a left-wing government might soon emerge in Paris ready to negotiate seriously with the Vietminh, was inclined to take the law into its own hands. In November 1946, a French gunboat shelled Haiphong, killing an estimated 6,000 civilians, an action that the French government neither sanctioned nor (tellingly) repudiated. When, the following month, French forces contested Vietminh control of Hanoi, the battle-lines were drawn. On 20 December, even Ho accepted the inevitable as he added his voice to a Vietminh call to arms (1.15). The Franco-Vietminh war had begun.

## 1.1  Ho Chi Minh and 'the path that led me to Leninism'

Vietnamese nationalism and communism in the twentieth century were dominated by the figure of Ho Chi Minh. In 1911, aged 21, Ho left Vietnam, working on a French liner operating out of Marseilles. After several years of travel, he settled in France, joining the French Socialist Party before becoming, in 1920, a founding member of the French Communist Party. Looking back in 1960, Ho recalled how his nationalist outlook came to be fused with Leninism.

After World War I, I made my living in Paris, now as a re-toucher at a photographer's, now as a painter of 'Chinese antiquities' (made in France!). I would distribute leaflets denouncing the crimes committed by the French colonialists in Viet-Nam.

At that time, I supported the October Revolution only instinctively, not yet grasping all its historic importance. I loved and admired Lenin because he was a great patriot who liberated his compatriots; until then, I had read none of his books.

The reason for my joining the French Socialist Party was that these 'ladies and gentlemen' – as I called my comrades at that moment – had shown their sympathy toward me, toward the struggle of the oppressed peoples. But I understood neither what was a party, a trade-union, nor what was Socialism or Communism.

Heated discussions were then taking place in the branches of the Socialist Party, about the question of whether the Socialist Party should remain in the Second International ... or should the Socialist Party join Lenin's Third International?[1] I attended the meetings regularly, twice or thrice a week, and attentively listened to the discussions. First, I could not understand thoroughly ...

What I wanted most to know – and this precisely was not debated in the meetings – was: Which International sides with the people of colonial countries?

I raised this question – the most important in my opinion – in a meeting. Some comrades answered: It is the Third, not the Second, International. And a comrade gave me Lenin's 'Theses on the National and Colonial Questions,' published in *l'Humanité*, to read.

There were political terms difficult to understand in this thesis. But by dint of reading it again and again, finally I could grasp the main part of it.

> Lenin's thinking, which so impressed Ho Chi Minh, has been summarised thus by the historian William Duiker.

Because of the weakness of the bourgeoisie in most Asian societies, the revolution against feudalism and imperialism could be successfully carried out only through an alliance of several progressive classes, including the peasantry, the proletariat, the petty bourgeoisie, and the national bourgeoisie. This gave an opening to the formation of Communist parties. Although the proletariat in most Asian societies was considered too weak and immature to lead a socialist revolution, it could aid other progressive classes in a united front against the reactionary forces of feudalism and imperialism. Once this first stage of the revolution had succeeded, the Communists, with the support of the most revolutionary elements from the peasantry and the petty bourgeoisie, would break with moderate nationalists and attempt to seize power. The Asian revolution was thus viewed as a two-staged process – a first bourgeois democratic stage and a second proletarian socialist one.

For Ho Chi Minh, the impact of Lenin's ideas was far-reaching.

What emotion, enthusiasm, clear-sightedness, and confidence it instilled into me! I was overjoyed to tears. Though sitting alone in my room, I shouted aloud as if addressing large crowds: 'Dead martyrs, compatriots! This is what we need, this is the path to our liberation!'

After then, I had entire confidence in Lenin, in the Third International.

Formerly, during the meetings of the Party branch, I only listened to the discussion: I had a vague belief that all were logical, and could not differentiate as to who were right and who were wrong. But from then on, I also plunged into the debates and discussed with fervor. Though I was still lacking French words to express all my thoughts, I smashed the allegations attacking Lenin and the Third International with no less vigor. My only argument was: 'If you do not condemn colonialism, if you do not side with the colonial people, what kind of revolution are you waging?'

> At the Tours Congress in December 1920, the French Socialist Party split on the question of Comintern membership, with Ho siding with the radical minority that broke away to form the French Communist Party and align itself with the Soviet Union.

At first, patriotism, not yet Communism, led me to have confidence in Lenin, in the Third International. Step by step, along the struggle, by studying Marxism-Leninism parallel with participation in practical activities, I gradually came upon the fact that only Socialism and Communism can liberate the oppressed nations and the working people throughout the world from slavery.

Bernard B. Fall (ed.), *Ho Chi Minh on Revolution: Selected Writings, 1920–66* (New York: Praegar, 1967), pp. 23–5; William J. Duiker, *The Communist Road to Power in Vietnam* (Boulder: Westview Press, 1996 edn), pp. 16–17.

## 1.2 'Lenin and the Colonial Peoples'

This article by Ho Chi Minh was published in *Pravda* on 27 January 1924, shortly after Ho's arrival in Moscow for revolutionary training at Comintern headquarters and in the immediate wake of Lenin's death. Beneath the purple prose in praise of Lenin can be found a concern – well-merited as it happened – that the promotion of revolution in colonial areas of the world like Indochina would not be amongst the new Soviet leadership's priorities.

'Lenin is dead!' This news struck the people like a bolt from the blue. It spread to every corner of the fertile plains of Africa and the green fields of Asia. It is true that the black or yellow people do not yet know clearly who Lenin is or where Russia is. The imperialists have deliberately kept them in ignorance. Ignorance is one of the chief mainstays of capitalism. But all of them, from the Vietnamese peasants to the hunters in the Dahomey forests, have secretly learned that in a faraway corner of the earth there is a nation that has succeeded in overthrowing its exploiters and is managing its own country with no need for masters and Governors General. They have also heard that that country is Russia, that there are courageous people there, and that the most courageous of them all was Lenin. This alone was enough to fill them with deep admiration and warm feelings for that country and its leader.

But this was not all. They also learned that that great leader, after having liberated his own people, wanted to liberate other peoples too. He called upon the white peoples to help the yellow and black peoples to free themselves from the foreign aggressors' yoke, from all foreign aggressors, Governors General, Residents, etc. And to reach that goal, he mapped out a definite program.

At first they could not believe that anywhere on earth could there exist such a man and such a program. But later they heard, although vaguely, of the Communist Parties, of the organization called the Communist International which is fighting for the exploited peoples, for all the exploited peoples including themselves. And they learned that Lenin was the leader of that organization.

And this alone was enough to make these peoples ... wholeheartedly respect Lenin. They look upon Lenin as their liberator. 'Lenin is dead, so what will happen to us? Will there be other courageous and generous people like Lenin who will not spare their time and efforts in concerning themselves with our liberation?' This is what the oppressed colonial peoples are wondering.

As for us, we are deeply moved by this irretrievable loss and share the common mourning of all the peoples with our brothers and sisters. But we believe that the Communist International and its branches, which include branches in colonial countries, will succeed in implementing the lessons and teachings the leader has left behind for us. To do what he advised us, is that not the best way to show our love for him?

In his lifetime he was our father, teacher, comrade, and adviser. Nowadays, he is the bright star showing us the way to the socialist revolution.

Eternal Lenin will live forever in our work.

Fall (ed.), *Ho Chi Minh on Revolution*, pp. 39–40.

### 1.3  Ho Chi Minh on rural revolution

As Ho feared, Lenin's successors reverted to more orthodox Marxist views, championing the proletariat as the true vanguard of revolution and downgrading the revolutionary value of the peasantry. For Ho, however, the Leninist viewpoint retained its validity, not least because peasants accounted for almost 90 per cent of Vietnam's native population.

[T]he aim of the proletarian party with respect to the peasants is clear. It must win leadership of the movement, organize it, moblize the peasant masses around certain class slogans which accord with the character of the revolution, and in short must lead the entire movement toward realizing those slogans. The party of the proletariat must coordinate the peasant movement with the revolutionary aims and operations of the proletariat in the industrial centres ... Victory of the proletarian revolution is impossible in rural and semi-rural countries if the revolutionary proletariat is not actively supported by the mass of the peasant population ... In China, in India, in Latin America, in many European countries (Balkan countries, Rumania, Poland, Italy, France, Spain etc.) the decisive ally of the proletariat in the revolution will be the peasant population. Only if the revolutionary wave sets in

motion the rural masses under the leadership of the proletariat, will
the revolution be able to triumph. Hence the exceptional importance
of Party agitation in the countryside.

Ho Chi Minh, *The Party's Military Work among the Peasantry* (1927),
cited in Duiker, *Communist Road to Power*, pp. 21–2.


## 1.4 The Vietnamese Communist Party

Disillusioned with the limited importance attached to revolution in colonial areas by the French communists and the
Comintern, in February 1930 Ho Chi Minh presided over the
creation in Hong Kong of a Vietnamese Communist Party. The
Party's founding programme gave greater prominence to patriotic themes and the redress of socio-economic grievances than
to strict ideological aims, a reflection of Ho's pragmatic outlook: an overtly communist manifesto would alienate non-
communist Vietnamese nationalists and bourgeois elements
when, in Ho's view, the overthrow of the French would require
a broad-based class alliance.


The Vietnamese revolution has made the French imperialists tremble
with fear. On the one hand, they utilise the feudalists and comprador
bourgeois in our country to oppress and exploit our people. On the
other, they terrorize, arrest, jail, deport, and kill a great number of
Vietnamese revolutionaries. If the French imperialists think that they
can suppress the Vietnamese revolution by means of terrorist acts,
they are utterly mistaken. Firstly, it is because the Vietnamese revolution is not isolated but enjoys the assistance of the world proletarian
class in general and of the French working class in particular. Secondly, while the French imperialists are frenziedly carrying out terrorist acts, the Vietnamese Communists, formerly working separately,
have now united into a single Party, the Communist Party ... to lead
our entire people in their revolution ...

It is the party of the working class. It will help the proletarian class
to lead the revolution in order to struggle for all the oppressed and
exploited people. From now on we must join the Party, help it and
follow it in order to implement the following slogans.

1) To overthrow French imperialism, feudalism, and the reaction-

ary Vietnamese capitalist class.

2) To make Indochina completely independent.

3) To establish a worker–peasant and soldier government.

4) To confiscate the banks and other enterprises belonging to the imperialists and put them under the control of the worker–peasant and soldier government.

5) To confiscate the whole of the plantations and property belonging to the imperialists and the Vietnamese reactionary capitalist class and distribute them to poor peasants.

6) To implement the eight-hour working day.

7) To abolish public loans and poll tax. To waive unjust taxes hitting the poor people.

8) To bring back all freedoms to the masses.

9) To carry our universal education.

10) To implement equality between man and woman.

Fall (ed.), *Ho Chi Minh on Revolution*, pp. 129–31.

### 1.5   Ho Chi Minh and the Comintern

In October 1930, the Comintern ordered the Party to change its name to the Indochinese Communist Party (ICP) and bring its aims more into line with those of Moscow; hence ideological objectives were prioritised at the expense of nationalist-patriotic goals, and the Party itself was 'Bolshevised' – recruiting from and principally representing the interests of the proletariat. It was at this point that the ICP split into two broad factions, one dominated by Moscow-trained ideologues, the other representing the pragmatic nationalist outlook. Ho, speaking for the latter faction, particularly questioned whether revolution in Vietnam could succeed if the Party relied so heavily on the small industrial proletariat. The Comintern's objection to such a deviationist viewpoint was explained in an article in *Bolshevik*, the official organ of Comintern's External Direction Bureau.

We are in debt to Nguyen Ai Quoc [Ho Chi Minh] but our comrades should not forget the nationalist legacy of Nguyen Ai Quoc and his erroneous instructions on the fundamental questions of the bourgeois democratic revolutionary movement in Indochina, and his opportun-

17

ist theories ... Nguyen Ai Quoc also advocated such erroneous and collaborationist tactics as 'neutrality with regard to the bourgeois and rich peasants,' 'alliances with the middle and small landowners,' and so forth. It is because of such errors from January to October 1930 that the ICP followed a policy which in many respects was in opposition to the instructions of the Communist International even though it had energetically led the masses in revolutionary struggle.

> The continuing efforts of Ho to extol the revolutionary virtues of the peasantry brought only further reprimands from Moscow.

There are still some comrades in Tonkin [northern Vietnam] who believe that the peasants constitute the principal force of the Indochinese revolutionary movement and not the proletarians, on the pretext that the rural masses constitute nine-tenths of the population. We recognize that the peasants are numerous, but quantity should not be confused with command. In effect, if we consider the peasants as the leading force, one must believe that the directing role of the revolutionary movement should be in their hands and not in that of the workers. Such a judgment is mistaken, because the peasantry is a heterogeneous class anxious to retain its land, very amorphous and slow from an ideological and practical point of view, and very disunited – and thus very poorly qualified to assume the direction of a revolutionary movement.

Extracts from *Bolshevik*, c. 1930, 1934, cited in Duiker, *Communist Road to Power*, pp. 50–1.

## 1.6   The founding of the Vietminh

By 1941, the nationalist-pragmatic faction had regained control of ICP decision-making and was instrumental in the creation of the Vietnamese Independence League (Viet Nam Doc Lap Dong Minh), or Vietminh for short. The Vietminh was a throw-back to the broad-based class alliance Ho had favoured in 1930 when the ICP was formed. The breadth of the constituency he hoped to attract is clear from an open letter written to the Vietnamese people in the spring of 1941.

Rich people, soldiers, workers, peasants, intellectuals, employees, traders, youth, and women who warmly love your country! At the present time national liberation is the most important problem. Let us unite together! As one in mind and strength we shall overthrow the Japanese[2] and French and their jackals in order to save people from the situation between boiling water and burning heat.

Dear Compatriots!

National salvation is the common cause to the whole of our people. Every Vietnamese must take part in it. He who has money will contribute his money, he who has strength will contribute his strength, he who has talent will contribute his talent. I pledge to use all my modest abilities to follow you, and am ready for the last sacrifice.

Revolutionary fighters!

The hour has struck! Raise aloft the insurrectionary banner and guide the people throughout the country to overthrow the Japanese and French! The sacred call of the Fatherland is resounding in your ears; the blood of our heroic predecessors who sacrificed their lives is stirring in your hearts! The fighting spirit of the people is displayed everywhere before you! Let us rise up quickly! United with each other, unify your action to overthrow the Japanese and the French.

Victory to Viet-Nam's Revolution!

Victory to the World's Revolution!

> In sponsoring a broad class alliance, the ICP had not lost sight of its ideological goals. On the contrary, as a secret Party resolution made clear, the social revolution would follow on from the national revolution.

This does not mean that our Party is ignoring the problem of class struggle in the Indochinese revolution. No, the problem of class struggle will continue to exist. But in the present stage, the nation has prime importance, and all demands which are of benefit to a specific class but which are harmful to the national interest must be subordinated to the survival of the nation and the race. At this moment, if we do not resolve the problem of national liberation, and do not demand independence and freedom for the entire people, then not only will the entire people of our nation continue to live the life of beasts, but also the particular interests of individual social classes will not be achieved for thousands of years.

Fall (ed.), *Ho Chi Minh on Revolution*, pp. 132–4; ICP resolution, May 1941, cited in Duiker, *Communist Road to Power*, p. 73.

## 1.7  A call to arms, August 1945

With the entry of the United States into the Second World War in December 1941, Ho and his colleagues worked on the assumption that the defeat of Japan was only a matter of time. In the event, Japan's abrupt surrender in August 1945 caught the Vietminh off-guard: having anticipated a seizure of power in the wake of an Allied invasion, the Vietminh leadership had quickly to alter its strategy. The new aim became the swift establishment of a functioning revolutionary government throughout Vietnam in advance of the arrival of any Allied forces.

Dear compatriots

Four years ago, in one of my letters [see 1.6], I called on you to unite together. Because unity is strength, only strength enables us to win back independence and freedom.

At present, the Japanese army is crushed. The National Salvation movement has spread to the whole country. The Revolutionary Front for the Independence of Viet-Nam (Viet Minh) has millions of members from all social strata ... Recently, the Viet Minh Front convened the Viet-Nam People's Congress and appointed the National Liberation Committee to lead the entire people in the resolute struggle until national salvation is won.

This is a great advance in the history of the struggle waged for nearly a century by our people for their liberation.

This is a fact that enraptures our compatriots and fills me with great joy.

However, we cannot consider this as good enough. Our struggle will be a long and hard one. Because the Japanese are defeated, we shall not be liberated overnight. We still have to make further efforts and carry on the struggle. Only a united struggle will bring us independence.

The Viet Minh Front is at present the basis of the struggle and solidarity of our people. Join the Viet Minh Front, support it, make it greater and stronger!

At present, the National Liberation Committee is, so to speak, in itself our provisional government. Unite around it and see to it that its policies and orders are carried out throughout the country!

In this way, our Fatherland will certainly win independence and our people will certainly win freedom soon.

The decisive hour in the destiny of our people has struck. Let us stand up with all our strength to free ourselves!

Many oppressed peoples the world over are vying with each other in the march to win back their independence. We cannot allow ourselves to lag behind.

Forward! Forward! Under the banner of the Viet Minh Front, move forward courageously.

Ho Chi Minh, 'Appeal for General Insurrection', 16–17 August 1945, in Fall (ed.), *Ho Chi Minh on Revolution*, pp. 140–1.


## 1.8 The August Revolution

What followed has become known as the August Revolution – more an assumption than a seizure of power by the Vietminh. The revolution was undoubtedly aided by the absence of French resistance (in March 1945 the Japanese had ended their four-year marriage of convenience to the French and imprisoned the entire colonial administration), but its success was also due to effective Vietminh politico-military preparations. Contemporary testimony underlines the notion of a popular revolution. In this extract, a villager from Thai Binh province, in the Red River Delta of north-east Vietnam, recalls the scene in late August 1945.

The village marketplace was jammed. A man in brown pants and a cloth shirt climbed onto a chair, and guards armed with machetes, spears, and sticks surrounded him. He delivered a speech, saying that the Japanese had capitulated to the Allies, and that the time had come for the Vietminh to seize power. I was just a teenager in ragged clothes, and I asked a schoolmate, 'Now that we've seized power, who will be the mandarin?' He replied, 'Get this. The mandarin is just a peasant – really ordinary.'

Other accounts confirm the relatively bloodless nature of the Vietminh victory, a corollary of its popularity. But as the same source chronicles, violence was not wholly absent, nor was it confined to opponents of the Vietminh. Witness this account of the trial of a village official, conducted by the Vietminh before the whole village.

They read out the charges. He had been an accomplice of the Japanese pirates. He had forced the peasants to pull up their rice and plant jute and peanuts, enriching himself even though the people were miserable and dying. He admitted that he had worked for the Japanese, but claimed that he was just carrying out orders. But they announced that his crime was very serious because he had opposed the revolution and helped the enemy. So they sentenced him to death and shot him right there ... This really fired up the people. They went after the henchmen of the Japanese, dragging them out of their houses, making them lower their heads and beating them. That finished their prestige, and the fervor of the masses kept rising.

Extracts from Stanley Karnow, *Vietnam: A History* (London: Penguin, 1984 edn), pp. 145–6.


### 1.9   The Democratic Republic of Vietnam

On 2 September 1945, Ho Chi Minh addressed a crowd of 500,000 in Hanoi and announced the birth of an independent Democratic Republic of Vietnam (DRV). Historians have often commented on the irony in Ho's choice of opening words, given all that lay ahead for Vietnamese–American relations.

All men are created equal; they are endowed by their Creator with certain inalienable Rights; among these are Life, Liberty, and the pursuit of Happiness.

This immortal statement was made in the Declaration of Independence of the United States of America in 1776. In a broader sense, this means: All the peoples on the earth are equal from birth, all the peoples have a right to live, to be happy and free.

The Declaration of the French Revolution in 1791 on the Rights of Man and the Citizen also states: 'All men are born free and with equal rights, and must always remain free and have equal rights.'

Those are undeniable truths.

Nevertheless, for more than eighty years, the French imperialists, abusing the standard of Liberty, Equality, and Fraternity, have violated our Fatherland and oppressed our fellow citizens. They have acted contrary to the ideals of humanity and justice.

> Ho followed with a history of French crimes against the Vietnamese people, before returning to the present.

Notwithstanding all this, our fellow citizens have always manifested toward the French a tolerant and humane attitude. Even after the Japanese *putsch* of March, 1945,[3] the Viet Minh League helped many Frenchmen to cross the frontier, rescued some of them from Japanese jail, and protected French lives and property.

From the autumn of 1940, our country had in fact ceased to be a French colony and had become a Japanese possession.

After the Japanese had surrendered to the Allies, our whole people rose to regain our national sovereignty and to found the Democratic Republic of Viet-Nam.

The truth is that we have wrested our independence from the Japanese and not from the French.

The French have fled, the Japanese have capitulated, Emperor Bao Dai[4] has abdicated. Our people have broken the chains which for nearly a century have fettered them and have won independence for the Fatherland. Our people at the same time have overthrown the monarchic regime that has reigned supreme for dozens of centuries. In its place has been established the present Democratic Republic.

For these reasons, we, members of the Provisional Government, representing the whole Vietnamese people, declare that from now on we break off all relations of a colonial character with France; we repeal all the international obligations that France has so far subscribed to on behalf of Viet-Nam, and we abolish all the special rights the French have unlawfully acquired in our Fatherland.

The whole Vietnamese people, animated by a common purpose, are determined to fight to the bitter end against any attempt by the French colonialists to reconquer their country.

We are convinced that the Allied nations, which at Teheran and San Francisco[5] have acknowledged the principles of self-determination and equality of nations, will not refuse to acknowledge the independence of Viet-Nam.

> Ho ended with a warning which, if heard in Paris or Washington, went unheeded.

A people who have courageously opposed French domination for more than eighty years, a people who have fought side by side with the Allies against the fascists during these last years, such a people must be free and independent.

For these reasons, we, members of the Provisional Government of the Democratic Republic of Viet-Nam, solemnly declare to the world that Viet-Nam has the right to be a free and independent country – and in fact it is so already. The entire Vietnamese people are determined to mobilize all their physical and mental strength, to sacrifice their lives and property in order to safeguard their independence and liberty.

Ho Chi Minh, 'Declaration of Independence of the Democratic Republic of Viet-Nam', 2 September 1945, in Fall (ed.), *Ho Chi Minh on Revolution,* pp. 141–3.


### 1.10   Ho Chi Minh: the man and the myth

> Efforts to identify and understand Ho Chi Minh the 'man' are hampered by a paucity of reliable documentary material, particularly for this period of his life. However, the following extracts offer a variety of opinion from different perspectives. The first is by the French communist, Joseph Ducoux, who met Ho in Hong Kong in 1931.

He looked astonishingly thin and lithe. He was clean-shaven at the time, apart from a few hairs on his upper lip. His face was sharp and seemed almost charred ... I've seldom met a human being who lived so frugally and was so disdainful of every comfort. The energy he showed! He was taut and quivering ... He had only one thought in his head – and it has, I think, obsessed him all his life long. His country. Vietnam. I won't say he wasn't a sincere internationalist, a true revolutionary. But to him, Vietnam has always come first ... He devoted little time to doctrinal wrangling. He was first and foremost a militant, an organizer.

> Nguyen Manh Ha, President of the Association of Catholic Students, was appointed Minister of National Economy in the first Vietminh government in 1945. Like most Vietnamese, Ha had little first-hand knowledge of the leader of the Vietminh, although Ho was widely known by reputation.

It seemed to us that the man called Ho Chi Minh, who was rumoured to be in command of the uprising, was one and the same person as Nguyen Ai Quoc, the revolutionary whose name had haunted and fired our imagination when we were young ... Giap,[6] whom we had known at the university, and who appeared to have been directing the insurrection since 20 August, used to call us together every evening from eight until midnight for meetings of the inner cabinet, at which public affairs were discussed. One evening he told us: 'Tomorrow Ho Chi Minh will be present.' That was on 25 or 26 August.

Next day, as we stood chatting in the corridors, we saw a strange-looking figure coming towards us, clad in shorts, carrying a walking stick and wearing a most peculiar brown-painted colonial helmet. He looked a real old character. Who was he? A rural '*can bo*' (cadre) fresh from the paddy-fields? A scholar from some outlying part? Our attention was caught by a detail which in those days was altogether unusual, and which made it obvious that he was no ordinary party member: a packet of American cigarettes was sticking out of his shirt-pocket ...

Ho was very easy-going at cabinet meetings. On 1 September, the eve of the declaration of independence, he arrived with a scrap of paper on which he had drafted his proclamation to the people. He laid it before us, passing it round, accepting amendments ...

Only twice did I ever see him lose his temper. The first time was after the Minister of Propaganda, Tran Huy Lieu, the most bigoted of the Vietminh ministers, had caused a violently anti-French proclamation to be broadcast by loudspeakers in the streets of Hanoi. Ho upbraided him at the cabinet meeting: 'All right, so it's fun abusing the colonialists. And where does it get you?' On another occasion, the minister in charge of the postal services admitted that he was unable to produce the special stamps which the President had called for. Ho went for the poor man with surprising sharpness: 'There! People clamour for independence, and yet it's too much bother to print a stamp!'

In 1991, Bui Tin, a former colonel in the North Vietnamese army and one of Vietnam's most prominent journalists, offered the following retrospective.

[W]hen I became a newspaperman, I had the opportunity on many occasions to observe Ho Chi Minh when he gave interviews to journalists from the Soviet Union, China and several other countries. He was always relaxed and natural, without any affectation. It is true he lived simply and honestly. He loved children and sympathised with women as well as the poor. He hated vanity, ostentation and formality. He was also very discerning and subtle with everybody, no matter what their experience and standing. But I entirely reject any suggestion that he was a clever actor. It has to be recognised that he was a cultured and well-travelled man as well as somebody who was very human. In fact he was very much a human being and certainly not a saint. I was therefore extremely interested to learn from the French scholar Daniel Hemery that Ho Chi Minh probably had two wives. One was Marie Briere, a French Socialist Party member whom he met in Paris during the early 1920s. The other was Tang Tuyet Minh, a midwife whom he married in Canton on October 18, 1926. Yet when a report about this latter marriage was printed in the Saigon youth newspaper *Tuoi Tre* in May 1991, its editor Kim Hanh was disciplined and dismissed from her post.

What is wrong with saying that when he was young Ho Chi Minh fell in love like any other ordinary mortal? ... It is stupid to extol Ho as a saint who led an exemplary life without a thought for love, marriage or the joys of having a family.

Ducoux and Nguyen Manh Ha cited in Jean Lacouture, *Ho Chi Minh* (London: Allen Lane, 1968), pp. 47–8, 82–4; Bui Tin, *Following Ho Chi Minh: The Memoirs of a North Vietnamese Colonel* (London: Hurst & Co., 1995), pp. 16–17.

## 1.11 Vietnamese independence unravels

Ten days after Ho's declaration, British-Indian forces arrived in Saigon. Although his orders were quite specific – to take the

Japanese surrender, repatriate prisoners of war, but otherwise avoid entanglement in local politics – the British commander, Major-General Douglas Gracey, was determined to contribute to the full restoration of French rule. In particular, he sought to circumvent the Vietminh and work with the residual colonial administration, his first step being to release French military and political personnel from jail. Gracey himself was unrepentant about his actions.

On the arrival of the Allied Control Commission on September 13th, the situation was appreciated afresh and it was quite evident that unless the puppet [Vietminh] government was evicted and the French government reinstated almost immediately ... not only would the puppet government's hold on the country be consolidated, and their plans for subversive action and hooliganism be made firm, but also landing by air and sea of troops and supplies would become daily more hazardous ... [I]t was clear that the situation of inactive mob rule then existing could not be allowed to continue: it was of the greatest importance, not only to Saigon and Cholon[7] but also to the remainder of French Indo China, that administrative services should be made to function properly as soon as possible and that, therefore, law and order and proper security must first be reestablished in the Saigon–Cholon area. It was therefore inevitable that the French should reestablish control with, as a first step, the assumption of police responsibilities and the necessary disarmament of [Vietnamese] armed elements.

In later oral testimony, Gracey was altogether blunter.

I went out there [Vietnam] after the war and saw the French after they had been through a most uncomfortable time with the Japanese ... I was welcomed on arrival by the Viet Minh, who said 'Welcome' and all that sort of thing. It was a very unpleasant situation, and I promptly kicked them out. They are obviously Communists.

Gracey situation reports, 1945–46, in Peter M. Dunn, *The First Vietnam War* (London: Hurst & Co., 1985), pp. 170, 186–7; Gracey recollection from 1953, in John Saville, *The Politics of Continuity: British Foreign Policy and the Labour Government, 1945–46* (London: Verso, 1993), p. 252, note 51.

## 1.12   Ho Chi Minh looks to America

Anxious for Vietnam's independence to be confirmed by the
international community and so prevent a restoration of
French rule, Ho appealed directly to the United States, which,
during the Second World War, had publicly championed self-
determination and colonial freedom. But whatever chance
there might have been of a positive American response fell victim to the emerging Cold War in Europe. By September 1945,
the cultivation of good US–French relations, and the participation of France in any future alliance against Soviet expansion-
ism in Europe, had become a US foreign policy priority.
Consequently, the Truman administration distanced itself from
President Roosevelt's earlier wartime policy of blocking a
French restoration and placing Indochina's future in the hands
of the United Nations.

Within a month of President Truman's entry into office, the French
raised the subject of Indochina at the United Nations Conference at
San Francisco. Secretary of State [Edward] Stettinius reported the
following conversation to Washington:

'... Indo-China came up in a recent conversation I had with [French
Foreign Minister] Bidault and [French Ambassador to Washington]
Bonnet ... It was made quite clear to Bidault that the record is entirely
innocent of any official statement of this government questioning,
even by implication, French sovereignty over Indo-China. Certain elements of American public opinion, however, condemned French governmental policies and practices in Indo-China. Bidault seemed
relieved and has no doubt cabled Paris that he received renewed assurances of our recognition of French sovereignty over that area.'

... In October 1945, the United States stated its policy in the following terms:

'US has no thought of opposing the reestablishment of French control in Indochina and no official statement by US GOVT has questioned even by implication French sovereignty over Indochina.
However, it is not the policy of this GOVT to assist the French to
reestablish their control over Indochina by force and the willingness
of the US to see French control reestablished assumed that French
claim to have the support of the population of Indochina is borne out
by future events.'

US Department of Defense, *The Pentagon Papers: The Defense Department History of United States Decision-making on Vietnam*, Senator Gravel edn, 5 vols (Boston: Beacon Press, 1971), Vol. I, pp. 15–17.

## 1.13   The Ho–Sainteny agreement

By the end of 1945, the French were back in southern Vietnam, while in the north the Chinese Nationalists were behaving like an occupying force. The priority for Ho Chi Minh was the removal of the Chinese – even a negotiated return of the French to the north was a lesser evil, especially if he could obtain assurances from France about future independence. In March 1946, Ho duly concluded an agreement with Jean Sainteny, the French government's representative in Vietnam.

1. The French Government recognizes the Vietnamese Republic as a Free State having its own Government, its own Parliament, its own Army and its own Finances, forming part of the Indochinese Federation and of the French Union. In that which concerns the reuniting of the three 'Annamite Regions', the French Government pledges itself to ratify the decisions by the populations consulted by referendum.[8]

2. The Vietnamese Government declares itself ready to welcome amicably the French Army when, conforming to international agreements, it relieves the Chinese Troops. A Supplementary Accord, attached to the present Preliminary Agreement, will establish the means by which the relief operations will be carried out.

3. The stipulations formulated above will immediately enter into force. Immediately after the exchange of signatures, each of the High Contracting Parties will take all measures necessary to stop hostilities in the field, to maintain the troops in their respective positions, and to create the favorable atmosphere necessary to the immediate opening of friendly and sincere negotiations. These negotiations will deal particularly with: a) diplomatic relations of Viet-Nam with Foreign States; b) the future law of Indochina; c) French interests, economic and cultural, in Viet-Nam.

There is evidence, however, that Ho was hard-pressed to sell an agreement to the ICP that appeared to give away the last remaining gains of the August Revolution.

You fools! Don't you realize what it means if the Chinese stay? Don't you remember your history? The last time the Chinese came, they stayed one thousand years!

The French are foreigners. They are weak. Colonialism is dying out. Nothing will be able to withstand world pressure for independence. They may stay for a while, but they will have to go because the white man is finished in Asia. But if the Chinese stay now, they will never leave.

As for me, I prefer to smell French shit for five years, rather than Chinese shit for the rest of my life.

*Pentagon Papers*, Vol. I, pp. 49–50, 18–19.


## 1.14   Deadlock in Paris

By the end of March 1946, the French army was back in northern Vietnam. In August, Franco-Vietminh independence talks in Paris collapsed. Ho stayed on in France in the hope of extracting last-minute concessions that would strengthen his position *vis-à-vis* the extremists in his government who had begun to question not just the point of negotiations, but also Ho's leadership. Ho was given the so-called *modus vivendi* of 14 September 1946.

I left for France over four months ago. Today I am back home. I am very happy to see the Fatherland and you again. I have the following statements to make ...

The Vietnamese–French Conference has not ended yet. It will resume next May, but the September 14 *modus vivendi* has, firstly, permitted the Vietnamese and French to carry out their business easily, and secondly, it has paved the way for the next Conference to be conducted in a friendly manner ...

The French Government has acknowledged the holding of a referendum by our southern compatriots to decide on the fate of the South. In the September 14 *modus vivendi*, the French Government agreed to implement the main points concerning the South as follows:

1) Political prisoners and those arrested for taking part in the resistance are to be released.

2) Our southern compatriots are to have freedom of organization,

of meeting, of the press, of movement, etc.

3) Both parties are to stop fighting.

Now, what must our southern compatriots have to do?

1) The Vietnamese army, like the French army, must simultaneously stop fighting.

2) Our compatriots must carry out political actions in a democratic way.

3) Close unity must be realized with no discrimination as to political parties, social classes, and creeds. Unity means strength. Division means weakness.

4) Acts of reprisal are forbidden. Toward those who went astray, our compatriots must display a generous policy. We must let them hear the voice of reason. Everybody loves his country. It is only for petty interests that they forget the great cause. If we use the right words, they will certainly listen to us. Violent actions are absolutely forbidden. This is what you have to do at present to create a peaceful atmosphere, paving the way democratically to reach the unification of our Viet-Nam.

Ho Chi Minh, 'Proclamation to the People upon Return from France after Negotiations', 23 October 1946, in Fall (ed.), *Ho Chi Minh on Revolution*, pp. 160–1.

## 1.15  War

The *modus vivendi* – essentially an agreement to talk again in the future – satisfied neither the war-party in the Vietminh nor the French colonial regime in Vietnam. Full-scale war was only an incident away: the shelling of Haiphong in November 1946 might have been the catalyst, but in the end if was a confrontation in Hanoi the following month that ignited the Franco-Vietminh war.

Compatriots all over the country!

As we desired peace, we made concessions. But the more we made concessions, the further the French colonialists went because they are resolved to invade our country once again. No! We would rather sacrifice all than lose our country. We are determined not to be enslaved.

Compatriots! Rise up! Men and women, old and young, regardless of creeds, political parties, or nationalities, all the Vietnamese must stand up to fight the French colonialists to save the Fatherland. Those who have rifles will use their rifles; those who have swords will use their swords; those who have no swords will use spades, hoes, or sticks. Everyone must endeavor to oppose the colonialists and save his country.

Armymen, self-defense guards, and militiamen! The hour for national salvation has struck! We must sacrifice even our last drop of blood to safeguard our country. Even if we have to endure hardship in the Resistance War, with the determination to make sacrifices, victory will surely be ours.

Long live an independent and unified Viet-Nam!

Long live the victorious Resistance!

Ho Chi Minh, 'Appeal to the Entire People to Wage the Resistance War', 20 December 1946, in Fall (ed.), *Ho Chi Minh on Revolution*, p. 162.

# 2

# The Franco-Vietminh war, 1946–1954

By 1948, the French found themselves mired in an enervating military struggle against an elusive but deadly enemy. From the very outset, Vietminh strategy, borrowing much from the military teachings of Mao Zedong, was specifically designed to frustrate the French and their superiority in conventional arms. The Vietminh's first objective was the construction of a secure rear base in the mountains of northern Vietnam, a task accomplished by the end of 1947; thereafter the Vietminh engaged in protracted guerrilla warfare that steadily debilitated the French; eventually the Vietminh planned to launch a general offensive in the countryside (with guerrilla warfare giving way to conventional large-scale engagements), while pre-planned political risings in urban areas would complement the military offensive and ensure the triumph of People's War, as Ho and his colleagues referred to this strategy (2.1). In practice, however, the Vietminh tended to confine themselves to attritional guerrilla warfare for much of 1946–54.

What had begun as a colonial war of reconquest took on a new and potentially incendiary character at the start of 1950 when the United States inaugurated a military assistance programme for France which by 1954 was underwriting almost 80 per cent of the total financial cost of the war effort (2.3). At the same time, the newly established People's Republic of China (PRC) extended military aid and advice to the Vietminh, helping to transform a 'peasant army' into an effective and well-armed fighting force (2.16). Thus, from 1950 onwards, the Franco-Vietminh war was simultaneously a colonial conflict and a major Cold War issue – a Sino-American war-by-proxy with the potential to escalate into a direct confrontation. This danger was particularly clear and present in 1954, when the war entered its climactic phase. Despite massive US assistance, the French had been unable to wrest the military initiative from the Vietminh, whose forces controlled large swathes of rural Vietnam. Politically, the Vietminh retained a high degree of popularity and nationalist legitimacy. In France itself, meanwhile, war weariness had led to a marked growth in political and public support for a negotiated solution (2.4). The impending crisis finally broke on 13 March 1954 when the Vietminh attacked Dien Bien Phu, a fortress in north-west Vietnam garrisoned by 16,000 French troops, in the start of what proved to be the decisive battle of the war.

French strategists had initially planned to lure the Vietminh into a set-piece confrontation where French firepower could – for once – be employed effectively; after inflicting a serious defeat on their enemy, the French could then approach negotiations from a position of military strength (an international conference was scheduled to open at Geneva on 26 April with Indochina among the top agenda items). This, at least, was the theory. But from the moment that the garrison's airstrip – its lifeline to the outside world – was put out of action, the Vietminh attackers had the French trapped in a deadly noose. For the US government, the Dien Bien Phu crisis posed an acute dilemma: policy-makers feared that defeat for the French could lead to a military rout throughout Vietnam and the loss of the keystone of Southeast Asia's Cold War security (2.5, 2.9); almost as worrying, defeat might spawn a French diplomatic capitulation to the Vietminh at the looming Geneva conference. It was against this backdrop that the Eisenhower administration issued a public call for 'united action' – military intervention by a 'free world' coalition to prop up the French position in Vietnam and, by extension, the French position at Geneva (2.6). In the event, there was no 'united action', only a humiliating French defeat at Dien Bien Phu on 7 May 1954. At Geneva, in July, the war was formally ended. Vietnam was partitioned pending nationwide elections in 1956, after which the residual French presence would be terminated and Vietnam would be reunited and independent under, in all probability, Ho Chi Minh and the Vietminh (2.13).

It is now clear that one of the reasons for the failure of US plans for 'united action' was the refusal of Britain – Washington's closest ally – to endorse a military solution. The British preferred to work instead for a political settlement at Geneva (2.7, 2.11). However, some historians have argued that the United States was never serious about military action, but *threatened* intervention in order to panic the Soviets and the Chinese into pressing the Vietminh to grant the French favourable terms. Leaving aside the question of American intent, the Vietminh certainly compromised at Geneva, and certainly did so under pressure from their more powerful communist allies (2.14, 2.15). Indeed in 1979, Hanoi would accuse the Chinese in particular of putting their own interests before those of the Vietnamese revolution in 1954. Of course, had the Geneva settlement been implemented, Hanoi would have taken a more sanguine view. But neither the United States nor the southern Vietnamese government of Ngo Dinh Diem (Bao Dai's Prime Minister) had any stomach for the projected 1956 elections (not least because the Vietminh were expected to win them), and preferred to work to ensure that the temporary partition became permanent. In doing so, they would sow the seeds of a new and even bloodier conflict in Vietnam.

## 2.1 People's War

The Vietminh always maintained that they were fighting a People's War – a war for and on behalf of the Vietnamese people. According to General Vo Nguyen Giap, the Vietminh's military commander, People's War was, in effect, 'total war'.

Our nationwide resistance war [against France], which was a people's war, was a new development; it was a *true revolutionary war, a war by the entire people, a total war*. A revolutionary war, because it was carried out on the basis of the mobilization and organization of the masses, with the aim of achieving a national democratic revolution. A war by the entire people, because it was a war in which our Party's correct revolutionary line succeeded in grouping all patriotic strata of the population in a broad front based on a strong worker–peasant alliance, and mobilizing them for the struggle. A total war, because armed struggle was frequently combined with political struggle, because at the same time as we engaged in a military struggle, we carried out reduction of land rent, land reform, political struggle in urban centers and enemy-occupied areas, and struggle in the economic and cultural fields.

In theory, the military struggle had to pass from the guerrilla war stage to regular war if victory was to be achieved.

To keep the offensive, [the revolutionaries] must ceaselessly develop guerrilla war and partial insurrection. From regional forces, they must build increasingly strong main force units, and incessantly develop the guerrilla war into a regular war. Only through *regular war* in which the main force troops fight in a concentrated manner and the armed services are combined and fighting in coordination with regional troops, militia guerrillas, and the political forces of the people, can they annihilate important forces of the enemy, liberate vast areas of land ... and create conditions for great strides in the war.

> Inevitably, French conventional military superiority left the Vietminh no alternative but to rely largely on guerrilla warfare for much of the war. Yet Ho, like Giap, remained convinced of eventual victory, likening the war to a struggle between a tiger (the Vietminh) and an elephant (France).

If the tiger ever stands still the elephant will crush him with his mighty tusks. But the tiger does not stand still. He lurks in the jungle by day and emerges by night. He will leap upon the back of the elephant, tearing huge chunks from his hide, and then he will leap back into the dark jungle. And slowly the elephant will bleed to death.

Giap cited in Marvin E. Gettleman *et al.* (eds), *Vietnam and America: The Most Comprehensive Documented History of the Vietnam War* (New York: Grove Press, 1995), pp. 195–6, and William J. Duiker, *The Communist Road to Power in Vietnam* (Boulder: Westview Press, 1996 edn), p. 306; Ho Chi Minh cited in Jean Lacouture, *Ho Chi Minh* (London: Allen Lane, 1968), p. 138.

## 2.2   Colonial war or Cold War battleground?

The French, in an attempt to secure American military assistance, increasingly emphasised the Vietminh's communist character, and argued that they were manning a vital Cold War battlement in Southeast Asia. The US government, wary about backing a European colonial enterprise, first sought proof that Ho was an agent of Moscow. But in the late 1940s, such proof was hard to come by.

U.S. attempts to discern the nature and extent of communist influence in Vietnam devolved to the seeming paradox that if Ho Chi Minh were communist, he seemed to have no visible ties with Moscow ... In the fall of 1948, the Office of Intelligence Research in the Department of State conducted a survey of communist influence in Southeast Asia. Evidence of Kremlin-directed conspiracy was found in virtually all countries except Vietnam ...

*Evaluation.* If there is a Moscow-directed conspiracy in Southeast Asia, Indochina is an anomaly so far. Possible explanations are:

1. No rigid directives have been issued by Moscow.

2. The Vietnam government considers that it has no rightist elements that must be purged.

3. The Vietnam Communists are not subservient to the foreign policies pursued by Moscow.

4. A special dispensation for the Vietnam government has been arranged in Moscow.

Of these possibilities, the first and fourth seem most likely.

> In May 1949, with the Cold War intensifying, US Secretary of State, Dean Acheson, issued an abrupt directive that ended the debate on Ho's political outlook.

Question whether Ho as much nationalist as Commie is irrelevant. All Stalinists in colonial areas are nationalists. With achievement [of] national state (i.e., independence) their objective necessarily becomes subordination [of] state to Commie purposes and ruthless extermination [of] not only opposition groups but all elements suspected [of] even slightest deviation.

US Department of Defense, *The Pentagon Papers: The Defense Department History of United States Decision-making on Vietnam*, Senator Gravel edn, 5 vols (Boston: Beacon Press, 1971), Vol. I, pp. 33–4, 51.

## 2.3  Two Vietnams

> Early in 1950, the DRV government issued an international appeal for diplomatic recognition.

Determined to safeguard their national independence from the French colonialists, the Vietnamese people and army are fighting heroically and are nearing final victory. Throughout these years of resistance, Viet Nam has won the sympathy and support of the people of the world. The Government of the Democratic Republic of Viet-Nam declares to the Governments of the countries of the world that it is the only lawful Government of the entire Vietnamese people. On the basis of common interests, it is ready to establish diplomatic relations with the Governments of all countries which respect the equality, territorial sovereignty, and national independence of Viet-Nam in order to contribute to safeguarding peace and building world democracy.

> Both the Soviet Union and the newly established People's Republic of China (PRC) responded positively to the DRV's appeal, an action that helped the Americans to locate Ho and the Vietminh firmly in the international communist camp and remove any lingering doubts in Washington about siding with French colonialism. In February 1950, the Truman administration formally recognised the so-called Associated States of Vietnam, Laos and Cambodia – French-sponsored native alternatives to the Vietminh – and acknowledged their 'independence' within the French Union.

Recognition by the United States of the three legally constituted governments of Vietnam, Laos and Cambodia appears desirable and in accordance with United States policy for several reasons. Among them are: encouragement to national aspirations under non-Communist leadership for peoples of colonial areas in Southeast Asia; the establishment of stable non-Communist governments in areas adjacent to Communist China; support to a friendly country which is also a signatory to the North Atlantic Treaty; and as a demonstration of displeasure with Communist tactics which are obviously aimed at eventual domination of Asia, working under the guise of indigenous nationalism.

> Although US policy-makers continued to harbour misgivings about the level of true independence enjoyed by the Associated States, in 1950 anti-communism had clearly superseded anti-colonialism as the principal determinant of US policy.

The choice confronting the United States is to support the French in Indochina or face the extension of Communism over the remainder of the continental area of Southeast Asia and, possibly, farther westward. We then would be obliged to make staggering investments in those areas and in that part of Southeast Asia remaining outside Communist domination or withdraw to a much-contracted Pacific line. It would seem a case of 'Penny wise, Pound foolish' to deny support to the French in Indochina.

DRV declaration, 14 January 1950, in Bernard B. Fall (ed.), *Ho Chi Minh on Revolution: Selected Writing, 1920–66* (New York: Praegar, 1967), pp. 182–3; Acheson memorandum to Truman, 2 February 1950, *Pentagon Papers*, Vol. I, pp. 64–5; *Foreign Relations of the United States (FRUS) 1950*, Vol. VI (Washington DC: Government Printing Office, 1976), p. 714, State Department memorandum, 1 February 1950.

## 2.4 War and peace, November 1953

By late 1953, the Vietminh held the military initiative in Vietnam, with the French, lacking the manpower for offensive operations, reduced to passive defensive measures. In France, meanwhile, political and public opinion was increasingly critical of the war, and by the autumn of 1953 talk of a negotiated settlement was in the air. Ho Chi Minh was quick to take advantage of such talk, his proposals below reflecting either a sincerely held view or his unswerving allegiance to Moscow (which was engaged in a 'peace offensive' following Stalin's death).

[Ho Chi Minh]: ... the war has been forced upon us by the French Government ... But if the French Government has learnt a lesson from these years of war and wishes to bring about an armistice and solve the Viet-Nam problem through negotiations, the [DRV] people and Government are ready ... The war has caused our people many hardships. It has also caused much suffering for the people of France. This is the reason why the French people oppose the war in Viet-Nam. I have always felt great sympathy and admiration for the people of France and the partisans of peace in France. It is not only the independence of Viet-Nam which is to-day exposed to severe attacks. The independence of France is also seriously threatened. On the one side American imperialism drives the French colonialists to continue and extend the war of reconquest in Viet-Nam with the object of making France weaker and weaker and overtaking her place in Viet-Nam. On the other side American imperialism forces France to sign the European Defence Pact which means the rebirth of German militarism.[1] The struggle of the French people for independence, democracy and peace and an end to the war in Viet-Nam forms one of the important factors in the endeavour to solve the Viet-Nam problem.

Ho Chi Minh, interview with S. Lofgren, published in Stockholm, 29 November 1953, in Cmnd 2834, *Documents Relating to British Involvement in the Indo-China Conflict 1945–1965*, Misc. No. 25 (London: HMSO, 1965), pp. 64–5.

## 2.5  1954 – year of decision

The crucial year in the Franco-Vietminh conflict came in 1954. At the beginning of the year, the National Security Council in Washington outlined the significance of Indochina to US national security. This assessment of the stakes involved adhered closely to the contours of similar assessments since 1950. In all analyses, Vietnam was posited as the trigger-domino in what would become known as the domino theory.

1. Communist domination, by whatever means, of all Southeast Asia would seriously endanger in the short term, and critically endanger in the long term, United States security interests.

a) In the conflict in Indochina, the Communist and non-Communist worlds clearly confront one another on the field of battle. The loss of the struggle in Indochina, in addition to its impact on Southeast Asia and in South Asia, would therefore have the most serious repercussions on U.S. and free world interests in Europe and elsewhere.

b) Such is the interrelation of the countries of the area that effective counteraction would be immediately necessary to prevent the loss of any single country from leading to submission to or an alignment with communism by the remaining countries of Southeast Asia and Indonesia. Furthermore, in the event all of Southeast Asia falls under communism, an alignment with communism of India, and in the longer term, of the Middle East (with the probable exceptions of at least Pakistan and Turkey) could follow progressively. Such widespread alignment would seriously endanger the stability and security of Europe.

c) Communist control of all of Southeast Asia and Indonesia would threaten the U.S. position in the Pacific offshore island chain and would seriously jeopardise fundamental U.S. security interests in the Far East.

d) The loss of Southeast Asia would have serious economic consequences for many nations of the free world and conversely would add significant resources to the Soviet bloc. Southeast Asia, especially Malaya and Indonesia, is the principal world source of natural rubber and tin, and a producer of petroleum and other strategically important commodities. The rice exports of Burma, Indochina and Thailand are critically important to Malaya, Ceylon and Hong Kong and are of considerable significance to Japan and India, all important areas of free Asia. Furthermore, this area has an important potential as a market for the industrialized countries of the free world.

e) The loss of Southeast Asia, especially of Malaya and Indonesia, could result in such economic and political pressures in Japan as to make it extremely difficult to prevent Japan's eventual accommodation to communism.

NSC 5405, 'United States Objectives and Courses of Action with Respect to Southeast Asia' (excerpts), 16 January 1954, in *Pentagon Papers,* Vol. I, pp. 434–43.

## 2.6  United action

On 13 March 1954, the decisive battle of the Franco-Vietminh war opened at Dien Bien Phu. Very early on, it was clear that the French were in trouble. After intensive inter-agency debate in Washington, the US government opted to create a coalition of powers to intervene in Vietnam to bolster the French position beyond Dien Bien Phu and insure against a French policy of scuttle at the forthcoming Geneva conference.

The Chinese Communists have ... avoided the direct use of their own Red Armies in open aggression against Indochina. They have, however, largely stepped up their support of the aggression in that area. Indeed, they promote that aggression by all means short of open invasion. Under all the circumstances it seems desirable to clarify further the United States position.

Under the conditions of today, the imposition on Southeast Asia of the political system of Communist Russia and its Chinese Communist ally, by whatever means, must be a grave threat to the whole free community. The United States feels that that possibility should not be passively accepted but should be met by united action. This might involve serious risks. But these risks are far less than those that will face us a few years from now if we dare not be resolute today.

The free nations want peace. However, peace is not had merely by wanting it. Peace has to be worked for and planned for. Sometimes it is necessary to take risks to win peace just as it is necessary in war to take risks to win victory. The chances for peace are usually bettered by letting a potential aggressor know in advance where his aggression could lead him.

Speech by US Secretary of State, John Foster Dulles, to the Overseas Press Club, New York, 29 March 1954, in *Department of State Bulletin No. 30* (12 April 1954), pp. 539–40.

## 2.7  An Anglo-American crisis

The crisis of 1954 was also an Anglo-American crisis, for just as the Eisenhower administration appeared to commit itself to a military solution, Winston Churchill's Conservative government was dedicating itself to the pursuit of a political settlement at Geneva.

Any direct intervention by the armed forces of any external nation ... would probably result in Chinese intervention, with the danger that this might ultimately lead to global war. Our influence should therefore be used against these more dangerous forms of deeper United States involvement ...

Recommendations:-

(a) Before and at Geneva we should continue to emphasise to the French Government the lamentable consequences which would flow from a capitulation to Communist demands. So long as there is any hope of success we should continue to urge the French to maintain their present policy of improving the military situation while satisfying the political aspirations of the Associate States.[2]

(b) Provided the French are willing to carry on, the provision by the United States of increased military aid and instructors appears to be the most hopeful military expedient. Any more dangerous form of United States involvement should be discouraged.

(c) If it becomes clear that the French are determined to reach a settlement, we should use our influence in favour of the solution least detrimental to our interests in South-East Asia.

Public Record Office (PRO), London, FO 371/112049/103G, Foreign Office memorandum, 'Policy Towards Indo-China', 31 March 1954.

## 2.8  The Americans court Churchill

Aware that congressional approval for warlike action in Vietnam depended on allied support in general and on London's support in particular, the US government put the British under great pressure to fall in behind 'united action', with President Eisenhower even playing on the ageing Churchill's vanity.

I have in mind in addition to our two countries, France, the Associated States, Australia, New Zealand, Thailand and the Philippines. The United States Government would expect to play its full part in such a coalition. The coalition we have in mind would not be directed against Communist China. But if, contrary to our belief, our efforts to save Indochina and the British Commonwealth position to the south should in any way increase the jeopardy to Hong Kong, we would expect to be with you there ...

The important thing is that the coalition must be strong and it must be willing to join the fight if necessary. I do not envisage any appreciable ground forces on your or our part. If the members of the alliance are sufficiently resolute it should be able to make clear to the Chinese Communists that the continuation of their material support to the Viet Minh will inevitably lead to the growing power of the resources arrayed against them.

My colleagues and I are deeply aware of the risks which this proposal may involve but in the situation which confronts us there is no course of action or inaction devoid of dangers and I know no man who has firmly grasped more nettles than you. If we grasp this one together I believe that we will enormously increase our chances of bringing the Chinese to believe that their interests lie in the direction of a discreet disengagement. In such a contingency we could approach the Geneva conference with the position of the free world not only unimpaired but strengthened.

Today we face the hard situation of contemplating a disaster brought on by French weakness and the necessity of dealing with it before it develops. This means frank talk with the French. In many ways the situation corresponds to that which you describe so brilliantly in the second chapter of *Their Finest Hour*,[3] when history made clear that the French strategy and dispositions before the 1940 breakthrough should have been challenged before the blow fell ...

If I may refer again to history, we failed to halt Hirohito, Mussolini and Hitler by not acting in unity and in time. That marked the beginning of many years of stark tragedy and desperate peril. May it not be that our nations have learned something from that lesson?

PRO, PREM 11/1074, Eisenhower letter to Churchill, 4 April 1954.


## 2.9  The domino theory unveiled

> Alongside its search for allies, the Eisenhower administration embarked on an education campaign designed to prepare the American people for possible military action in a faraway country of which they knew little. The President himself provided the most enduring image of Vietnam's importance in response to a question from a journalist about the country's 'strategic importance'.

You have, of course, both the specific and the general when you talk about such things. First of all, you have the specific value of a locality in its production of materials that the world needs. Then you have the possibility that many human beings pass under a dictatorship that is inimical to the free world. Finally, you have the broader considerations that might follow what you would call the 'falling domino' principle. You have a row of dominoes set up, you knock over the first one, and what will happen to the last one is the certainty that it will go over very quickly. So you could have a beginning of a disintegration that would have the most profound influences.

Eisenhower news conference, 7 April 1954, in *Public Papers of the Presidents of the United States: Dwight D. Eisenhower, 1954* (Washington DC: Government Printing Office, 1960), pp. 382–3.

## 2.10   Churchill stands firm

Churchill, though troubled by Anglo-American differences over Vietnam, remained steadfast in his opposition to military action, rebuffing yet another appeal delivered on the eve of the Geneva conference by the hawkish chairman of the US Joint Chiefs of Staff, Admiral Arthur Radford.

Radford said that the fall of Dien Bien Phu, and failure of the United States and Great Britain to take appropriate action, would be a great victory for the Communists and a turning point in history ... This was the critical moment to make a stand against China and he did not think that the Russians, who were frightened of war, would go openly to the aid of the Chinese ...

The Prime Minister said that he admitted the fall of Dien Bien Phu might be a critical moment in history ... [But the] British people would not be easily influenced by what happened in the distant jungles of S. E. Asia; but they did know that there was a powerful American base in East Anglia and that war with China, who would invoke the Sino-Russian Pact, might mean an assault by Hydrogen bombs on these islands. We could not commit ourselves at this moment, when all these matters were about to be discussed at Geneva, to a policy which might lead by slow stages to a catastrophe ...

PRO, FO 371/112057/360G, record of Churchill–Radford dinner, Chequers, 26 April 1954.

## 2.11   Dien Bien Phu and after ...

The resistance of the garrison at Dien Bien Phu ended on 7 May 1954. During the 54-day battle, the French lost 1,500 men killed, 4,000 wounded and 10,000 taken prisoner. Vietminh casualties amounted to some 8,000 dead and 15,000 wounded. In the aftermath of battle, the Americans appeared to revert to their earlier preference for a military solution in the hope of salvaging something from the wreck. For British Foreign Secretary Anthony Eden, the leading advocate of a peaceful solution at Geneva, American behaviour was decidedly unhelpful.

The American attitude becomes increasingly disturbing. It is no doubt true that they are irritated with their Allies – with the French because they won't fight without help, which in the end means troops, and with us because we want to give this conference a chance to reach agreement before we discuss in detail a Pacific pact.[4] I am doing everything I can to bring the real Asiatic powers along but the Americans are too impatient. Also I must say that I think they are jealous of our authority and following here. They like to give orders, and if they are not at once obeyed they become huffy. That is their conception of an alliance – of Dulles' anyway. Unhappily they have never really put their weight behind this conference and made an effort to get an agreement ... You know that Radford's policy has for some time been intervention in Indo-China, and in China too. Some aspects of American policy are only comprehensible to me if that view is held by others in addition to Radford.

> In contrast to the Americans, Eden was sceptical about the domino theory.

I do not personally agree with the people who suggest that if Indo-China were to go, Siam, Malaya etc., must be indefensible. They would obviously be much more difficult to defend, but that is not in itself a reason for intervening in Indo-China, even if we could do so effectively at this stage. If something could be saved from the wreck in that country, well and good. But we do not want to bring a greater disaster upon our heads by trying to avert the immediate one.

Eden (Geneva) letters to Lord Salisbury, 16 May 1954, and to Selwyn Lloyd, 21 May 1954, in the Avon Papers, University of Birmingham, AP20/17/118A and 15A.

## 2.12   Ho Chi Minh on the prospects for peace

During a recess at Geneva, Ho Chi Minh met the Chinese Prime Minister Zhou Enlai. Zhou evidently urged the Vietminh to compromise in the interests of a swift settlement. The recent advent of a French government under Pierre Mendès-France that was wholly dedicated to a peaceful solution offered the Vietminh the opportunity to secure most of their aims by means short of war whilst simultaneously extinguishing any remaining danger of American military intervention and a 'new' Korea (China's main concern). In reporting back to the Party Central Committee, Ho seemed persuaded of this logic.

Faced with the Geneva Conference and our victory at Dien Bien Phu, the United States plotted to issue a 'joint declaration' with France, Britain and a number of other countries to intimidate China, charging it with intervention in the Indochina war. But due to opposition from Britain and reluctance from the other countries, the move failed. Then the Americans proposed 'joint action' to save France at Dien Bien Phu but Britain and the other countries again disagreed, and this scheme also failed. The Americans have used every means to sabotage the Geneva Conference. The US Secretary of State attended the Conference for only a few days then left, but the Conference has continued none the less and has led to some results ...

Viet Nam, China and the Soviet Union are closely united. Owing to contradictions among the imperialists, to our own efforts and to those of our camp, we have managed to secure a few fairly important agreements. The French Government being now in the hands of those who stand for peace, there are better chances for an end to the Indochina war.

During the recess at the Geneva Conference, the chief delegates have returned home, leaving things in the hands of their deputies. Availing himself of this occasion, Comrade Chou En-lai, Prime Minister of the People's Republic of China, has visited India and Burma [where he met Ho] ... My meeting with Comrade Chou has also been fruitful. The friendly meetings between Comrade Chou En-lai and the representatives of India, Burma and Viet Nam have tightened solidarity among the Asian nations. This is a success for our camp.

The present situation in the world, in Asia and at home, holds out prospects of peace for our country. However, the US imperialists are bent on sabotage; in France there remain bellicose groups; the pro-American puppets also strive to wreck the peace; and so the war may still go on.

That is the characteristic feature of the new situation in our country.

> Turning to those in the Vietnam Workers' Party (as the ICP was renamed in 1951) who balked at the idea of a temporary parti-tion of Vietnam, the likely outcome of Geneva, Ho offered a warning.

The following ideological errors may be committed: *Leftist deviation.* Some people, intoxicated with our repeated victories, want to fight on at all costs, to a finish; they see only the trees, not the whole forest; with their attention focused on the withdrawal of the French they fail to detect their schemes; they see the French but they do not see the Americans; they are partial to military action and make light of diplo-macy. They are unaware that we are struggling in international con-ferences as well as on the battlefields in order to attain our goal. They will oppose the new slogans, which they deem to be rightist manifesta-tions and to imply too many concessions. They set forth excessive conditions unacceptable to the enemy. They want quick results, una-ware that the struggle for peace is a hard and complex one. Leftist deviation will cause one to be isolated, alienated from one's own peo-ple and those of the world, and suffer set-backs. *Rightist deviation* will lead to pessimism, inaction and unprincipled concessions. It causes one to lack confidence in the people's strength and to blunt their combative spirit; to lose the power to endure hardships and to aspire only to a quiet and easy life. Leftist and rightist tendencies are both wrong. They will be exploited by the enemy; they will benefit them and harm us.

Ho Chi Minh, Report to the Sixth Plenum of the Vietnam Workers' Party Central Committee, 15 July 1954, in Ho Chi Minh, *Selected Writ-ings, 1920–1969* (Hanoi: Foreign Languages Publishing House, 1973), pp. 174–7.

## 2.13   The Geneva settlement

On 21 July 1954, the Geneva conference ended. Apart from
the cease-fire articles signed on the ground in Vietnam, Laos
and Cambodia, the most important document was the Final
Declaration of the conference which chronicled the political
aspects of the settlement. Vietnam was to be divided at the seventeenth parallel, with the Vietminh regrouping to the north
and the French and their supporters to the south. Both zones
were to follow a foreign policy of neutrality until nationwide
elections were held in July 1956 to reunite the country under a
single government and thereby solemnise Vietnam's freedom.
Critically, the Final Declaration was not a signed and legally
binding treaty, and so offered disgruntled parties (like the
Americans) scope for evading its provisions in the future. The
following Articles are the key ones in terms of the subsequent
history of Vietnam.

ARTICLE 4
The Conference takes note of the clauses in the agreement on the cessation of hostilities in Vietnam prohibiting the introduction into Vietnam of foreign troops and military personnel as well as of all kinds of
arms and munitions ...

ARTICLE 5
The Conference takes note of the clauses in the agreement on the cessation of hostilities in Vietnam to the effect that no military base
under the control of a foreign State may be established in the
regrouping zones of the two parties, the latter having the obligation to
see that the zones allotted to them shall not constitute part of any
military alliance and shall not be utilised for the resumption of hostilities or in the service of an aggressive policy ...

ARTICLE 6
The Conference recognises that the essential purpose of the agreement
relating to Vietnam is to settle military questions with a view to ending hostilities and that the military demarcation line is provisional and
should not in any way be interpreted as constituting a political or
territorial boundary. The Conference expresses its conviction that the
execution of the provisions set out in the present declaration and in
the agreement on the cessation of hostilities creates the necessary basis

for the achievement in the near future of a political settlement in Vietnam.

ARTICLE 7
The Conference declares that, so far as Vietnam is concerned, the settlement of political problems, effected on the basis of respect for the principles of independence, unity and territorial integrity, shall permit the Vietnamese people to enjoy the fundamental freedoms, guaranteed by democratic institutions established as a result of free general elections by secret ballot. In order to ensure that sufficient progress in the restoration of peace has been made, and that all the necessary conditions obtain for free expression of the national will, general elections shall be held in July, 1956, under the supervision of an international commission composed of representatives of the member States of the International Supervisory Commission, referred to in the agreement on the cessation of hostilities.[5] Consultations will be held on this subject between the competent representative authorities of the two zones from 20 July, 1955, onwards.

Cmnd 2834, pp. 83–5.

## 2.14   Ho Chi Minh on the Geneva dénouement

The day after the Geneva conference ended, Ho Chi Minh offered a personal assessment of the settlement.

The Geneva Conference has come to an end. It is a great victory for our diplomacy. On behalf of the Government, I cordially make the following appeal.

For the sake of peace, unity, independence, and democracy of the Fatherland, our people, armymen, cadres, and Government have, during these eight years or so, joined in a monolithic bloc, endured hardship, and resolutely overcome all difficulties to carry out the Resistance; we have won many brilliant victories. On this occasion, on behalf of the Government, I cordially congratulate you, from North to South. I respectfully bow to the memory of the armymen and people who have sacrificed their lives for the Fatherland, and send my homages of comfort to the wounded and sick armymen.

This great victory is also due to the support given us in our just struggle by the peoples of our brother countries, by the French people, and by the peace-loving people of the world. Thanks to these victories and the efforts made by the delegation of the Soviet Union at the Berlin Conference,[6] negotiations were opened between our country and France at the Geneva Conference. At this conference, the struggle of our delegation and the assistance given by the delegations of the Soviet Union and China have ended in a great victory for us: The French Government has recognized the independence, sovereignty, unity, and territorial integrity of our country; it has agreed to withdraw French troops from our country, etc.

From now on, we must make every effort to consolidate peace and achieve reunification, independence, and democracy throughout our country ...

... We are resolved to abide by the agreements entered into with the French Government. At the same time, we demand that the French Government correctly implement the agreements they have signed with us.

We must do our utmost to strengthen peace and be vigilant to check the manoeuvres of peace wreckers. We must endeavor to struggle for the holding of free general elections throughout the country to reunify our territory. We must exert all our efforts to restore, build, strengthen, and develop our forces in every field so as to attain complete independence. We must do our utmost to carry out social reforms in order to improve our people's livelihood and realize genuine democracy.

We further tighten our fraternal relations with Cambodia and Laos. We strengthen the great friendship between us and the Soviet Union, China, and other brother countries. To maintain peace, we enhance our solidarity with the French people, and people all over the world ...

... If our people are as one, if thousands of men are like one, victory will certainly be ours.

Long live a peaceful, unified, independent, and democratic Viet-Nam.

Ho Chi Minh, 'Appeal Made After the Successful Conclusion of the Geneva Agreements', 22 July 1954, in Fall (ed.), *Ho Chi Minh on Revolution*, pp. 246–7.

## 2.15 The White Book

Ho's open expression of gratitude to Communist China and the Soviet Union, though not necessarily disingenuous, obscured what seems to have been Vietminh resentment at pressure from Beijing and Moscow to accept a settlement that failed to reflect their battlefield supremacy. In 1979, Hanoi published the White Book, a candid account of Sino-Vietminh relations which argued, *inter alia*, that the Vietminh had been betrayed at Geneva. Emerging at a time of unprecedented Sino-Vietnamese tension and enmity, the White Book is clearly partisan, but its value as a source is still considerable. The historian R. B. Smith has summarised the issues brought forth in its pages.

Ho Chi Minh accepted the [Geneva] settlement as a matter of international Communist discipline, and also because the military dependence of the Viet-Minh on China (and ultimately the Soviet Union) would not have allowed them to fight on alone in the face of greater United States involvement. But some Vietnamese Communist leaders resented the decision especially deeply, even though they remained silent. Twenty-five years later, in the 'White Book' of 1979, Le Duan[7] finally brought their resentment into the open, directing it specifically at Peking. He alleged that, during the months leading up to the Agreement, Zhou Enlai had brought pressure to bear on the Viet-Minh to accept a ceasefire at a time when they had the military advantage and ought to have continued the struggle until final victory. There seems to be general agreement amongst students of the diplomacy of Geneva that Zhou Enlai did indeed take the initiative in promoting a settlement, by urging the concessions which made agreement possible. But no mention was made in 1979 of the Soviet position, which had also been in favour of compromise at Geneva. Since Vietnam was essentially an Asian problem, the Soviet leaders probably took the view that Zhou should resolve it in his own way if a solution was possible – leaving the Russians free to present themselves to the Vietnamese as advocates of a 'harder' line than the one actually adopted ...

In reply [to the 'White Book'] the Chinese rejected the implication that they had positively encouraged the partition of Vietnam. The military realities of 1954 had left no alternative, since without an agreement the war would have escalated to a new level of violence.

There would have been no French withdrawal, and a much greater level of American involvement, which in turn would have required greater commitment from the Chinese. The Vietnamese 'White Book' played down the extent of Viet-Minh dependence on Chinese military aid, and it was left to the former Vietnamese Politburo-member Hoang Van Hoan (by 1979 an exile in Peking) to reveal that during the early 1950s the Viet-Minh had been assisted by a Chinese advisory mission headed by General Wei Guoqing and that the celebrated victory of Dien-Bien-Phu had only been achieved – as Western intelligence experts have always alleged – because the Vietnamese could rely on Chinese technical support. Without such assistance during the years 1952–4 ... the Viet-Minh would have been quite unable to counter the increase in French firepower resulting from the American aid programme inaugurated in 1950. If the war had continued beyond 1954, with direct United States intervention, this dependence on Chinese aid would have been even greater. Conceivably the war might eventually have been lost, whereas in 1954 it was at least being won in the North. In short, the Chinese were unwilling to make Indochina a cause for prolonged military confrontation with the United States; and without Chinese aid the Viet-Minh would have faced disaster.

R. B. Smith, *An International History of the Vietnam War: Volume I, Revolution versus Containment, 1955–61* (London: Macmillan, 1987 edn), pp. 24, 59–60.

### 2.16  Communist Chinese aid to the Vietminh

While the Vietminh may have been justified in their criticisms of Communist China's behaviour at Geneva, the fact remains – as noted in the previous extract – that without Chinese military advice and assistance from 1950 onwards, the Vietminh would not have been able to negotiate with the French from such a strong position in 1954. Recent scholarship, utilising Chinese sources, has contributed to our understanding of Beijing's motivation in supporting the Vietminh, as well as the scale of its largesse.

A mixture of geopolitical, ideological, and historical factors determined Beijing's decision to assist the Vietminh in the early 1950s.

After the establishment of the PRC in 1949, Mao perceived threats from the United States on three fronts: Taiwan, Korea, and Vietnam. The elimination of the French presence in Indochina would not only strengthen China's southern frontier against foreign intervention but also deny the Nationalist [Chinese] remnant a sanctuary. The CCP [Chinese Communist Party] and Vietminh leaders shared common ideological beliefs and similar anti-imperialist experiences. Ho Chi Minh had close personal relationships with many of the CCP leaders. The Beijing decision-makers felt an international obligation to support the Vietminh. Historically, Chinese rulers had regarded Vietnam as within China's sphere of influence. In seeking the CCP's assistance to fight the French, Ho Chi Minh was clearly following Vietnam's traditional practice of looking to China for models while trying to maintain independence ...

China played an important part in Ho's victory over the French. Beijing sent some of its most capable generals to Vietnam as military advisers, who helped the DRV professionalize and politicize its army, reorganize its administrative structure, and mobilize the masses. The CMAG [Chinese Military Advisory Group, established in April 1950] contributed greatly to the success of the Border, Northwest, and Dien Bien Phu engagements ... In November 1953, it was [General] Wei Guoqing and his group [the CMAG] who first proposed the Dien Bien Phu campaign and helped the Vietminh army command direct the whole operation.

The CMAG made some mistakes in advising the Vietminh. In early 1951, they encouraged Giap to attack the French strongholds in the Red River Delta. The Vietminh incurred heavy casualties. In the initial phase of the Dien Bien Phu campaign, Chinese advisers made a poor judgment by asking the Vietminh to launch an all-out assault against the French. They miscalculated the strength of the enemy. Despite these occasional misjudgments, China's strategy and tactics in general proved successful in Vietnam. Giap's fame as a superb military commander has been much inflated.

... Between 1950 and 1954, China provided substantial support for the Vietnamese revolution. Beijing supplied the Vietminh with 116,000 guns and 4,360 cannons, and equipped five infantry divisions, one engineering and artillery division, one antiaircraft regiment, and one guard regiment. It is true that the Vietnamese won the First Vietnam War because, as a French survivor of Dien Bien Phu [Lucien Bodard] admitted later on, 'they were fighting for an ideal'.

They were fighting for a just cause, national independence. But it is also true that without China's assistance the Vietnamese could not have defeated the French as soon as they did.

Qiang Zhai, 'Transplanting the Chinese Model: Chinese Military Advisers and the First Vietnam War, 1950–1954', *Journal of Military History*, Vol. 57 (1993), pp. 713–15.

# 3

# War renewed,
# 1954–1960

In the aftermath of the Geneva conference, the United States worked to establish a stable, anti-communist state in southern Vietnam. The man chosen to front this enterprise was Ngo Dinh Diem, an ardent Vietnamese nationalist (3.1). Although some in Washington were uneasy about Diem's overtly illiberal tendencies, there could be no doubting his militant anti-communism (3.2). The Diem regime thus became the recipient of massive US economic and military assistance in the years after 1954; 'nation building', as the American approach was dubbed, was hardly consistent with the terms of the Geneva settlement, but this mattered less than the Cold War security of the southern half of the trigger-domino of Southeast Asia. In north Vietnam, 'nation building' of a different kind took place, as the Vietnam Workers' Party (VWP) consolidated power and began laying the foundations of a socialist state. However, land reform, a key element in this process, was so crudely and violently implemented in 1954-56 that the Party's relationship with the peasantry, hitherto the bedrock of its popular support, was badly damaged. Indeed, if the 1956 elections had been held as planned, the Party's showing in rural north Vietnam might well have been adversely affected (3.6, 3.7). The elections, of course, were *not* held. Fearful of the outcome, the Diem regime, backed by the Americans, ignored the political provisions of the Geneva settlement and consequently the partition of Vietnam assumed an air of permanence (3.3). In Hanoi, Ho and his followers reacted with anger and dismay, but in the absence of international support for their position – even Beijing and Moscow offered only lukewarm backing for the reconvening of the Geneva conference – and lacking the power to reunite Vietnam by force, they were compelled to accept the situation (3.4, 3.5). From 1956, therefore, two Vietnams existed – Diem's Republic of Vietnam (RVN) and Ho's

Democratic Republic of Vietnam (DRV) – both of which claimed jurisdiction over the whole country.

American economic and military aid to South Vietnam increased steadily during the late 1950s, but instead of helping to build a model democracy, this assistance served to underpin a Diemist dictatorship in which all political opposition was outlawed and where enemies of the state – especially known or suspected communists and ex-Vietminh – were summarily imprisoned or executed. An embarrassed Eisenhower administration repeatedly urged Diem to institute demo-cratic reforms and liberalise his rule, but his dictatorship endured, not least because America's backing continued. Diem correctly calculated that as long as his anti-communist policies were producing results – by 1959 the communists in the south were on the verge of extinction – he could parry US demands for reform. As for North Vietnam, the suc-cess of Diem's anti-communist pogroms forced Hanoi to redefine its approach to the question of national reunification. Between 1956 and 1959, Hanoi had placed primary emphasis on building up North Viet-nam's economic, industrial and military base, while its followers in South Vietnam were instructed to avoid armed confrontation with Diemist forces and to work instead for a new Saigon government, one that would be responsive to popular and nationalist opinion and dedi-cated to the resurrection of the Geneva settlement (3.5). In January 1959, however, with the southern communist position crumbling, North Vietnam sanctioned a new strategy that accorded the liberation of the south equal importance alongside the consolidation of the north. The communist rump in South Vietnam was encouraged to increase anti-Diem political activity, and to engage in selective revolu-tionary violence against the Saigon government and armed forces; at the same time, southerners who had moved north in 1954 would be infiltrated back into South Vietnam to assist in the assault on Diemist rule (3.8).

Despite this greater level of identification with the struggle in the south, caution remained Hanoi's watchword. Precipitate action could provoke direct American intervention on Diem's behalf, a develop-ment that North Vietnam naturally was keen to avoid; so, too, were China and the Soviet Union, both of whom counselled restraint on the issue of reunification. However, during 1959–60, as the anti-Diem campaign escalated into a full-blown insurgency, Hanoi was again forced to reconsider its approach. Recognising that the Diem govern-ment's unpopularity had created a real revolutionary opportunity, the

VWP Central Committee voted in September 1960 to increase substantially its political and military support for the insurgency. The caution that had previously characterised Hanoi's policy was not entirely jettisoned: great efforts were to be taken to ensure that the struggle in the south retained the essential characteristics of a *civil* war, thus minimising the risk of US intervention in retaliation for external – that is to say North Vietnamese – aggression. In December 1960, the formation of the National Liberation Front (NLF) for South Vietnam – a spontaneous reaction by non-communist southerners to Diem's excesses – worked to North Vietnam's advantage (3.10, 3.11). Adopting the revolutionary methodology that had succeeded in the early years of the Vietminh, southern communists were able to wield a hidden but controlling influence over the Front that allowed Hanoi to exert a degree of direction over the political struggle. From the start of 1961, the military side of the insurgency would be conducted by the more overtly communist People's Liberation Armed Forces (PLAF), its activities overseen by the Central Office for South Vietnam (COSVN) – the communist 'jungle Pentagon' – and ultimately by the Party leadership in North Vietnam. For Diem and for America, the crisis that had been brewing since 1954, and more especially since 1959, had finally broken.

### 3.1 American support for Ngo Dinh Diem

In October 1954, the Eisenhower administration undertook to supply military and economic aid direct to the Diem government in southern Vietnam, bypassing the French through whom it had been channelled since 1950. Although his anti-communism made Diem an attractive standard-bearer for US 'nation building', American policy-makers were dubious about his credentials as a democrat.

Dear Mr President [Diem]

I have been following with great interest the course of developments in Vietnam, particularly since the conclusion of the conference at Geneva. The implications of the agreement concerning Vietnam have caused grave concern regarding the future of a country temporarily divided by an artificial military grouping, weakened by a long and exhausting war, and faced with enemies without and by their subversive collaborators within ...

We have been exploring ways and means to permit our aid to Vietnam to be more effective and to make a greater contribution to the welfare and stability of the Government of Vietnam. I am, accordingly, instructing the American Ambassador to Vietnam to examine with you in your capacity as Chief of Government, how an intelligent program of American aid given directly to your Government can serve to assist Vietnam in its present hour of trial, provided that your Government is prepared to give assurances as to the standards of performance it would be able to maintain in the event such aid were supplied.

> This last remark, and those that follow, testify to US unease about Diem.

The purpose of this offer is to assist the Government of Vietnam in developing and maintaining a strong, viable state, capable of resisting attempted subversion or aggression through military means. The Government of the United States expects that this aid will be met by performance on the part of the Government of Vietnam in undertaking needed reforms. It hopes that such aid, combined with your own continuing efforts, will contribute effectively toward an independent Vietnam endowed with a strong Government. Such a Government would, I hope, be so responsive to the nationalist aspirations of its people, so enlightened in purpose and effective in performance, that it will be respected both at home and abroad and discourage any who might wish to impose a foreign ideology on your free people.

Eisenhower letter to Diem, 1 October 1954, in *Public Papers of the Presidents of the United States: Dwight D. Eisenhower, 1954* (Washington DC: Government Printing Office, 1960) pp. 948–9.

## 3.2 Diem: early hopes

> Some Americans believed that Diem could be educated in the ways of democracy. General Edward Lansdale, an adviser to Diem in the early period of his rule, was among those whom time would prove wrong.

We were all invited to come down to [Saigon] airport to greet him, that is all of the foreign community leaders. I started off for the airport, saw immense throngs on the sidewalk and decided I would watch the people rather than the man arriving and see what their reaction was as they saw him. I stopped and waited with the people on the sidewalk – a very long wait of hours, and finally sirens in the distance and a limousine all closed up with outriders and police, motorcycle police, came along and zipped by the people. They were all ready to cheer and holding their kids up to see him, and, zing, he went right by and they were terribly disappointed at not having a chance to cheer and so on.

I felt if this was going to be the leader on our side 'God help us', because he had no instincts at all of politics and the people he was going to lead. So I jotted down some notes on how to be a Prime Minister of Vietnam at that moment, and saw the Ambassador, and said I'd like to show these to this man. The Ambassador said alright, if you make sure that he doesn't think these are official US views, but are strictly your own. I said, 'I'll do that'.

At the Palace people were running around. There wasn't a receptionist, it didn't seem to be organized in any way. I asked someone who was carrying a bundle of papers along the hall: I said, there's a new Prime Minister around and where is his office please? He said you go upstairs and at the head of the stairs you ask the man in the room there and he'll show you. So I went upstairs, there was a little room with a door open off to the left and a man sitting at a desk there and I asked for the Prime Minister, and he said 'Well that's me'. I told him about watching him come into Saigon, and the disappointment of the people, and the fact that I had my own personal ideas of some of the things that a Prime Minister might do. I said that all of these ideas were generated from my time out among Vietnamese, and I thought this was what his own people were looking for. With that I sat down and gave him the papers, and we became close friends afterwards. He even liked some of the ideas and started asking me to come in and see him on concepts of things that foreigners had told him about. We finally came to see each other almost daily.

Lansdale quoted in Michael Charlton and Anthony Moncrieff (eds), *Many Reasons Why: The American Involvement in Vietnam* (New York: Hill & Wang, 1989 edn), pp. 55–6.

## 3.3 Diem boycotts the 1956 elections

In August 1955 the Diem regime issued a public statement clarifying its position on the projected 1956 elections.

Faced now with a regime of oppression as practiced by the Vietminh, we remain skeptical concerning the possibility of fulfilling the conditions of free elections in the North. We shall not miss any opportunity which would permit the unification of our homeland in freedom, but it is out of the question for us to consider any proposal from the Vietminh if proof is not given that they put the superior interests of the national community above those of Communism, if they do not cease violating their obligation as they have done by preventing our countrymen of the North from going South or by recently attacking, together with the Communist Pathet Lao, the friendly state of Laos ...

The Government does not consider itself bound in any way by the Geneva Agreements which it did not sign. It affirms once again that, placing the interests of the nation as its first consideration, it is determined, in any circumstances, to reach the obvious goal of its policy – the unity of the country in peace and freedom.

The Vietminh authorities sent a letter dated July 19 [1955] to the Government in which they asked for a pre-election consultation conference, thus, for propaganda purposes, seeking to give credence to the false idea that they would be defenders of territorial unity ...

The policy of the Government remains unchanged toward the partitioning of the country accomplished against its will. Serving the cause of true democracy, the Government is anxious that all Vietnamese throughout the entire country may live without fear and that they be totally free from all dictatorship and oppression. The Government considers the principle of essentially free elections a democratic and peaceful institution, but believes that conditions of freedom of life and of voting must be assured beforehand. From this point of view, nothing constructive will be done as long as the Communist regime of the North does not permit each Vietnamese citizen to enjoy democratic freedoms and the basic fundamental rights of man.

RVN statement, in Marvin E. Gettleman *et al.* (eds), *Vietnam and America: The Most Comprehensive Documented History of the Vietnam War* (New York: Grove Press, 1995), pp. 103–5.

### 3.4 'Consolidate the north and keep in mind the south'

With the cancellation of the 1956 elections, North Vietnam's leaders resigned themselves to a protracted period of partition. National reunification remained the ultimate goal, but the immediate priority was to complete the socialist transformation of the north. Though logical, this strategy dismayed those southerners who had regrouped in the north in 1954, and whose families now faced an uncertain future in Diem's South Vietnam. In June 1956, Ho Chi Minh spoke to their concerns.

It is often said that 'north and south belong to the same family and are brothers.' These words have a deep significance. They testify to the firm, unshakeable solidarity of our people from North to South. Your presence here testifies to this solidarity. Since the day you were regrouped here, you have regarded the North as your home, you have overcome all difficulties, and eagerly taken part in the construction of the North ... In the name of the Party and the Government, I congratulate you all and urge you to make continuous efforts and constant progress. Our policy is: to consolidate the North and to keep in mind the South. To build a good house, we must build a strong foundation. To have a vigorous plant with green leaves, beautiful flowers and good fruit, we must take good care of it and feed the root.

The North is the foundation, the root of the struggle for complete national liberation and the reunification of the country. That is why everything we are doing in the North is aimed at strengthening both the North and the South. Therefore, to work here is the same as struggling in the South: it is to struggle for the South and for the whole of Viet-Nam.

> Ho repeatedly emphasised that political – hence peaceful – reunification was the preferred approach to the national question.

From the moral aspect, if everybody understands that our political struggle will be victorious but will be a long and hard struggle, then the tendency to become impatient, pessimistic, and to succumb to other cares will disappear.

The political struggle will certainly be victorious, national reunification will certainly be achieved ...

The Americans and their agents are endeavoring to sabotage the Geneva Agreement. They refuse to hold political consultations with us or to organize in due time free general elections as has been stipulated in the Geneva Agreement; they are scheming to divide our country permanently. They are betraying the people's interests and their ranks are being torn by internal strife. That is why, despite their arrogant attitude, their strength is unstable, like that of a palace built on sand.

As to our struggle, it is a just struggle; the peace-loving of the world support us. Our people from North to South ... hate and oppose the American–Diem clique. The North is being increasingly consolidated to become a firm support, a strong base for our entire people's struggle. For these reasons, our political struggle will certainly be victorious ...

Ho Chi Minh, letter to southern cadres, 19 June 1956, in Bernard B. Fall (ed.), *Ho Chi Minh on Revolution: Selected Writings, 1920–66* (New York: Praegar, 1967), pp. 272–4.

### 3.5 'The Path of Revolution in the South'

In November 1956, Ho's message – 'consolidate the north and keep in mind the south' – was codified in an important study paper, written by Le Duan, the Party's General Secretary and (formerly) the Party's leader in the south. Subsequently sanctioned by the VWP Central Committee, Le Duan's paper reinforced Hanoi's belief that, at this point, the struggle in the south should be political and peaceful. This was to be Hanoi's position for the next three years.

In order to cope with that situation created by the U.S.–Diem [regime], and in order to complete the work of national liberation, to liberate the Southern people from the imperialist-feudalist yoke, the Party Central Committee has put forward three main tasks to make a general line for the whole revolution ...

1. Firmly consolidate the North
2. Strongly push the Southern revolutionary movement
3. Win the sympathy and support of the people who love peace,

democracy and national independence in the world ...

... There are those who think that the U.S.–Diem's use of violence is now aimed fundamentally at killing the leaders of the revolutionary movement in order to destroy the Communist Party and if the Communist Party is worn away to the point that it doesn't have the capacity to lead the revolution, the political struggle of the masses cannot develop.

This judgment is incorrect. Those who lead the revolutionary movement are determined to mingle with the masses, to protect and serve the interests of the masses and to pursue correctly the mass line. Between the masses and Communists there is no distinction any more. So how can the U.S.–Diem destroy the leaders of the revolutionary movement, since they cannot destroy the masses? Therefore they cannot annihilate the cadres leading the mass movement.

> Le Duan's analysis was informed by external realities: American support for Diem, which could manifest itself in US military intervention if North Vietnam adopted a non-political approach; Beijing's lack of enthusiasm for any action that could precipitate a clash with the United States; and Moscow's belief – expressed in Khrushchev's 'secret speech' of February 1956 – that the transition to socialism could and probably should take peaceful form.

We believe that: the peaceful line is not only appropriate to the general situation in the world but also to the situation within the country, both nation-wide and in the South ... We believe that the people's will for peace and the forces of peace and democracy will defeat the cruel, dictatorial and fascist policy of U.S.–Diem and will advance to smashing the imperialist, feudalist U.S.–Diem government. Using love and righteousness to triumph over force is a tradition of the Vietnamese nation. The aspiration for peace is an aspiration of the world's people in general and in our own country, including the people of the South, so our struggle line cannot be apart from the peaceful line.

Le Duan, 'The Path of Revolution in the South', November 1956, in Gareth Porter (ed.), *Vietnam: The Definitive Documentation of Human Decisions*, 2 vols (London: Heyden, 1979), Vol. 2, pp. 24–30.

### 3.6 'All this has caused us to commit errors'

The VWP's land reform programme of 1954–56 was disas-
trously executed: estimates of lives lost range from several
thousand to more than 100,000, with critics of Vietnamese
communism seizing on the latter figure and more dispassionate
analysts inclining towards the former. So concerned was the
VWP leadership at the damage done to relations with the
peasantry that Ho Chi Minh was compelled to issue a public
apology in August 1956.

Land reform is a class struggle against the feudalists; an earth-shak-
ing, fierce, and hard revolution. Moreover, the enemy has frenziedly
carried out sabotage work. A number of our cadres have not thoroughly grasped the land-reform policy or correctly followed the mass
line. The leadership of the Party Central Committee and of the Government is sometimes lacking in concreteness, and control and
encouragement are disregarded. All this has caused us to commit errors and meet with shortcomings in carrying out land reform: in realizing the unity of the countryside, in fighting the enemy, in readjusting
the organization, in applying the policy of agricultural taxes, etc.

The Party Central Committee and the Government have rigorously
reviewed these errors and shortcomings and drawn up plans resolutely to correct them with a view to uniting the cadres and the people,
stabilizing the countryside, and promoting production.

We have to correct such short-comings as: not relying fully on the
poor and landless peasants, not uniting closely with the middle peasants, and not establishing a sincere alliance with the rich peasants.

The status of those who have been wrongly classified as landlords
or as rich peasants should be reviewed.

Party membership, rights, and honor should be restituted to Party
members, cadres, and others who have been wrongly convicted.

With regard to landlords, we should abide by the eight-point regu-
lation when dealing with them and pay attention to those landlords
who have taken part in the Resistance and supported the revolution or
those whose children are enrolled in the army or working as cadres.

Wherever land area and production output have been erroneously
estimated, a readjustment is required.

The correction of errors should be resolute and planned. What can
be corrected immediately should be dealt with without delay. What

cannot be corrected forthwith should be done in combination with the checking-up operation. It is necessary to further the achievements we have made, and at the same time resolutely to right the wrongs committed.

Ho Chi Minh, open letter, 18 August 1956, in Fall (ed.), *Ho Chi Minh on Revolution*, pp. 275–7.

### 3.7 'Ho Chi Minh was to blame'

The Party's rural rectification campaign was generally successful: by the end of the 1950s, agricultural output was up, and full-scale collectivisation had commenced. But the scars of 1954–56 lingered. One Vietnamese communist who participated in the land reform programme has lately sought to explain how it went so badly wrong.

Land reform occurred after we had heard hundreds of Chinese advisers introduce the process on the basis of experience in their own country. I recall eight lectures on the subject given to all middle-level cadres. Not a single one of us could escape them. They were a hurdle we had to jump in order to 'grow up and become a genuine revolutionary'. The eight stages of growing up involved numerous sessions of team discussions and debate to help one another criticise mistakes. Then there were sessions to air the grievances of the peasants and tell stories illustrating the cruelty of landlords and imperialists. We were also taught that cases which seemed correct could be a divergence from the truth. So we watched films and plays about landlords and peasants. Everything was cut and dried. He is a landlord even though he owns only 10 square metres. Therefore he is bad, greedy, cruel and the evil hand of imperialism. All peasants are good. They have a revolutionary spirit and are disciplined ...

To find only two cruel landlords in any one village was not enough. One had to try again, even though the system of land tenure in northern Vietnam was different from that in China and few people owned more than a few hectares ... In 1954 and 1955 those who were supreme were the leaders of the land reform brigades. In their hands the power of life and death was absolute. They applied the rules and used the people's courts to make a judgement with a simple show of hands. There were no lawyers, and in fact there was no law. Sentences were carried out by a rifle section selected from local guerrillas who were landless peasants with no relatives among the middle peasantry or landlords. As for the leaders of the land reform brigades, they always went around with solemn faces, wearing blue Mao jackets in summer and felt ones in winter. They did not wear Ho Chi Minh sandals but rather leather shoes which creaked authoritatively. They also carried shiny briefcases and travelled in Chinese jeeps ...

But the real problem was posed by the mistakes of land reform which caused the deaths of more than ten thousand people. Most of them were Party members or patriots who had supported the Revolution but nonetheless were reasonably well off. They were shot having been condemned by what amounted to kangaroo courts, although they were called people's tribunals. This was the result of the mechanistic application of Chinese experience imposed by their advisers. In my opinion, Ho Chi Minh was to blame. Initially he was very hesitant about land reform, then at the beginning of 1952 he was criticised by Stalin for pursuing a policy based on nationalism rather than class warfare. But it was Mao Tse-tung who really forced his hand ... [T]he mistakes of land reform have still not been summed up in a serious and constructive way. And its leaders were never really disciplined.

Bui Tin, *Following Ho Chi Minh: The Memoirs of a North Vietnamese Colonel* (London: Hurst & Co., 1995), pp. 23–30.

## 3.8 Hanoi's 'milestone' decision

At the Fifteenth Plenum of the VWP Central Committee in Hanoi in January 1959, agreement was reached that political struggle alone would be insufficient to destroy the Saigon regime and reunite Vietnam, and that a degree of revolutionary violence would be required. The decision – later described by Party historians as an 'extremely important milestone' – was enshrined in a Central Committee resolution.

The fundamental path of development for the revolution in South Vietnam is that of violent struggle. Based on the concrete conditions and existing requirements of revolution, then, the road of violent struggle is: use the strength of the masses, with the political strength as the main factor, combined with military strength to a greater or lesser degree depending on the situation, in order to overthrow the ruling power of the imperialist and feudalist forces and build the revolutionary power of the people.

> It would be wrong, however, to see January 1959 as the point at which Hanoi opted for all-out revolutionary war. Political struggle remained the key, with violence only sanctioned in self-defence.

In the process of difficult and complicated struggle, political struggle will be the main form, but because the enemy is determined to drown the revolution in blood, and because of the ... extraordinary mood in the South, it will be necessary to a certain extent to adopt methods of self-defense and armed propaganda activities to assist the political struggle ... But in the process of using self-defense and armed propaganda units, it is necessary to grasp thoroughly the principle of emphasizing political strength.

> The 'milestone' decision was not communicated to the Party at large until May 1959, when a communiqué was issued, and it was probably not until the end of 1959 that its contents were fully disseminated at rice-roots level in the south. Again the emphasis was on political struggle.

The Central Committee of the Vietnam Lao Dong [Vietnam Workers'] Party has held its 15th enlarged session ... After hearing reports on the development of the nationwide struggle for reunification since the reestablishment of peace, the session noted:

1. The long, hard and heroic war of resistance of the Vietnamese people defeated the French colonialists, the U.S. interventionists and their henchmen and completely liberated the northern part of our country ... North Vietnam, now completely liberated, has carried through its task of national people's democratic revolution and is carrying out the socialist revolution and building socialism. This is an extremely important change which determines the direction of the development of the Vietnamese revolution in the new stage. Meanwhile, the southern part of our country is still under the domination of the American imperialists and their lackey – Ngo Dinh Diem. They have turned South Vietnam into a new-type colony and a military base for

preparing war. The characteristics of the present situation in our country are that North Vietnam is advancing toward socialism, while the task of the national people's democratic revolution is not yet achieved throughout the country.

2. Peace and national reunification are the most earnest aspirations of the whole Vietnamese people at present for the revolutionary cause of the fatherland and in the highest interests of the people ... However, the interventionist policy of the U.S. imperialists and the South Vietnam authorities' policy of dependence on the United States have undermined and deliberately continue to undermine the implementation of the Geneva agreements and the cause of peaceful national reunification, thus cutting across the desire and interests of the Vietnamese people. The U.S. imperialists and their followers are scheming to perpetuate the division of our country and prepare a new war.

To carry out this perfidious scheme, over the past few years, the U.S.–Diem clique has been actively increasing its military forces, carrying out a policy of ruthless exploitation of the people, abolishing all democratic freedoms, repressing and terrorizing the people in a most barbarous manner, causing ever more serious dislocation of the South Vietnam economy, and making the life of the local people more and more precarious and wretched ...

3. Since the restoration of peace, under the leadership of the party, our people in North Vietnam have overcome all difficulties and hardships, carried through the land reform, and successfully completed the period of economic rehabilitation ... To take North Vietnam toward socialism is the most urgent task, and this task is directly related to the struggle of the Vietnamese people for completing the achievement of independence and democracy throughout the country and winning national reunification.

While our people in the north are making all-out efforts to build the North in all fields, our compatriots in the south are developing their tradition of solidarity and heroic struggle ... The policies of demagogy, national division, and barbarous terror and massacre applied by the U.S.–Diem clique certainly cannot subdue our southern compatriots. On the contrary, the patriotic movement in South Vietnam will become broader and deeper day by day. The aggressive character of the U.S. imperialists and the traitorous nature of Ngo Dinh Diem have been laid bare before the people throughout the country and before wide public opinion in the world, making them alone and more isolated.

4. To achieve national reunification on the basis of independence and democracy, the session mapped out the following tasks: The entire people will unite and strive to struggle for national reunification on the basis of independence and democracy; to endeavor to consolidate the north and actively take it step by step toward socialism; to build a peaceful, unified, independent, democratic, prosperous and strong Vietnam; and to contribute to the safe-guarding of peace in Southeast Asia and the world.

VWP resolution, January 1959, in William J. Duiker, *The Communist Road to Power in Vietnam* (Boulder: Westview Press, 1996 edn), p. 200; 'Communiqué of the 15th Enlarged Session of the VWP Central Committee', 13 May 1959, in Porter (ed.), *Vietnam*, Vol. 2, pp. 44–6.

## 3.9 The nanifesto

Diem's political and religious intolerance, together with the brutality of his security forces, alienated large sections of the South Vietnamese population – from the peasant masses in the countryside to the democracy-hungry urban intelligentsia. The best indication of how badly Diem mismanaged political affairs is the unhappiness of those urban, professional, educated, patriotic *non-communists* who might otherwise have been an important prop of support to his government. In April 1960, eighteen disaffected South Vietnamese, some of them former government ministers, issued the Caravelle manifesto, so-named from the Caravelle Hotel in Saigon where the group based itself. Despite their relatively modest demands – to be allowed, in effect, to form a 'loyal opposition' – all eighteen were subsequently arrested and imprisoned.

Mr President:

We the undersigned, representing a group of eminent citizens and personalities, intellectuals of all tendencies, and men of good will, recognize in the face of the gravity of the present political situation that we can no longer remain indifferent to the realities of life in our country.

Therefore, we officially address to you today an appeal with the aim of exposing to you the whole truth in the hope that the government will accord it all the attention necessary so as to urgently modify its polices, so as to remedy the present situation and lead the people out of danger ...

... [In 1954] The whole people thought that you would be the man of the situation and that you would implement its hopes. That is the way it was when you returned. The Geneva Accords of 1954 put an end to combat and to the devastations of war. The French Expeditionary Corps was progressively withdrawn, and total independence of South Viet Nam had become a reality. Furthermore, the country had benefited from moral encouragement and a substantial increase of foreign aid from the free world. With so many favorable political factors, in addition to the blessed geographic conditions of a fertile and rich soil yielding agricultural, forestry, and fishing surpluses, South Viet Nam should have been able to begin a definitive victory in the historical competition with the North, so as to carry out the will of the people and to lead the country on the way to hope, liberty, and happiness. Today, six years later, having benefited from so many undeniable advantages, what has the government been able to do? Where has it led South Viet Nam? What parts of the popular aspirations have been implemented?

> Although the manifesto pinpointed government failure in a number of areas – Administration, Army, Economic and Social Affairs – its most devastating critique came under the simple heading 'Policies'.

In spite of the fact that the bastard regime created and protected by colonialism has been overthrown and that many of the feudal organizations of the factions and parties which oppress the population were destroyed, the people do not know a better life or more freedom under the republican regime which you have created.[1] A constitution has been established in form only; a National Assembly exists whose deliberations always fall into line with the government; antidemocratic elections – all those are methods and 'comedies' copied from the dictatorial Communist regimes, which obviously cannot serve as terms of comparison with North Viet Nam.

Continuous arrests fill the jails and prisons to the rafters, as at this precise moment; public opinion and the press are reduced to silence. The same applies to the popular will as translated in certain open elections, in which it is insulted and trampled ... All these have provoked the discouragement and resentment of the people.

Political parties and religious sects have been eliminated. 'Groups' or 'movements' have replaced them. But this substitution has only brought about new oppressions against the population without protecting it for that matter against Communist enterprises ...

Today the people want freedom. You should, Mr. President, liberalize the regime, promote democracy, guarantee minimum civil rights, recognize the opposition so as to permit the citizens to express themselves without fear, thus removing grievances and resentments, opposition to which now constitutes for the people their sole reason for existence. When this occurs, the people of South Viet Nam, in comparing their position with that of the North, will appreciate the value of true liberty and of authentic democracy. It is only at that time that the people will make all the necessary efforts and sacrifices to defend that liberty and democracy.

US Department of Defense, *The Pentagon Papers: The Defense Department History of United States Decision-making on Vietnam*, Senator Gravel edn, 5 vols (Boston: Beacon Press, 1971), Vol. I, pp. 316–21.

## 3.10   The National Liberation Front of South Vietnam

The National Liberation Front (NLF) of South Vietnam came into being in December 1960. Later, both the Saigon regime and the Americans would depict the NLF as a northern construct, whilst Hanoi, and the Front itself, maintained that it was an independent, indigenous political grouping. The truth lies somewhere in between: the NLF was of southern origin and composition, but it was encouraged and, after formation, directed clandestinely by Hanoi through the medium of the Party in the south. Truong Nhu Tang, a *non-communist* southerner from a prosperous commercial background and a founding member of the NLF, has recalled the Front's genesis.

By the end of 1958, Diem had succeeded brilliantly in routing his enemies and arrogating power.[2] But he had also alienated large segments of the South Vietnamese population, creating a swell of animosity throughout the country. Almost unknown at first, in a few short years he had made himself widely detested, a dictator who could look for support only to the Northern Catholic refugees and to those who made money from his schemes. Most damning of all, he had murdered many patriots who had fought in the struggle against France and had tied his existence to the patronage of the United States, France's successor. To many nationalist-minded Vietnamese, whose emotions were those of people just emerging from a hundred years of subjugation to foreigners, Diem had forfeited all claims to loyalty.

In light of Diem's conduct of the presidency, two facts were clear: First, the country had settled into an all too familiar pattern of oligarchic rule and utter disregard for the welfare of the people. Second, subservience to foreigners was still the order of the day. We had a ruler whose overriding interest was power and who would use the Americans to prop himself up – even while the Americans were using him for their own strategic purposes.

As far as I was concerned, this situation was intolerable. Replacing the French despots with a Vietnamese one was not a significant advance. It would never lead to either the broad economic progress or the national dignity which I (along with many others) had been brooding about for years. Among my circle of friends there was anger and profound disappointment over this turn of events. We were living, we felt, in historic times. A shameful, century-long era had just been violently closed out, and a new nation was taking shape before our eyes. Many of us agreed that we could not acquiesce in the shape it was taking. If we were not to be allowed a say about it from within the government, we would have to speak from without.

By the end of 1958, those of us who felt this way decided to form an extralegal political organization, complete with a program and a plan of action. We had not moved toward this decision quickly; it was an undertaking of immense magnitude, which would require years of effort before giving us the strength to challenge Diem's monopoly on power. To some, that prospect seemed quixotic at best. But most of us felt we had little choice.

> Truong Nhu Tang and his co-conspirators were fully aware that they would have to work with the southern communists and seek support from North Vietnam.

At each stage we discussed carefully the ongoing search for allies, wary about how to gather support and still retain our own direction and freedom. It was a delicate and crucial problem of the utmost complexity. The overwhelming strength of our enemy urged us to acquire whatever assistance we could, from whatever source. In addition, the anticolonial war had not simply ended in 1954; a residual Vietminh infrastructure was still in place and was beginning to come alive again. For better or worse, our endeavor was meshed into an ongoing historical movement for independence that had already developed its own philosophy and means of action. Of this movement, Ho Chi Minh was the spiritual father, in the South as well as the North, and we looked naturally to him and to his government for guidance and aid ... And yet, this struggle was also our own. Had Ngo Dinh Diem proved a man of breadth and vision, the core of people who filled the NLF and its sister organizations would have rallied to him. As it was, the South Vietnamese nationalists were driven to action by his contempt for the principles of independence and social progress in which they believed. In this sense, the Southern revolution was generated of itself, out of the emotions, conscience, and aspirations of the Southern people.

The complexity of the struggle was mirrored in the makeup of our group. Most were not Lao Dong ('Workers' Party' – the official name of the Vietnamese Communist Party) members; many scarcely thought of themselves as political, at least in any ideological way. Our allies among the resistance veterans were also largely nationalist rather than political (though they had certainly been led and monitored by the Party.) But we also had Party activists among us, some open, some surreptitious ... But I was not overly concerned at that point about potential conflicts between the Southern nationalists and the [VWP] ideologues. We were allies in this fight, or so I believed. We needed each other, and the closest ties of background, family, and patriotism united us in respect for each other's purposes. This was my reading of the situation in 1959 as the yet-to-be-named National Liberation Front gathered momentum ...

> Members of the nascent NLF made contact with Hanoi in 1959–60. As Truong Nhu Tang recalls, the NLF's manifesto, prepared in late 1960, bore the subtle but unmistakable imprimatur of Ho Chi Minh.

Reading through the finished documents [relating to the NLF manifesto], I was impressed by the analysis they presented of the South's political situation and the balance of forces within the country as well as in Southeast Asia and throughout the world. It was clear that these works had been finely crafted to appeal to the broadest spectrum of people in the South and to marshal the anticolonial emotions that animated almost everyone. At the same time, the manifesto and program responded forcefully and specifically to the interests of the various elements of South Vietnamese society – the intellectuals, students, middle class, peasants and workers.

As I read, I had the distinct sense that these historical documents could not have been the work of just the [NLF] leadership group. They had too much depth, they showed too expert a grasp of politics, psychology, and language. I suspected I was seeing in them the delicate fingerprints of Ho Chi Minh. There seemed nothing strange about this. Ho's experience with revolutionary struggle was not something alien, to arouse suspicion and anxiety. It was part and parcel of our own background.

Truong Nhu Tang (with David Chanoff and Doan Van Toai), *A Vietcong Memoir* (New York: Harcourt Brace Jovanovich, 1985), pp. 65–72.


### 3.11   The NLF's political programme

The NLF's manifesto eschewed ideological goals (much as the founding programme of the Vietminh had), and instead emphasised national/patriotic themes and social justice in an effort (as Truong Nhu Tang observes in the previous reading) to appeal to 'the broadest spectrum of people'. In this regard, it was to prove remarkably successful.


1. Overthrow the camouflaged colonial regime of the American imperialists and the dictatorial power of Ngo Dinh Diem, servant of the Americans, and institute a government of national democratic union.

*The present South Vietnamese regime is a camouflaged colonial regime dominated by the Yankees, and the South Vietnamese Government is a servile government, implementing faithfully all the policies of the American imperialists. Therefore, this regime must be overthrown and a government of national and democratic union put in its place composed of representatives of all social classes, of all nationalities, of the various political parties, of all religions; patriotic, eminent citizens must take over for the people the control of economic, political, social, and cultural interests and thus bring about independence, democracy, well-being, peace, neutrality, and efforts toward the peaceful unification of the country.*

2. Institute a largely liberal and democratic regime.

(i) *Abolish the present constitution of the dictatorial powers of Ngo Dinh Diem, servant of the Americans. Elect a new National Assembly through universal suffrage.*

(ii) *Implement essential democratic liberties: freedom of opinion, of press, of assembly, of movement, of trade-unionism; freedom of religion without any discrimination; and the right of all patriotic organizations of whatever political tendency to carry on normal activities.*

(iii) *Proclaim a general amnesty for all political prisoners and the dissolution of concentration camps of all sorts; abolish fascist law 10/59[3] and all the other antidemocratic laws; authorize the return to the country of all persons persecuted by the American–Diem regime who are now refugees abroad.*

(iv) *Interdict all illegal arrests and detentions; prohibit torture; and punish all the Diem bullies who have not repented and who have committed crimes against the people.*

3. Establish an independent and sovereign economy, and improve the living conditions of the people.

(i) *Suppress the monopolies imposed by American imperialists and their servants; establish an independent and sovereign economy and finances in accordance with the national interests; confiscate to the profit of the nation the properties of the American imperialists and their servants.*

(ii) *Support the national bourgeoisie in the reconstruction and development of crafts and industry; provide active protection for national products through the suppression of production taxes and the limitation or prohibition of imports that the national economy is capable of producing; reduce customs fees on raw materials and machines.*

(iii) *Revitalize agriculture; modernize production, fishing, and cattle raising; help the farmers in putting to the plow unused land and in developing production; protect the crops and guarantee their disposal.*

(iv) *Encourage and reinforce economic relations between the city and country, the plain and the mountain regions; develop commercial exchanges with foreign countries, regardless of their political regime, on the basis of equality and mutual interests.*

(v) *Institute a just and rational system of taxation; eliminate harassing penalties.*

(vi) *Implement the labor code; prohibition of discharges, of penalties, of ill-treatment of wage earners; improvement of the living conditions of workers and civil servants; imposition of wage scales and protective measures for young apprentices.*

(vii) *Organize social welfare: find work for jobless persons; assume the support and protection of orphans, old people, invalids; come to the help of the victims of natural calamities.*

(viii) *Come to the help of displaced persons desiring to return to their native areas and to those who wish to remain permanently in the South; improve their working and living conditions.*

(ix) *Prohibit expulsions, spoliation, and compulsory concentration of the population; guarantee job security for the urban and rural working populations.*

4. Reduce land rent; implement agrarian reform with the aim of providing land to the tillers.

(i) *Reduce land rent; guarantee to the farmers the right to till the soil; guarantee the property right of accession to fallow lands to those who have cultivated them; guarantee property rights to those farmers who have already received land.*

(ii) *Dissolve 'prosperity zones', and put an end to recruitment for the camps that are called 'agricultural development centers'.*[4] *Allow those compatriots who already have been forced into 'prosperity zones' and 'agricultural development centers' to return freely to their own lands.*

(iii) *Confiscate the land owned by American imperialists and their servants, and distribute it to poor peasants without any land or with insufficient land; redistribute the communal lands on a just and rational basis.*

(iv) *By negotiation and on the basis of fair prices, repurchase for distribution to landless peasants or peasants with insufficient land those surplus lands that the owners of large estates will be made to relinquish if their domain exceeds a certain limit, to be determined in accordance with regional peculiarities. The farmers who benefit from such land distribution will not be compelled to make any payment or to submit to any other conditions.*

5. Develop a national and democratic culture and education.

(i) *Combat all forms of culture and education enslaved to Yankee fashions; develop a culture and education that is national, progressive, and at the service of the Fatherland and people.*

(ii) *Liquidate illiteracy; increase the number of schools in the fields of general education as well as in those of technical and professional education, in advanced study as well as in other fields; adopt Vietnamese as the vernacular language; reduce the expenses of education and exempt from payment students who are without means; resume the examination system.*

(iii) *Promote science and technology and the national letters and arts; encourage and support the intellectuals and artists so as to permit them to develop their talents in the service of national reconstruction.*

(iv) *Watch over public health; develop sports and physical education.*

6. Create a national army devoted to the defense of the Fatherland and the people.

(i) *Establish a national army devoted to the defense of the Fatherland and the people; abolish the system of American military advisers.*

(ii) *Abolish the draft system; improve the living conditions of the simple soldiers and guarantee their political rights; put an end to illtreatment of the military; pay particular attention to the dependants of soldiers without means.*

(iii) *Reward officers and soldiers having participated in the struggle against the domination by the Americans and their servants; adopt a policy of clemency toward the former collaborators of the Americans and Diemists guilty of crimes against the people but who have finally repented and are ready to serve the people.*

(iv) *Abolish all foreign military bases established on the territory of Vietnam.*

7. Guarantee equality between the various minorities and between the two sexes; protect the legitimate interests of foreign citizens established in Vietnam and of Vietnamese citizens residing abroad.

(i) *Implement the right to autonomy of the national minorities: found autonomous zones in the areas with minority population, those zones to be an integral part of the Vietnamese nation. Guarantee equality between the various nationalities: each nationality has the right to use and develop its language and writing system, to maintain or to modify its mores and customs; abolish the policy of the Americans and the Diemists of racial discrimination and forced assimilation. Create conditions permitting the national minorities to reach the general level of progress of the population: development of their economy and culture; formation of cadres of minority nationalities.*

(ii) *Establish equality between the two sexes; women shall have equal rights with men from all viewpoints (political, economic, cultural, social, etc.).*

(iii) *Protect the legitimate interests of foreign citizens established in Vietnam.*

(iv) *Defend and take care of the interests of Vietnamese citizens living abroad.*

8. Promote a foreign policy of peace and neutrality.

(i) *Cancel all unequal treaties that infringe upon the sovereignty of the people and that were concluded with other countries by the servants of the Americans.*

(ii) *Establish diplomatic relations with all countries, regardless of their political regime, in accordance with the principles of peaceful coexistence adopted at the Bandung Conference.[5]*

(iii) *Develop close solidarity with the nations of Southeast Asia, in particular with Cambodia and Laos.*

(iv) *Stay out of any military bloc; refuse any military alliance with another country.*

(v) *Accept economic aid from any country willing to give us help without attaching conditions to such help.*

9. Re-establish normal relations between the two zones, and prepare for the peaceful reunification of the country.

*The peaceful reunification of the country constitutes the dearest desire of all our compatriots throughout the country. The National Liberation Front of South Vietnam advocates the peaceful reunification by stages on the basis of negotiations and through seeking of ways and means in conformity with the interests of the Vietnamese nation. While awaiting this reunification, the governments of the two zones will, on the basis of negotiations, promise to banish all separatist and warmongering propaganda and not to use force to settle differences between the zones. Commercial and cultural exchanges between the two zones will be implemented; the inhabitants of the two zones will be free to move about throughout the country as their family and business interests indicate. The freedom of postal exchanges will be guaranteed.*

10. Struggle against all aggressive war; actively defend universal peace.

(i) *Struggle against all aggressive war and against all forms of imperialist domination; support the national emancipation movements of the various peoples.*

(ii) *Banish all warmongering propaganda; demand general disarmament and the prohibition of nuclear weapons; and advocate the utilization of atomic energy for peaceful purposes.*

(iii) *Support all movements of struggle for peace, democracy, and social progress throughout the world; contribute actively to the defense of peace in Southeast Asia and the world.*

NLF manifesto, in Gettleman *et al.* (eds), *Vietnam and America*, pp. 188–92.

# 4

# The struggle for South Vietnam, 1960–1965

As the anti-Diem insurgency gathered pace, the new US administration of John F. Kennedy publicly reaffirmed its commitment to a non-communist South Vietnam (4.2). Between 1961 and 1963, this commitment manifested itself in vastly increased military aid to the Saigon government, the despatch of more than 16,000 military advisers, and the ill-fated Strategic Hamlet initiative. The overall programme was labelled 'counter-insurgency'; instead of viewing the crisis as a weakening preliminary to an invasion from the north (as the Eisenhower administration had), the Kennedy team regarded the insurgency as the main event. As for the insurgents themselves, they were labelled 'Vietcong' (Vietnamese communists) by Saigon, an accurate enough description of the PLAF but one that denied the pluralistic political nature of the NLF. Moreover, despite Hanoi's efforts to conceal the extent of its commitment to the southern revolution, both Washington and Saigon looked upon the insurgents as North Vietnamese proxies, another partially accurate assessment that failed to acknowledge the southern-indigenous roots and complexion of the insurgency.[1] By 1963, although counter-insurgency measures seemed to have arrested the Vietcong military advance, politically the NLF retained widespread popularity (4.1). Indeed Washington increasingly questioned whether the insurgency could ever be won while Diem's dictatorial practices continued to alienate large sections of the population. By the autumn of 1963, many senior US policy-makers had reluctantly arrived at an answer in the negative: on 1–2 November, Diem was overthrown and killed in a military coup, the rebel generals having received implicit encouragement from a US government keen to procure a new regime committed both to the vigorous prosecution of the war effort and to an imaginative political strategy (4.3). Yet the southern Republic's fortunes continued to decline until, in early 1965, the country appeared to be on the verge of collapse. In Washington, Kennedy's successor, Lyndon B. Johnson, reacted by ordering a major escalation in the US commitment, beginning in March 1965 with an air war against North Vietnam (4.12, 4.16).

Because US escalation (including the subsequent influx of ground troops into South Vietnam) produced not victory but entrapment, historians have sought to locate the point at which the American descent into the abyss became irreversible. One such is the death of President Kennedy in 1963. In the last months of his life, it is argued, Kennedy approved plans that would have led to US disengagement from a conflict that he had decided was unwinnable; his assassination was thus a double tragedy in that it also killed the withdrawal plan, for under Johnson there would be escalation where there should have been disengagement. Although evidence exists to buttress these claims, on balance the case for Johnson as a continuation rather than a break with the Kennedy strategy is the stronger. It was only in the weeks after Diem's death that the true gravity of the situation in South Vietnam began to reveal itself. Hitherto such withdrawal plans as existed had been based on optimistic assessments of military progress which, on Diem's removal, were shown to be exaggerated (4.4 to 4.10). Moreover, however bad matters were in autumn 1963, they would soon get worse. In December 1963, Hanoi, sensing an opportunity to achieve a military and political breakthrough, decided to step up its material support for the insurgency, and by late 1964 units of the North Vietnamese army (the People's Army of Vietnam, PAVN) would be operating for the first time south of the seventeenth parallel (4.11). By 1965, as a consequence of Hanoi's escalation, the Saigon regime appeared to be facing certain doom. It was of course President Johnson, not Kennedy, who had to decide on America's response, opting – after a period of protracted deliberation – on drastic remedial measures, beginning with the bombing of North Vietnam in the hope that, by such coercive action, the DRV would cease its support for the southern insurgents. To argue that Kennedy, in this crisis situation, would have done otherwise is probably wishful thinking, but the nature of counter-factual history being what it is, this debate will no doubt run and run.

In recent years, historians have scrutinised anew President Johnson's part in the escalation process. Although often depicted as an unreformed hawk, with a wider war always his chosen course, new scholarship offers an alternative picture. Wracked with doubts about escalation, questioning of Vietnam's importance to America, and worried about the possibility of a confrontation with Communist China and even the Soviet Union, Johnson postponed any major decisions for eighteen months until, in early 1965, the consequence of further inaction appeared to be the complete collapse of the Republic of Vietnam (4.14). Also of central importance to this revised view of Johnson is the Great Society, his domestic reform programme. The war that Johnson really wanted to fight was against poverty and social injustice in America, and this provided him with a powerful impulse to seek an alternative to greater involvement in Vietnam. In the end, he could find none; a wider war might divert attention and resources from the Great Society, but allowing South Vietnam to fall would generate a conservative backlash in America that would destroy the Great Society anyway (4.15). Ultimately, whether Johnson went to war reluctantly or willingly, go to war he did. The bombing of North Vietnam began the Americanisation of the war; the despatch of ground troops to South Vietnam would complete the process.

### 4.1   The source of NLF and Vietcong popularity

Active support and sympathy for the NLF–Vietcong grew steadily during 1961–62, particularly in rural areas where the intrinsic appeal of their patriotic and reformist programme melded with widespread fear and loathing of the Diem regime. In her celebrated memoir on the war, Le Ly Hayslip has recalled how, as a young girl growing up in rural South Vietnam in the late 1950s and early 1960s, she became politicised.

Everything I knew about the war I learned as a teenaged girl from the North Vietnamese cadre leaders in the swamps outside Ky La.[2] During these midnight meetings, we peasants assumed everything we heard was true because what the Viet Cong said matched, in one way or another, the beliefs we already had ...

First we were taught that Vietnam was *con rong chau tien* – a sovereign nation which had been held in thrall by Western imperialists for over a century. That all nations had a right to determine their own destiny also seemed beyond dispute, since we farmers subsisted by our own hands and felt we owed nothing to anyone but god and our ancestors for the right to live as we saw fit. Even the Chinese, who had made their own disastrous attempt to rule Vietnam in centuries past, had learned a painful lesson about our country's zeal for independence. 'Vietnam,' went the saying, 'is nobody's lapdog.'

Second, the cadres told us that the division of Vietnam into North and South in 1954 was nothing more than a ploy by the defeated French and their Western allies, mainly the United States, to preserve what influence they could in our country ...

After these initial 'lessons,' the cadre leaders introduced us to the two Vietnamese leaders who personified each view – the opposite poles of our tiny world. On the South pole was President Ngo Dinh Diem, America's staunch ally, who was Catholic like the French. Although he was idolized by many who said he was a great humanitarian and patriot, his religion alone was enough to make him suspicious to Buddhists on the Central Coast. The loyalty we showed him, consequently, was more duty to a landlord than love for a founding father ...

In the North, on the other pole, was Ho Chi Minh, whom we were encouraged to call *Bac Ho* – Uncle Ho – the way we would refer to a trusted family friend. We knew nothing of his past beyond stories of his compassion and his love for our troubled country – the independence of which, we were told, he had made the mission of his life.

Given the gulf between these leaders, the choice of whom we should support again seemed obvious. The cadre leaders encouraged our natural prejudices (fear of outsiders and love of our ancestors) with stirring songs and tender stories about Uncle Ho in which the Communist leader and our ancient heroes seemed to inhabit one congenial world. Like an unbroken thread, the path from our ancestors and legends seemed to lead inevitably to the Northern leader – then past him to a future of harmony and peace.

But to achieve that independence, Ho said, we must wage total war. His cadremen cried out 'We must hold together and oppose the American empire. There is nothing better than freedom, independence, and happiness!'

... Although most of us thought we knew what the Viet Cong meant by freedom, independence, and happiness, a few of us dared to ask what life the Northerners promised when the war was over. The answer was always the same: 'Uncle Ho promises that after our victory, the Communist state will look after your rights and interests. Your highest interest, of course, is the independence of the fatherland and the freedom of our people. Our greatest right is the right to determine our own future as a state.' This always brought storms of applause from the villagers because most people remembered what life was like under the French.

Nonetheless, despite our vocal support, the Viet Cong never took our loyalty for granted. They rallied and rewarded and lectured us sternly, as the situation demanded, while the Republicans assumed we would be loyal because we lived south of a line some diplomats had drawn on a map. Even when things were at their worst – when the allied forces devastated the countryside and the Viet Cong themselves resorted to terror to make us act the way they wanted – the villagers clung to the vision the Communists had drummed into us. When the Republicans put us in jail, we had the image of 'Communist freedom' – freedom from war – to see us through. When the Viet Cong executed a relative, we convinced ourselves that it was necessary to bring 'Communist happiness' – peace in the village – a little closer. Because the Viet Cong encouraged us to voice our basic human feelings through patriotic songs, the tortured, self-imposed silence we endured around the Republicans only made us hate the government more. Even on those occasions when the Republicans tried to help us, we saw their favors as a trick or sign of weakness. Thus, even as we accepted their kindness, we despised the Republicans for it.

As the war gathered steam in the 1960s, every villager found his or her little world expanded – usually for the worse. The steady parade of troops through Ky La meant new opportunities for us to fall victim to outsiders. Catholic Republicans spurned and mistreated Buddhists for worshipping their ancestors. City boys taunted and cheated the 'country bumpkins' while Vietnamese servicemen from other provinces made fun of our funny accents and strange ways. When the tactics on both sides got so rough that people were in danger no matter which side they favored, our sisters fled to the cities where they learned about liquor, drugs, adultery, materialism, and disrespect for their ancestors. More than one village father died inside when a 'stranger from Saigon' returned in place of the daughter he had raised.

In contrast to this, the Viet Cong were, for the most part, our neighbors. Even though our cadre leaders had been trained in Hanoi, they had all been born on the Central Coast. They did not insult us for our manners and speech because they had been raised exactly like us. Where the Republicans came into the village overburdened with American equipment designed for a different war, the Viet Cong made do with what they had and seldom wasted their best ammunition – the goodwill of the people. The cadremen pointed out to us that where the Republicans wore medals, the Viet Cong wore rags and never gave up the fight. 'Where the Republicans pillage, rape, and plunder,' they said, 'we preserve your houses, crops, and family'; for they knew that it was only by these resources – our food for rations, our homes for hiding, our sons and brothers for recruits – that they were able to keep the field.

Le Ly Hayslip (with Jay Wurts), *When Heaven and Earth Changed Places: A Vietnamese Woman's Journey from War to Peace* (New York: Doubleday, 1989), pp. x–xiv.

## 4.2   The Kennedy administration and Diem

> In December 1961, the Kennedy administration publicly dedicated itself to the preservation of a non-communist South Vietnam, and undertook to increase its assistance to the Diem regime to help counter the insurgency.

Dear Mr. President [Diem]

I have received you recent letter in which you described so cogently the dangerous condition caused by North Viet-Nam's efforts to take over your country. The situation in your embattled country is well known to me and the American people. We have been deeply disturbed by the assault on your country. Our indignation has mounted as the deliberate savagery of the Communist program of assassination, kidnapping and wanton violence becomes clear.

Your letter underlines what our own information has convincingly shown – that the campaign of force and terror now being waged against your people and your Government is supported and directed from the outside by the authorities at Hanoi. They have thus violated the provisions of the Geneva Accords designed to ensure peace in Viet-Nam and to which they bound themselves in 1954 ...

[W]e are prepared to help the Republic of Viet-Nam to protect its people and to preserve its independence. We shall promptly increase our assistance to your defense effort ... I have already given the orders to get these programs underway.

The United States, like the Republic of Viet-Nam, remains devoted to the cause of peace and our primary purpose is to help your people maintain their independence. If the Communist authorities in North Viet-Nam will stop their campaign to destroy the Republic of Viet-Nam, the measures we are taking to assist your defense efforts will no longer be necessary. We shall seek to persuade the Communists to give up their attempts of force and subversion. In any case, we are confident that the Vietnamese people will preserve their independence and gain the peace and prosperity for which they have sought so hard and so long.

Kennedy letter to Diem, 14 December 1961, in *Public Papers of the Presidents of the United States: John F. Kennedy, 1961* (Washington DC: Government Printing Office, 1962), p. 801.


### 4.3   The overthrow of Diem: American complicity?

Over the next two years, the US increased substantially its military assistance to South Vietnam and despatched around 16,000 advisers to the Saigon army. By 1963, however, many policy-makers began to doubt whether the insurgency would ever be crushed while the unpopular Diem remained in power. The extent to which the US government – and in particular the White House – encouraged the November 1963 coup against Diem has been a matter of fierce historical disputation. Although no obvious encouragement was given, the Kennedy administration did inform the rebel generals that it supported South Vietnam, not any particular leader, a subtle but unmistakable green light to proceed against Diem.


CAP 63560. In conjunction with decisions and recommendations in separate [telegram], President today approved recommendation that no initiative should now be taken to give any active covert encouragement to a coup. There should, however, be urgent covert effort with closest security under broad guidance of Ambassador to identify and build contacts with possible alternative leadership as and when it appears. Essential that this effort be totally secure and fully deniable and separated entirely from normal political analysis and reporting of country team. We repeat that this effort is not to be aimed at active promotion of a coup but only at surveillance and readiness. In order to provide plausibility to denial suggest you and no one else in

Embassy issue these instructions orally to Acting Station Chief and hold him responsible to you alone for making appropriate contacts and reporting to you alone.

McGeorge Bundy telegram to Ambassador Henry Cabot Lodge, Saigon, 5 October 1963, in *Foreign Relations of the United States (FRUS) 1961–1963,* Vol. IV (Washington DC: Government Printing Office, 1991), p. 379.

## 4.4 JFK: the withdrawal debate

Three weeks after Diem's death, Kennedy was himself assassinated. Is there any substance to the claim that, had he lived, Kennedy would have terminated the US commitment to South Vietnam? Those historians who propound the withdrawal thesis tend to rely on the recollections of former Kennedy friends and associates. Robert McNamara, Kennedy's Secretary of Defense, has lately made his contribution to the debate.

Having reviewed the record in detail, and with the advantage of hindsight, I think it highly probable that, had President Kennedy lived, he would have pulled us out of Vietnam. He would have concluded that the South Vietnamese were incapable of defending themselves, and that Saigon's grave political weaknesses made it unwise to try to offset the limitations of South Vietnamese forces by sending U.S. combat troops on a large scale. I think he would have come to that conclusion even if he had reasoned, as I believe he would have, that South Vietnam and, ultimately, Southeast Asia would then be lost to Communism. He would have viewed that loss as more costly than we see it now. But he would have accepted that cost because he would have sensed that the conditions he had laid down – i.e., it was a South Vietnamese war, that it could only be won by them, and to win it they needed a sound political base – could not be met. Kennedy would have agreed that withdrawal would cause the fall of the 'dominoes' but that staying in would ultimately lead to the same result, while exacting a terrible price in blood.

Robert S. McNamara, *In Retrospect: The Tragedy and Lessons of Vietnam* (New York: Times Books/Random House, 1995), pp. 95–6.

## 4.5 'All we can do is help'

Critics of the withdrawal thesis contend that it lacks firm evidential foundations. The documentary record is certainly limited and ambiguous: the transcript of a televised interview given by Kennedy in September 1963, for example, offers support for both sides in the argument.

MR. CRONKITE. Do you think this [South Vietnamese] government still has time to regain the support of the people?

THE PRESIDENT. I do. With changes in policy and perhaps with personnel I think it can. If it doesn't make those changes, I would think that the chances of winning it would not be very good.

MR. CRONKITE. Hasn't every indication from Saigon been that President Diem has no intention of changing his pattern?

THE PRESIDENT. If he does not change it, of course, that is his decision. He has been there 10 years and, as I say, he has carried the burden when he has been counted out on a number of occasions.

Our best judgment is that he can't be successful on this basis. We hope that he comes to see that, but in the final analysis it is the people and the government [of South Vietnam] itself who have to win or lose this struggle. All we can do is help, and we are making it very clear, but I don't agree with those who say we should withdraw. That would be a great mistake. I know people don't like Americans to be engaged in this kind of an effort. Forty-seven Americans have been killed in combat with the enemy, but this is a very important struggle even though it is far away.

We took all this – made this effort to defend Europe. Now Europe is quite secure. We also have to participate – we may not like it – in the defense of Asia.

Cronkite–Kennedy interview, 2 September 1963, in *FRUS 1961–1963*, Vol. IV, pp. 93–4.

## 4.6 NSAM-263

Probably the most important piece of evidence in support of withdrawal is a brief National Security Action Memorandum in which Kennedy, six weeks before his death, authorised the removal of 1,000 US advisers from South Vietnam by the end of 1963. This, some historians argue, would have been the future. Instead, America – and Vietnam – got Lyndon Johnson and escalation.

At a meeting on October 5, 1963, the President considered the recommendations contained in the report of Secretary McNamara and General Taylor on their mission to South Vietnam.

The President approved the military recommendations contained in Section I B (1–3) of the report, but directed that no formal announcement be made of the implementation of plans to withdraw 1,000 U.S. military personnel by the end of 1963.

NSAM-263, 11 October 1963, in *FRUS 1961–1963*, Vol. IV, pp. 395–6.

## 4.7 The McNamara–Taylor report

Yet even NSAM-263 is open to variable interpretation. What the document actually *approved* was Section I B (1–3) of a report drawn up by Defense Secretary McNamara and General Maxwell D. Taylor, chairman of the Joint Chiefs of Staff, following a fact-finding mission to South Vietnam. This, Kennedy's critics insist, attached a key condition to withdrawal plans.

I.

B. *Recommendations*

We recommend that:

1. General Harkins[3] review with Diem the military changes necessary to complete the military campaign in Northern and Central areas … by the end of 1965 …

2. A program to be established to train Vietnamese so that essential functions now performed by U.S. military personnel can be carried out by Vietnamese by the end of 1965. It should be possible to withdraw the bulk of U.S. personnel by that time.

3. In accordance with the program to train progressively Vietnamese to take over military functions, the Defense Department should announce in the very near future presently prepared plans to withdraw 1000 U.S. military personnel by the end of 1963. This action

should be explained in low key as an initial step in a long-term program to replace U.S. personnel with trained Vietnamese *without impairment of the war effort* [emphasis added].

McNamara–Taylor report, 2 October 1963, in *FRUS 1961–1963*, Vol. IV, pp. 336–8.

## 4.8 Reality dawns?

Hence, whilst not denying the existence of putative withdrawal plans, critics of Kennedy maintain that their implementation was dependent upon a favourable battlefield situation. Following Diem's death, however, reporting from Saigon assumed a more realistic, hence more worrying tone.

The Prime Minister [of South Vietnam, Nguyen Ngoc Tho] said that he had been told by people in the Government who had worked in the Strategic Hamlet Program before and by the Generals that I was the American to see about the Strategic Hamlets. He said he wanted my frank views and he would give me his ...

He said it was difficult for the Americans to understand what had happened in the [Mekong] Delta and how the support of the population had been lost but they must understand this now. The truth was that the Government had been losing the war against the VC [Vietcong] in the Delta for some time because it had been losing the population. If one wanted to cite statistics, he said, all one needed to do was mention the fact that the total number of VC in the area was greater now than two years ago, yet around 20,000 had supposedly been killed during this same period. But beyond that, he said, he knew first hand what had been happening because he personally knew the people of this region, his region, and they had told him clearly over the past two years why more and more people were turning to the VC.

Nguyen Ngoc Tho meeting with Rufus C. Phillips, US Assistant Director for Rural Affairs, Saigon, 13 November 1963, in *FRUS 1961–1963*, Vol. IV, p. 596.

## 4.9   NSAM-273

Even before Kennedy's assassination, therefore, the signs were that the essential condition for US withdrawal – 'without impairment of the war effort' – did not exist. On 26 November 1963, NSAM-273, authorised by Kennedy's successor, Lyndon Johnson, put withdrawal on hold. Johnson has often been accused of sabotaging Kennedy's plans, but NSAM-273 adheres in almost every particular to a draft drawn up for Kennedy in the expectation that he would sign it.

1. It remains the central object of the United States in South Vietnam to assist the people and Government of that country to win their contest against the externally directed and supported Communist conspiracy. The test of all U.S. decisions and actions in this area should be the effectiveness of their contribution to this purpose.

2. The objective of the United States with respect to the withdrawal of U.S. military personnel remain as stated in the White House statement of October 2, 1963.[4]

3. It is a major interest of the United States Government that the present provisional government of South Vietnam should be assisted in consolidating itself and in holding and developing increased public support.[5] All U.S. officers should conduct themselves with this objective in view.

4. The President expects that all senior officers of the Government will move energetically to insure the full unity of support for established U.S. policy in South Vietnam ...

5. We should concentrate our own efforts, and insofar as possible we should persuade the Government of South Vietnam to concentrate its efforts, on the critical situation in the Mekong Delta. This concentration should include not only military but political, economic, social, educational and informational effort. We should seek to turn the tide not only of battle but of belief, and we should seek to increase not only the control of hamlets but the productivity of this area, especially where the proceeds can be held for the advantage of anti-Communist forces ...

NSAM-273, 26 November 1963, in *FRUS 1961–1963*, Vol. IV, pp. 637–8.

## 4.10 'Distorted Vietnamese reporting'

A month after Johnson sanctioned NSAM-273, the rectitude of postponing withdrawal plans was confirmed by McNamara, following another fact-finding trip to South Vietnam.

In accordance with your request this morning, this is a summary of my conclusions after my visit to Vietnam on December 19–20.

The situation is very disturbing. Current trends, unless reversed in the next 2–3 months, will lead to neutralization at best and more likely to a Communist-controlled state ...

Viet Cong progress has been great during the period since the coup [against Diem], with my best guess being that the situation has in fact been deteriorating in the countryside since July to a far greater extent than we realized because of our undue dependence on distorted Vietnamese reporting. The Viet Cong now control very high proportions of the people in certain key provinces, particularly those south and west of Saigon. The Strategic Hamlet Program was seriously over-extended in these provinces, and the Viet Cong has been able to destroy many hamlets, while others have been abandoned or in some cases betrayed or pillaged by the Government's own Self Defense Corps. In these key provinces, the Viet Cong have destroyed almost all major roads, and are collecting taxes at will.

McNamara memorandum to Johnson, 21 December 1963, in *FRUS 1961–1963*, Vol. VI, pp. 732–5.

## 4.11 Hanoi ups the stakes

By the end of 1963, the conditions under which the US government could safely commence disengagement did not exist – nor, following Hanoi's decision to escalate North Vietnam's commitment to the insurgency in the hope of producing a swift and decisive victory, would they ever exist.

The U.S. imperialists waged the *special war* in SVN [South Vietnam] and established the Southeast Asia aggressive bloc[6] in order to achieve the following three objectives.

– Repress the national liberation movement and carry out the

neocolonialist policy
- Build up military bases and prepare to attack our side
- Keep socialism from spreading throughout Southeast Asia.

If the U.S. imperialists are after the third objective, it is because all national liberation movements tend unavoidably to develop into socialist revolutions, especially in Southeast Asia in general and in South Viet-Nam in particular. In these areas, the national democratic revolutions are being conducted by the strong Marxist-Leninist parties ...

The U.S. imperialists are determined to pursue the three objectives mentioned above. However, the third goal is the most important to them, because it includes preventing the decline and collapse of imperialist capitalism in Southeast Asia and over the world. To attain this goal, the American imperialists do not hesitate to wage a 'special war', and if they are not successful, they may wage a limited war ...

> The term 'special war' denoted America's preference for working indirectly through proxies, like the Saigon government and armed forces, limiting its own involvement to military advice and support. However, Hanoi was aware that 'special war' could give way to 'limited war' involving direct US participation.

We must and have the capability to check and defeat the enemy in his 'special war.' This capability will increase if we are determined to fight the U.S. imperialists and their henchmen, if we have a clever strategem, and know how to exploit the contradictions between the U.S. imperialists and the other imperialists, especially the French imperialists,[7] contradictions between the U.S. and their henchmen in South Viet-Nam and the bourgeois ruling clique in Southeast Asia. In this way, we can cause difficulties for the U.S in using the aggressive force of the Southeast Asia bloc to escalate the war in South Viet-Nam ... However, we must always be vigilant and prepared to cope with the U.S. if she takes the risk of turning the war in South Viet-Nam into a limited war ...

In the framework of the 'special war', there are two possibilities:
- First, the Americans would carry on the war at the present or slightly higher level.
- Second, the Americans would intensify the war by bringing in

troops many times larger [than the present number of approximately 16,000] or both American troops and troops from the Southeast Asian aggressive bloc will intervene in the war.

If the U.S. takes a stronger part in the Viet-nam war but still uses the troops of the satellite countries to play the main role, this war is still considered a 'special war'. If they use their own troops as the main force, and deploy the armed forces of the Southeast Asia aggressive bloc into Viet-Nam, the Viet-Nam war will no longer be a 'special war' but a limited war, although it is going on within South Viet-Nam. This may occur in the following cases:

– First, faced with their numerous difficulties in South Viet-Nam, the U.S. Imperialists believe that they will be successful if they fight more violently.

– Second, the U.S. believes that the North will not strongly react.

– Third, if they believe their increased involvement in the war in South Viet-Nam will not raise a strong opposition from the people of the U.S. and the world.

However, the above are only remote possibilities because the U.S. cannot evaluate all the disastrous consequences she might bear if she wages the war on a larger scale. She realizes that if she is bogged down in a large-scale and protracted war, she will be thrown into a very passive position in the world. However, the above possibilities may become more probable if the revolutionary movement in South Viet-Nam is not strong enough.

Through our subjective efforts, let us strive to deal with the first eventuality; at the same time, let us positively prepare to defeat the enemy should the second eventuality materialize.

We have sufficient conditions to quickly change the balance of forces in our favor. And whether the U.S. maintains its combat strength at the present level or increases it, she must still use her henchman's army as a main force. However, this army becomes weaker day by day due to the serious decline of its quality, the demoralization of its troops and the disgust of the latter for the Americans and their lackeys. These are the factors that cause the collapse of Americans' and their lackeys' troops. No U.S. financial assistance or weapons can prevent this collapse.

As for us, we become more confident in the victory of our armed forces ... To create a basic change in the balance of forces between the enemy and us is within our grasp. In the days ahead, our force will be increasingly developed, whereas the enemy will certainly encounter a great deal of difficulties and he will be demoralized ... A strong development of the Revolution will cause many more troubles for the enemy and bring about a quicker disorganization of his armed forces and government. The Revolution in SVN will inevitably evolve into a General Offensive and Uprising to achieve the complete victory.[8]

If the U.S. imperialists send more troops to Viet-Nam to save the situation after suffering a series of failures, the Revolution in Viet-Nam will meet more difficulties, the struggle will become stronger and harder but it will certainly succeed in attaining the final victory ...

VWP Central Committee resolution, December 1963, in Gareth Porter (ed.), *Vietnam: The Definitive Documentation of Human Decisions*, 2 vols (London: Heyden, 1979), Vol. 2, pp. 223–7.

## 4.12   Graduated overt military pressure

Reacting to gloomy reports about South Vietnam's prospects for survival, President Johnson in the spring of 1964 author-ised the fine-tuning of various plans for deeper American involvement. Most of his senior advisers had concluded that bombing North Vietnam was the key to a solution in South Vietnam if, as a result, Hanoi gave up its support for the insurgency.

[US policy is] to prepare immediately to be in a position on 72 hours' notice to initiate ... 'Retaliatory Actions' against North Vietnam, and to be in a position on 30 days' notice to initiate the program of 'Graduated Overt Military Pressure' against North Vietnam ...

We seek an independent non-Communist South Vietnam. We do not require that it serve as a Western base or as a member of a Western Alliance. South Vietnam must be free, however, to accept outside assistance as required to maintain its security. This assistance should be able to take the form not only of economic and social measures but also police and military help to root out and control insurgent elements.

Even in 1964, the domino theory retained its relevance for US policy-makers.

Unless we can achieve the objective in South Vietnam, almost all of Southeast Asia will probably fall under Communist dominance (all of Vietnam, Laos and Cambodia), accommodate to Communism so as to remove effective U.S. and anti-Communist influence (Burma), or fall under the domination of forces not now explicitly Communist but likely then to become so (Indonesia taking over Malaysia). Thailand might hold for a period without help, but would be under grave pressure. Even the Philippines would become shaky, and the threat to India on the West, Australia and New Zealand to the South, and Taiwan, Korea, and Japan to the North and East would be greatly increased.

NSAM-288, 17 March 1964, in Porter (ed.), *Vietnam*, Vol. 2, pp. 258–9.

### 4.13   The Gulf of Tonkin resolution

Reluctant to authorise any escalation in Vietnam without domestic political support, President Johnson approved the drawing up of a congressional resolution that would grant him effective war powers in the Southeast Asian region. At the start of August 1964, the notorious Gulf of Tonkin incident provided the US government with an opportunity to table the resolution. It was passed almost unanimously and would provide the legal basis upon which the later massive US escalation in Vietnam was undertaken.

*To Promote the Maintenance of International Peace and Security in Southeast Asia.*
Whereas naval units of the Communist regime in Vietnam, in violation of the principles of the Charter of the United Nations and of international law, have deliberately and repeatedly attacked United States naval vessels lawfully present in international waters, and have thereby created a serious threat to international peace; and

Whereas these attacks are part of a deliberate and systematic campaign of aggression that the Communist regime in North Vietnam has been waging against its neighbors and the nations joined with them in the collective defense of their freedom; and

Whereas the United States is assisting the peoples of southeast Asia to protect their freedom and has no territorial, military or political ambitions in that area, but desires only that these peoples should be left in peace to work out their own destinies in their own way: Now, therefore, be it

Resolved by the Senate and House of Representatives of the United States of America in Congress assembled.

That the Congress approves and supports the determination of the President as Commander in Chief, to take all necessary measures to repel any armed attack against the forces of the United States and to prevent further aggression.

SEC.2. The United States regards as vital to its national interest and to world peace the maintenance of international peace and security in southeast Asia. Consonant with the Constitution of the United States and the Charter of the United Nations and in accordance with its obligations under the Southeast Asia Collective Defense Treaty, the United States is, therefore, prepared, as the President determines, to take all necessary steps, including the use of armed force, to assist any member or protocol state of the Southeast Asia Collective Defense Treaty requiring assistance in defense of its freedom.[9]

SEC. 3. This resolution shall expire when the President shall determine that the peace and security of the area is reasonably assured by international conditions created by action of the United Nations or otherwise, except that it may be terminated earlier by concurrent resolution of the Congress.

The Gulf of Tonkin resolution, 7 August 1964, *Department of State Bulletin*, 24 August 1964.

### 4.14   Johnson the hawk: a revised assessment

For Johnson's critics, the resolution was the necessary means to the end which he, like his advisers, had been working towards all along: a major escalation in the US commitment to South Vietnam, and an air war against North Vietnam. In recent years, this image of Johnson as a hawk has been questioned. The transcripts of his telephone conversations in 1964, for example, reveal Johnson's profound doubts about the wisdom of escalation.

*27 May 1964, 10.55 am, conversation with Democratic Senator Richard Russell*

LBJ: I spend all my days with Rusk and McNamara and Bundy and Harriman and Vance and all those folks that are dealing with it [Vietnam] and I would say that it pretty well adds up to them now that we've got to show some power and some force, that they do not believe – they're kinda like MacArthur in Korea – they don't believe that the Chinese Communists will come into this thing. But they don't know and nobody can really be sure. But their feeling is that they won't. And in any event, that we haven't got much choice, that we are treaty-bound [through SEATO], that we are there, that this will be a domino that will kick off a whole list of others, that we've just got to prepare for the worst. Now I have avoided that for a few days. I don't think the American people are for it ... I don't think the people of the country know much about Vietnam and I think they care a hell of a lot less.

Later the same day, Johnson again revealed his anxieties.

*27 May 1964, 11.24 am, conversation with McGeorge Bundy*
LBJ: ... it looks to me like we're getting into another Korea. It just worries the hell out of me. I don't see what we can ever hope to get out of there with, once we're committed. I believe that the Chinese Communists are coming into it. I don't think that we can fight them ten thousand miles away from home ... I don't think it's worth fighting for and I don't think that we can get out. It's just the biggest damned mess that I ever saw ...

But then Johnson's Cold War orthodoxy reasserted itself.

Of course if you start running from the Communists, they may just chase you right into your own kitchen.

Michael R. Beschloss (ed.), *Taking Charge: The Johnson White House Tapes, 1963–1964* (New York: Touchstone, 1997), pp. 364–5, 370.

## 4.15  Johnson, Vietnam and the Great Society

In recent years, the importance of President Johnson's domestic reform programme has come to feature prominently in a number of works on his Vietnam decision-making. Increasingly, he is depicted as a reluctant warrior, worried that a wider war in Vietnam would destroy his cherished Great Society. In this extract, Johnson himself describes his dilemma, namely that the Great Society would be equally imperilled, and his presidency ruined, if he 'lost' South Vietnam.

I knew from the start that I was bound to be crucified either way I moved. If I left the woman I really loved – the Great Society – in order to get involved with that bitch of a war on the other side of the world, then I would lose everything at home. All my programs. All my hopes to feed the hungry and shelter the homeless. All my dreams to provide education and medical care to the browns and the blacks and the lame and the poor. But if I left that war and let the Communists take over South Vietnam, then I would be seen as a coward and my nation would be seen as an appeaser and we would both find it impossible to accomplish anything for anybody anywhere on the entire globe.

Oh, I could see it coming all right. History provided too many cases where the sound of the bugle put an immediate end to the hopes and dreams of the best reformers ... Once the [Vietnam] war began, then all those conservatives in the Congress would use it as a weapon against the Great Society. You see, they'd never wanted to help the poor or the Negroes in the first place. But they were having a hard time figuring out how to make their opposition sound noble in a time of great prosperity. But the war. Oh, they'd use it to say they were against my programs, not because they were against the poor ... but because the war had to come first. First, we had to beat those Godless Communists and then we could worry about the homeless Americans. And the generals. Oh, they'd love the war, too ... Oh, I could see it coming. And I didn't like the smell of it. I didn't like anything about it, but I think the situation in South Vietnam bothered me most. They never seemed able to get themselves together down there. Always fighting with one another. Bad. Bad.

Yet everything I knew about history told me that if I got out of Vietnam and let Ho Chi Minh run through the streets of Saigon, then I'd be doing exactly what Chamberlain did in World War II. I'd be giving a big fat reward to aggression. And I knew that if we let Communist aggression succeed in taking over South Vietnam, there would follow in this country an endless national debate – a mean and destructive debate – that would shatter my Presidency, kill my administration, and damage our democracy. I knew that Harry Truman and Dean Acheson had lost their effectiveness from the day that the Communists took over in China. I believed that the loss of China had played a large role in the rise of Joe McCarthy. And I knew that all these problems, taken together, were chickenshit compared with what might happen if we lost Vietnam.

Doris Kearns, *Lyndon Johnson and the American Dream* (London: André Deutsch, 1976), pp. 251–3.

### 4.16  Pleiku: prelude to Rolling Thunder

By the end of 1964, even Johnson had come to accept the need to bomb North Vietnam. All that was now required was a Vietcong 'spectacular' to justify launching an air war. It came on the night of 6–7 February 1965 with an attack on a US base at Pleiku in South Vietnam. Johnson authorised immediate reprisal raids against North Vietnam, a process that quickly evolved into the sustained bombing of the DRV – Operation Rolling Thunder. By coincidence, Johnson's close aide, McGeorge Bundy, was in South Vietnam at the time of the Pleiku raid, and his forceful reaction was probably decisive in ending Johnson's vacillation over firm action.

The situation in Vietnam is deteriorating, and without new U.S. action defeat appears inevitable – probably not in a matter of weeks or perhaps even months, but within the next year or so. There is still time to turn it around, but not much.

The stakes in Vietnam are extremely high. The American investment is very large, and American responsibility is a fact of life which is palpable in the atmosphere of Asia, and even elsewhere. The international prestige of the United States, and a substantial part of our influence, are directly at risk in Vietnam. There is no way of unloading the burden on the Vietnamese themselves, and there is no way of negotiating ourselves out of Vietnam which offers any serious promise at present ...

The policy of graduated and continuing reprisal ... is the most promising course available, in my judgment. That judgment is shared by all who accompanied me from Washington, and I think by all members of the country team.

The events of the last twenty-four hours have produced a practicable point of departure for this policy of reprisal, and for the removal of U.S. dependants. They may also have catalyzed the formation of a new Vietnamese government. If so, the situation may be at a turning point.

> In an annex to his memorandum, Bundy described in detail the nature of the reprisal policy he advocated. When, however, he considered its likely effects, Bundy reversed one of the premises upon which US policy had rested: hitherto political stability in South Vietnam was deemed to be a prerequisite to bombing the North; now Bundy argued that this elusive stability could actually be *generated* by bombing the DRV. Most officials in Washington seemed to agree. The American war in Vietnam was about to begin.

We emphasize that our primary target in advocating a reprisal policy is the improvement of the situation in *South* Vietnam. Action against the North is usually urged as a means of affecting the will of Hanoi to direct and support the VC. We consider this an important but longer-range purpose. The immediate and critical targets are in the South – in the minds of the South Vietnamese and in the minds of the Viet Cong cadres.

Predictions of the effect of any given course of action upon the states of mind of people are difficult. It seems very clear that if the United States and the Government of Vietnam join in a policy of reprisal, there will be a sharp immediate increase in optimism in the South, among nearly all articulate groups. The Mission believes – and our own conversations confirm – that in all sectors of Vietnamese opinion there is a strong belief that the United States could do much more it if would, and that they are suspicious of our failure to use more of our obviously enormous power. At least in the short run, the reaction to reprisal policy would be very favorable.

McGeorge Bundy memorandum and annex to Johnson, 7 February 1965, in *FRUS 1964–1968*, Vol. II (Washington DC: Government Printing Office, 1996), pp. 174–85.

# 5

# The American war, 1965–1968

Alongside Operation Rolling Thunder, the Johnson administration launched a vigorous public relations exercise designed to educate the American people about the situation in Vietnam, justify the bombing, and advertise the terms upon which Hanoi could have peace (5.2). Although North Vietnam also professed interest in a negotiated settlement, the aims of the two sides were so far apart that talk of compromise was – and would remain – little more than public posturing, the Johnson administration playing to domestic opinion and the DRV government to the wider international community (5.3). As for the war itself, Hanoi had responded to the onset of Rolling Thunder by increasing its support for the Vietcong, with manpower and material assistance funnelled into South Vietnam via the Ho Chi Minh Trail (5.1). For their part, US strategists began arguing that more time was needed for the bombing to take effect. Time, though, was not on South Vietnam's side, a fact confirmed in July 1965 when the US Field Commander, General William C. Westmoreland, urgently requested major American reinforcements to forestall the imminent collapse of the Saigon government and army in the face of concerted Vietcong pressure. After intense inter-agency debate in Washington, President Johnson agreed to furnish Westmoreland with whatever manpower resources he needed. However, as with the decision to launch an air war against the DRV, evidence now suggests that Johnson, far from willingly embracing an aggressive policy, continued to harbour deep misgivings about escalation (5.5). Yet, in the final analysis, Johnson's Cold War orthodoxy proved decisive, with both his decision to meet Westmoreland's immediate request and his commitment to look positively on similar requests in the future predicated on the need to prevent the loss of the trigger-domino of Southeast Asia and so insulate his government from the inevitably negative domestic political consequences of a do-nothing approach (5.6).

North Vietnam's leaders, meanwhile, sensing that Washington might be on the brink of moving from 'special' to 'limited' war, determined to match any American escalation in the south with greater escalation of their own. Interestingly, in reaching this decision, Hanoi was conscious that US public opinion might yet be an important ally: if the United States could be drawn into a protracted war of attrition, American opinion might come to tire of the struggle; if or when that happened, the US government would be forced to negotiate on Hanoi's terms (5.4). Therefore, as the American build-up in South Vietnam got under way (by 1968, 500,000 US ground troops would be committed), the Vietcong and its northern backer prepared themselves for the long haul. Victory would come, they believed, if they simply avoided defeat for long enough. In practical terms, this philosophy translated itself into an avoidance of large-scale engagements with US and South Vietnamese forces in favour of guerrilla warfare that allowed the Vietcong to dictate the pace and nature of the war (of the numerous small unit engagements in the war, 90 per cent were initiated by the communists), and gradually to erode enemy strength and morale (5.7, 5.8).

By 1967, the United States found itself in a quagmire, unable to win the war in South Vietnam, only perpetuate it. Yet publicly the Johnson administration maintained that good progress was being made and that an end was in sight. This optimism was partly sincere (statistical indicators pointed in the right direction) and partly insincere (by holding out the prospect of victory, the administration was able to keep a lid on the simmering pressure cooker of domestic discontent with the war) (5.10). Then, at the end of January 1968, came the great communist Tet offensive. According to traditional accounts, Tet was a military disaster for the communists (they suffered enormous losses) but ultimately a strategic victory in that it brought about an end to US escalation in Vietnam – the offensive, by exposing the 'credibility gap' between Johnson's assurances of progress and battlefield reality, effectively left the US government without public support for further escalation. In recent years, however, this interpretation has been refined. For example, the emphasis on US public opinion (itself a more nuanced phenomenon than often depicted) tends to obscure the post-Tet revolt of many of Johnson's hitherto most hawkish advisers. Suddenly isolated within his own administration, Johnson, whose initial preference had been to provide Westmoreland with additional troops in order to keep the pressure on the communists, had no choice but to bring the curtain down on escalation (5.13). Vietnamese communist documentation also offers important insights; whereas Westmoreland maintained at the time that Tet was a last gasp action by an exhausted enemy, Vietcong sources suggest the opposite – that the communists regarded it as the practical implementation of their long-standing general offensive/general uprising revolutionary methodology (5.11, 5.12).

Although the debate surrounding the Tet offensive will go on, there can be no doubting its importance as a turning point in the American war. On 31 March 1968, Johnson announced a near total end to the bombing of the DRV, an effective cap on US troop levels in South Vietnam, and his government's readiness to engage in meaningful peace talks. For the United States, it was no longer a question of getting on in Vietnam, but of getting out (5.14).

## 5.1   The Ho Chi Minh Trail

As North Vietnam stepped up its support for the struggle in South Vietnam, men, weaponry and other supplies made their way down the Ho Chi Minh Trail – the network of jungle paths that snaked through Laos and Cambodia. It is easy to think of the Trail as some kind of a conveyor belt, with soldiers or arms placed on it in the north and safely deposited shortly after in the south. The reality was altogether different, as one who experienced the Trail has recalled.

I twice travelled south down the Ho Chi Minh Trail. The first time was in 1961 when it really was a trail and we literally had to hack or crawl our way through the jungle carrying only a rucksack with our personal effects.

In early 1964 it was easier. The trail was still narrow and only passable by bicycle, although it could carry a large load. Nor was the trip as dangerous as it became during the early 1970s when the trail was intensively bombed. Even so, quite a large number of deaths occurred. At each military staging-post – and they were 20 to 30 kilometers apart – there was a cemetery for those who had sacrificed their lives on the Trail. They died from a variety of causes. Some soldiers lost their way in the jungle and died of starvation. Small groups sleeping alone at night were pounced on by tigers or attacked by bears. On one occasion, I and three of my companions shot and killed a black bear staggering drunkenly down a hill towards us after it had raided a bee-hive and eaten all the honey. And in the rainy season there were those who, unable to see clearly, stepped on poisonous snakes and were bit-ten to death. Then there were stomach upsets and severe attacks of yellow fever to contend with. Others swung their hammocks up in the trees, only to be killed when the branches were torn off in high winds. During such storms when the water ran fast in the streams, it was also easy to lose one's footing on a slippery bridge and fall in without hope of rescue. Another hazard was jungle leeches; we encountered hundreds and thousands of them on our march, and they attached themselves not only to one's legs but also to certain vital organs, caus-ing a haemorrhage and threatening one's future family life. Sometimes too, as one climbed mountains covered in moss on a rainy day, the ground was as slippery as if it was covered with oil, so it was easy to lose one's footing and fall into a deep hollow, rucksack and all. Worst of all was eating poisonous mushrooms and leaves. For that there was no cure.

... In early 1964, following the death of the Ngo brothers and Kennedy, the atmosphere was different. We felt a new opportunity was opening up to despatch larger units to the South ... During this trip through such difficult terrain, we rested only after every nine or ten days to wash our clothes. Otherwise we woke every morning at 4 o'clock to cook rice, which we ate with roasted sesame mixed with salt. Sometimes we were able to catch fish in the streams. We dried and salted them, although often there was more salt than fish. Then when we ran out of salt, we licked the banana leaves used to wrap the dried fish. What we really lacked was vegetables and fruit. Occasion-ally we would find an orange tree close to a deserted house and really treasured its fruit. In the same way, whenever we saw any edible leaves we stopped to pick them to make a soup for the evening meal, which we usually ate at about 4 or 5 before it got dark.

At night it was very cold in the jungles of Laos and the Central Highlands, especially in the winter months when we shivered in the damp and cloudy atmosphere. To keep warm, we tried to dig holes instead of sleeping in hammocks as usual. The worst thing was cross-ing streams. It needed the entire effort of one's mind to keep going because the rest of one's body was paralysed with cold. On the other hand, in summer a different discipline was necessary. We became so thirsty we began to see stars and had to drink very slowly whenever we reached a stream.

Bui Tin, *Following Ho Chi Minh: The Memoirs of a North Vietnamese Colonel* (London: Hurst & Co., 1995), pp. 48–51.

## 5.2 'Why are we in South Vietnam?'

Coinciding with start of Operation Rolling Thunder, the Johnson administration launched a public relations drive to explain its Vietnam policy. The President himself led from the front.

Over this war, and all Asia, is the deepening shadow of Communist China. The rulers in Hanoi are urged on by Peking. This is a regime which has destroyed freedom in Tibet, attacked India, and been condemned by the United Nations for aggression in Korea.[1] It is a nation which is helping the forces of violence in almost every continent. The contest in Vietnam is part of a wider pattern of aggressive purpose.

Why are these realities our concern? Why are we in South Vietnam? We are there because we have a promise to keep. Since 1954 every American President has offered support to the people of South Vietnam. We have helped to build, and we have helped to defend. Thus, over many years, we have made a national pledge to help South Vietnam defend its independence. And I intend to keep our promise.

To dishonor that pledge, to abandon this small and brave nation to its enemy, and to the terror that must follow, would be an unforgivable wrong.

We are also there to strengthen world order. Around the globe, from Berlin to Thailand, are people whose well-being rests, in part, on the belief that they can count on us if they are attacked. To leave Vietnam to its fate would shake the confidence of all these people in the value of America's word. The result would be increased unrest and instability, and even wider war.

We are also there because there are great stakes in the balance. Let no one think for a moment that retreat from Vietnam would bring an end to conflict. The battle would be renewed in one country and then another. The central lesson of our time is that the appetite of aggression is never satisfied. To withdraw from one battlefield means only to prepare for the next. We must say in Southeast Asia, as we did in Europe, in the words of the Bible: 'Hitherto shalt thou come, but no further.'

> The justification for escalation was followed by Johnson's terms for peace.

Our objective is the independence of South Vietnam, and its freedom from attack ... We will not withdraw, either openly or under the cloak of a meaningless agreement ... Once this is clear, then it should also be clear that the only path for reasonable men is the path of peaceful settlement.

Such peace demands an independent South Vietnam securely guaranteed and able to shape its own relationships to all others, free from outside interference, tied to no alliance, a military base for no other country.

These are the essentials of any final settlement.

Johnson speech, 7 April 1965, *Public Papers of the Presidents of the United States: Lyndon B. Johnson, 1965* (Washington DC: Government Printing Office, 1966), p. 395.

## 5.3 Hanoi's four points

> In his insistence that Hanoi accept the principle of a separate South Vietnam, Johnson can hardly have expected a positive response; indeed his real target audience was in America where there was mounting unease at the recent turn of events. Hanoi duly countered with a four-point proposal of its own. For both sides, the key issue was who would rule in Saigon in the future; North Vietnam hoped for an NLF-led coalition dedicated to eventual national reunification, but Hanoi's hope was precisely Washington's fear. Hence talk of peace remained just that – talk.

The unswerving policy of the DRV Government is to respect strictly the 1954 Geneva agreements on Vietnam and to implement correctly their basic provisions as embodied in the following points:

1. Recognition of the basic national rights of the Vietnamese people – peace, independence, sovereignty, unity, and territorial integrity. According to the Geneva agreements, the U.S. Government must withdraw from South Vietnam U.S. troops, military personnel, and weapons of all kinds, dismantle all U.S. military bases there, and cancel its military alliance with South Vietnam. According to the Geneva agreements, the U.S. Government must stop its acts of war against North Vietnam and completely cease all encroachments on the territory and sovereignty of the DRV.

2. Pending the peaceful reunification of Vietnam, while Vietnam is still temporarily divided into two zones the military provisions of the 1954 Geneva agreements on Vietnam must be strictly respected. The two zones must refrain from entering into any military alliance with foreign countries and there must be no foreign military bases, troops, or military personnel in their respective territory.

3. The internal affairs of South Vietnam must be settled by the South Vietnamese people themselves in accordance with the program of the National Liberation Front of South Vietnam without any foreign interference.

4. The peaceful reunification of Vietnam is to be settled by the Vietnamese people in both zones, without foreign interference.

DRV statement, in Marvin E. Gettleman *et al.* (eds), *Vietnam and America: The Most Comprehensive Documented History of the Vietnam War* (New York: Grove Press, 1995), pp. 277–8.

## 5.4 'US imperialism could be adventurous'

By July 1965 there were around 75,000 US ground troops in South Vietnam, most having arrived since the start of Rolling Thunder. For Hanoi, the question now was whether this US commitment – adequate for defensive purposes – would be increased. The VWP leadership chose to work on the worst assumption: gone was the earlier optimism that America would never contemplate a major ground force commitment and in its place was a grim conviction that the revolution in the south would succeed no matter what the United States did. Note again that American public opinion is posited as a potential ally in the struggle.

The US is still strong enough to enter into a limited war in Vietnam, by sending not only 200,000–250,000 but 300,000–400,000 troops to South Vietnam. But if it switches to limited war, the US still will have weaknesses which it cannot overcome. The US rear area is very far away, and American soldiers are 'soldiers in chains', who cannot fight like the French, cannot stand the weather conditions, and don't know the battlefield but on the contrary have many weaknesses in their opposition to people's war ...

The Southern revolution can fight a protracted war, while the US can't, because American military, economic and political resources must be distributed throughout the world. If it is bogged down in one place and can't withdraw, the whole effort will be violently shaken. The US would lose its preeminence in influential sectors at home and create openings for other competing imperialists, and lose the American market. Therefore at present, although the US can immediately send 300,000 to 400,000 troops at once, why must the US do it step by step? Because even if it does send many troops like that, the US would still be hesitant; because that would be a passive policy full of contradictions; because of fear of protracted war, and the even stronger opposition of the American people and the world's people, and even of their allies who would also not support widening the war.

> The use of American atomic weapons against North Vietnam was thought possible but unlikely, while a direct US invasion of the DRV, though somewhat more likely, could be insured against.

If they reach a stage of desperation, would the US use the atomic bomb? Our camp also has the atomic bomb. The Soviet Union has sufficient atomic strength to oppose any imperialists who wish to use the atomic bomb in order to attack a socialist country, and threaten mankind. If US imperialism uses the atomic bomb in those circumstances they would be committing suicide. The American people themselves would be the ones to stand up and smash the US government when that government used atomic bombs. Would the US dare to provoke war between the two blocks, because of the Vietnam problem [?] ... But the possibility of broadening the direct war to the North is a possibility [to] which we must pay utmost attention, because US imperialism could be adventurous. We must be vigilant and prepared to cope with each worst possibility. The best way to cope, and not to let the US broaden the direct warfare in the South or in the North, is to fight even more strongly and more accurately in the South, and make the puppet military units – the primary mainstay of the US – rapidly fall apart, push military and political struggle forward, and quickly create the opportune moment to advance to complete defeat of US imperialism and its lackeys in the South.

Le Duan, speech to a cadre conference, 6–8 July 1965, in Gareth Porter (ed.), *Vietnam: The Definitive Documentation of Human Decisions*, 2 vols (London: Heyden, 1979), Vol. 2, pp. 383–5.

## 5.5   Johnson hesitates

Just as Le Duan was making these observations, the Johnson administration was indeed wrestling with the issue of escalation. The inter-agency debate in Washington on a ground troop commitment to South Vietnam reached a climax between 21 and 27 July 1965. The transcripts of the meetings between the President and his top politico-military advisers suggest that Johnson retained grave misgivings about escalation.

*Meeting, White House Cabinet room, 21 July 1965*
PRESIDENT: What makes you think if we put in 100,000 men Ho Chi Minh won't put in another 100,000?
   WHEELER [General Earl G., Chairman of the US Joint Chiefs of Staff]: This means greater bodies of men, which will allow us to cream them.
   PRESIDENT: But what are the chances of more NVN [North Vietnam] men coming?
   WHEELER: 50–50 chance. He [Ho] would be foolhardy to put ¼ of his forces in SVN [South Vietnam]. It would expose him too greatly in NVN.

*Meeting, White House Cabinet room, 22 July 1965, mainly with military leaders*
PRESIDENT: I asked McNamara to invite you here to counsel with you on these problems and the ways to meet them. Hear from the Chiefs the alternatives open to you and then recommendations on those alternatives from a military point [of view]. Options open to us:

(1) leave the country – with as little loss as possible – the 'bugging out' approach; (2) maintain present force and lose slowly; (3) add 100,000 men – recognizing that may not be enough – and adding more next year. Disadvantages of #3 – risk of escalation, casualties will be high – may be a long war without victory ... I would like you to start out by stating our present position and where we can go.

McDONALD [Admiral David L., chief of naval operations]: Sending Marines has improved [the] situation. I agree with McNamara that we are committed to [the] extent that we can't move out. If we continue the way we are, it will be a slow, sure victory for the other side. By putting more men in it will turn the tide and let us know what further we need to do. I wish we had come to this long before.

PRESIDENT: But you don't know if 100,000 will be enough. What makes you conclude that if you don't know where we are going – and what will happen – we shouldn't pause and find this out?

McDONALD: Sooner or later we will force them to the conference table ...

PRESDIENT: But if we put in 100,000 men won't they put in an equal number?

McDONALD: No, if we step up our bombing ...

PRESIDENT: Is this a chance we want to take?

McDONALD: Yes, when I view the alternatives. Get out now or pour in more men.

PRESIDENT: Is that all?

McDONALD: I think our allies will lose faith in us.

PRESIDENT: We have few allies really helping us.

McDONALD: Thailand, for example. If we walk out of Vietnam, the whole world will question our word. We don't have much choice.

The meeting moved on, but Johnson's doubts remained.

JOHNSON [General Harold K., army chief of staff]: Least desirable alternative is getting out. Second least is doing what we are doing. Best is to get in and get the job done.

PRESIDENT: But I don't know how we are going to get that job done. There are millions of Chinese. I think they are going to put their stack in. Is this the best place to do this? We don't have the allies we had in Korea.

Finally, Johnson asked the crucial question: there was no clear answer to it.

PRESIDENT: Are we starting something that in 2–3 years we simply can't finish?

*Foreign Relations of the United States (FRUS) 1964–1968*, Vol. III (Washington DC: Government Printing Office, 1996), pp. 193, 210–11, 213.


## 5.6 Johnson decides

For all his doubts, Johnson in the end sanctioned a major increase in the American commitment, announcing his decision publicly on 28 July 1965.

What are our goals in that war-stained land? First, we intend to convince the Communists that we cannot be defeated by force of arms or by superior power. They are not easily convinced. In recent months they have greatly increased their attacks and the number of incidents. I have asked the Commanding General, General Westmoreland, what more he needs to meet this mounting aggression. He has told me. We will meet his needs.

I have today ordered to Viet-Nam the Air Mobile Division and certain other forces which will raise our fighting strength from 75,000 to 125,000 men almost immediately. Additional forces will be needed later, and they will be sent as required.

Johnson address to the Nation, 29 July 1965, in *Public Papers of the Presidents, 1965*, p. 795.


## 5.7 The American ground war in South Vietnam

For the next three years, the United States, in conjunction with the Saigon army, waged a savage ground war in South Vietnam. Although numerous military histories chronicle the US descent into stalemate – a stalemate which the 500,000 American troops committed to the war by 1968 could not reverse – comparatively few accounts consider the reality of life (and death) for the ordinary American soldier. Philip Caputo has done as much as anybody to rectify this omission in his graphic recollection of his tour of duty in South Vietnam in 1965.

For Americans who did not come of age in the early sixties, it may be hard to grasp what those years were like -- the pride and overpowering self-assurance that prevailed. Most of the thirty-five hundred men in our brigade, born during or immediately after World War II, were shaped by that era, the age of Kennedy's Camelot. We went overseas full of illusions, for which the intoxicating atmosphere of those years was as much to blame as our youth.

War is always attractive to young men who know nothing about it, but we had also been seduced into uniform by Kennedy's challenge to 'ask what you can do for your country' and by the missionary idealism he had awakened in us. America seemed omnipotent then: the country could still claim it had never lost a war, and we believed we were ordained to play cop to the Communists' robber and spread our own political faith around the world. Like the French soldiers of the late eighteenth century, we saw ourselves as the champions of 'a cause that was destined to triumph.' So, when we marched into the rice paddies on that damp March afternoon [in 1965], we carried, along with our packs and rifles, the implicit convictions that the Viet Cong would be quickly beaten and that we were doing something altogether noble and good. We kept the packs and rifles; the convictions, we lost.

The discovery that the men we had scorned as peasant guerrillas were, in fact, a lethal, determined enemy and the casualty lists that lengthened each week with nothing to show for the blood being spilled broke our early confidence. By autumn [1965], what had begun as an adventurous expedition had turned into an exhausting, indecisive war of attrition in which we fought for no cause other than our own survival.

Writing about this kind of warfare is not a simple task. Repeatedly, I have found myself wishing that I had been the veteran of a conventional war, with dramatic campaigns and historic battles for subject matter instead of a monotonous succession of ambushes and fire-fights. But there were no Normandies or Gettysburgs for us, no epic clashes that decided the fates of armies or nations. The war was mostly a matter of enduring weeks of expectant waiting and, at random intervals, of conducting vicious manhunts through jungles and swamps where snipers harassed us constantly and booby traps cut us down one by one.

The tedium was occasionally relieved by a large scale search-and-destroy operation, but the exhilaration of riding the lead helicopter into a landing zone was usually followed by more of the same hot walking, with the mud sucking at our boots and the sun thudding against our helmets while an invisible enemy shot at us from distant tree lines. The rare instances when the VC chose to fight a set-piece battle provided the only excitement; not ordinary excitement, but the manic ecstasy of contact. Weeks of bottled-up tensions would be released in a few minutes of orgiastic violence, men screaming and shouting obscenities above the explosions of grenades and the rapid, rippling bursts of automatic rifles.

Beyond adding a few more corpses to the weekly body count, none of these encounters achieved anything ... Still, they changed us and taught us, the men who fought in them; in those obscure skirmishes we learned the old lessons about fear, cowardice, courage, suffering, cruelty, and comradeship. Most of all, we learned about death at an age when it is common to think of oneself as immortal. Everyone loses that illusion eventually, but in civilian life it is lost in instalments over the years. We lost it all at once and, in the span of months, passed from boyhood through manhood to a premature middle age. The knowledge of death, of the implacable limits placed on a man's existence, severed us from our youth as irrevocably as a surgeon's scissors had once severed us from the womb. And yet, few of us were past twenty-five. We left Vietnam peculiar creatures, with young shoulders that bore rather old heads.

Philip Caputo, *A Rumor of War* (London: Macmillan, 1977), pp. xii–xiv.

## 5.8 'looking at our future selves'

The ordinary North Vietnamese soldier shared more in common with his American counterpart than either probably realised at the time. The common denominator was fear.

On our way to the south we often met groups of wounded who were going North. Some had lost their arms or legs, some had been burned by napalm. Some had malaria. They all looked like skeletons. Every day we would meet them walking or riding in the opposite direction, groups of two or six or ten of them. We told each other that some day we would be like that. We began to feel the war.

Sometimes the men asked the lower-ranking cadres questions. The answer was that war always brings death and that we shouldn't bother ourselves with morbid thoughts. No one argued with the cadres. But everyone was frightened, especially when we met those men for the first time. It was horrifying. It was like looking at our future selves.

Recollections of Nguyen Trong Nghi (PAVN) in David Chanoff and Doan Van Toai, *Portrait of the Enemy* (London: I. B. Tauris, 1987), p. 68.

## 5.9   Surviving the US air war

The resilience of the Vietnamese population in the face of the US air war is well known. Even so, eyewitness accounts add substance to such generalisations. Here, Truong Nhu Tang recalls bombing raids against North Vietnamese/Vietcong enclaves in the border area with Cambodia.

From a kilometer away, the sonic roar of the B-52 explosions tore eardrums, leaving many of the jungle dwellers permanently deaf. From a kilometer, the shock waves knocked their victims senseless. Any hit within a half kilometer would collapse the walls of an unreinforced bunker, burying alive the people cowering inside. Seen up close, the bomb craters were gigantic – thirty feet across and nearly as deep. In the rainy seasons they would often fill up with water and often saw service as duck or fishponds, playing their role in the guerrillas' never-ending quest to broaden their diet. But they were treacherous then too. For as the swamps and lowland areas became flooded under half a foot of standing water, the craters would become invisible. Not infrequently some surprised guerrilla, wading along what he had taken to be a familiar route, was suddenly swallowed up.

... The first few times I experienced a B-52 attack it seemed, as I strained to press myself into the bunker floor, that I had been caught in the Apocalypse. The terror was complete. One lost control of bodily functions as the mind screamed incomprehensible orders to get out. On one occasion a Soviet delegation was visiting our ministry when a particularly short-notice warning came through. When it was over, no one had been hurt, but the entire delegation had sustained considerable damage to its dignity – uncontrollable trembling and wet pants the all-too-obvious outward signs of inner convulsions. The visitors could have spared themselves their feelings of embarrassment; each of their hosts was a veteran of the same symptoms.

Truong Nhu Tang (with David Chanoff and Doan Van Toai), *A Vietcong Memoir* (New York: Harcourt Brace Jovanovich, 1985), pp. 167–71.

### 5.10 Anti-war protest in America

Although by 1967 the war appeared stalemated, the Johnson administration sought to place a positive construction on events in its public statements. One reason was the need to neutralise burgeoning domestic criticism, a task assisted by reiteration of the *prospect* of success. In April 1967, however, Martin Luther King Jr. delivered a speech in New York that exposed the hidden reality of the war. Emphasising the conflict's disastrous impact on American as well as Vietnamese society, King's words stand as a withering indictment of US policy.

I come to this platform to make a passionate plea to my beloved nation. This speech is not addressed to Hanoi or to the National Liberation Front. It is not addressed to China or Russia ... but rather to my fellow Americans who, with me, bear the greatest responsibility in ending a conflict that has exacted a heavy price.

... Since I am a preacher by trade, I suppose it is not surprising that I have ... major reasons for bringing Vietnam into the field of my moral vision. There is at the outset a very obvious and almost facile connection between the war in Vietnam and the struggle I, and others, have been waging in America. A few years ago there was a shining moment in that struggle. It seemed as if there was a real promise of help for the poor – both black and white – through the Poverty Program.[2] Then came the build-up in Vietnam, and I watched the program broken and eviscerated as if it were some idle plaything of a society gone made on war, and I knew America would never invest the necessary funds or energies in rehabilitation of its poor so long as

Vietnam continued to draw men and skills and money like some demonic, destructive suction tube. So I was increasingly compelled to see the war as an enemy of the poor and to attack it as such.

Perhaps the more tragic recognition of reality took place when it became clear to me that the war was doing far more than devastating the hopes of the poor at home. It was sending their sons and their brothers and their husbands to fight and to die in extraordinarily high proportions relative to the rest of the population. We were taking the young black men who had been crippled by our society and sending them 8,000 miles away to guarantee liberties in Southeast Asia which they had not found in Southwest Georgia and East Harlem. So we have been repeatedly faced with the cruel irony of watching Negro and white boys on TV screens as they kill and die together for a nation that has been unable to seat them together in the same schools. So we watch them in brutal solidarity burning the huts of a poor village, but we realize they would never live on the same block. I could not be silent in the face of such cruel manipulation of the poor.

[Another reason for opposing the war] grows out of my experience in the ghettos of the North over the last three years – especially the last three summers. As I have walked among the desperate, rejected and angry young men, I have told them that Molotov cocktails and rifles would not solve their problems. I have tried to offer them my deepest compassion while maintaining my conviction that social change comes most meaningfully through non-violent action. But, they asked, what about Vietnam? They asked if our own nation wasn't using massive doses of violence to solve its problems, to bring about the changes it wanted. Their questions hit home, and I knew that I could never again raise my voice against the violence of the oppressed in the ghettos without having first spoken clearly to the greatest purveyor of violence in the world today – my own government ...

... We must find new ways to speak for peace in Vietnam and justice throughout the developing world – a world that borders on our doors. If we do not act we shall surely be dragged down the long, dark and shameful corridors of time reserved for those who possess power without compassion, might without morality, and strength without sight.

Dr Martin Luther King Jr., address to Riverside Church, Manhattan, New York, 4 April 1967, in Gettleman *et al.* (eds), *Vietnam and America*, pp. 310–18.

## 5.11  The Tet offensive

When the Tet offensive opened on 31 January 1968, the US
military sought to depict it as a desperate gamble by an enemy
on the verge of defeat. This interpretation retains support
amongst historians, although there are just as many who argue
the opposite – that the offensive represented a conviction on
the part of the communists that victory could be theirs. The
recollections of General Tran Van Tra, commander of the
Vietcong at the time of Tet, although partisan and coloured by
hindsight, offer a firm rebuttal of the 'desperate gamble thesis

We were winning [in 1967] and we held the initiative despite the diffi
culties and weaknesses we had in replenishing our forces, building our
political strength and conducting mass movements in urban areas,
and ensuring material and technical supplies. However, these were
difficulties in the context of a favorable situation. As for the United
States, its numerous difficulties resulted from a war that had reached
its peak but still offered no way out. President Johnson had to make a
definite and important decision: either yield to the military and escalate the war, expanding it to the whole of Indochina (including an
invasion of North Vietnam), or listen to McNamara and several high-
level civilian officials, and de-escalate the war and negotiate with
Hanoi and the Viet Cong.[3] He could not afford to stay at the cross-
roads any longer ... [T]he entire United States could not help but
sicken of the deadlock in South Vietnam and the fact that their heavy
losses in the air war over North Vietnam were not compensated by
any tangible political or military results. Differences within the United
States and Saigon ranks were widening. The anti-war movement of
the American people intensified. So did the world's condemnation of
the war. All of this forced an extremely cautious stand on Johnson
who was further frustrated by the gloomy prospects for the 1968
presidential elections.

This provided us with a very important opportunity to push
Johnson into making a decision which would lead to a strategic shift
in our favor ... In judging this situation, the Political Bureau of the
[Vietnam Workers'] Party Central Committee noted, 'the situation
allows us to shift our revolution to a new stage, that of decisive victory.' It adopted a resolution [in the autumn of 1967) on the immediate goals and tasks.

'Our great and urgent task now is to mobilize the greatest efforts of our Party, armed forces and people in both regions [North and South Vietnam] to move our revolutionary war to the highest level and achieve decisive victory through a General Offensive and General Uprising, and realize the strategic objectives set by the Party.'

These objectives were:

– To break down and destroy the bulk of the puppet troops [of the Saigon army], topple the puppet administration [in Saigon] at all levels, and take power into the hands of the people.

– To destroy the major part of the U.S. forces and their war material, and render then unable to fulfil their political and military duties in Vietnam.

– On this basis, to break the U.S. will of aggression, force it to accept defeat in the South and put an end to all acts of war against the North. With this, we will achieve the immediate objectives of our revolution – independence, democracy, peace, and neutrality for the South – and we can proceed to national reunification.

General Tran Van Tra, 'Tet: The 1968 General Offensive and General Uprising', in Jayne S. Werner and Luu Doan Huynh (eds), *The Vietnam War: Vietnamese and American Perspectives* (New York: M. E. Sharpe, 1993), pp. 38–41.


## 5.12   Tet: the view from Hanoi

In terms of pure profit-and-loss on the battlefield, the Tet offensive proved to be a resounding military defeat for the communists. More than this, it was also a political defeat, insofar as the predicted popular uprising – the critical accompaniment to the general military offensive – did not materialise. According to a captured document, the VWP leadership privately acknowledged 'deficiencies and weak points' in its strategy.

We have won great successes but still have many deficiencies and weak points:

1) In the military field – from the beginning, we have not been able to annihilate much of the enemy's live force and much of the reactionary clique. Our armed forces have not fulfilled their role as 'lever' and have not created favorable conditions for motivating the masses to

arise in towns and cities.

2) In the political field – organized popular forces were not broad and strong enough. We have not had specific plans for motivating the masses to the extent that they would indulge in violent armed uprisings in coordination with and supporting the military offensives.

3) The puppet [Saigon] troops proselytising failed to create a military revolt movement in which the troops would arise and return to the people's side. The enemy troop proselytising task to be carried out in coordination with the armed struggle and political struggle has not been performed, and inadequate attention had been paid to this in particular.

4) There has not been enough consciousness about specific plans for the widening and development of liberated rural areas and the appropriate mobilization of manpower, material resources and the great capabilities of the masses to support the front line.

5) The building of real strength and particularly the replenishment of troops and development of political forces of the infrastructure has been slow and has not met the requirements of continuous offensives and uprisings of the new phase.

6) In providing leadership and guidance to various echelons, we failed to give them a profound and thorough understanding of the Party's policy, line and strategic determination so that they have a correct and full realization of this phase of General Offensive and General Uprising. The implementation of our policies has not been sharply and closely conducted. We lacked concreteness, our plans were simple, our coordination poor, control and prodding were absent, reporting and requests for instructions were much delayed.

The above-mentioned deficiencies and weak points have limited our successes and are, at the same time, difficulties which we must resolutely overcome.

VWP assessment of Tet, March 1968, in George Katsiaficas (ed.), *Vietnam Documents: American and Vietnamese Views of the War* (New York: M. E. Sharpe, 1992), pp. 102–4.

## 5.13 The revolt of the 'wise men'

On the face of it, Westmoreland's claim that the communists were on the military – and arguably the political – defensive by

March 1968 has something to recommend it. Indeed President Johnson was at first inclined to meet Westmoreland request for 206,000 extra troops, even though this would have b en in defiance of American public opinion. However, his new Secretary of Defense, Clark Clifford, along with a number of other previously hawkish advisers, seeing no way to win the war, only to perpetuate it, counselled de-escalation, an end to the bombing of North Vietnam, and negotations Their decision shocked Johnson, but in the end, as George Ball later recalled, he felt unable to contest it.

He [Johnson] called a meeting of the so-called senior advisers or wise men or whatever, a bunch of superannuated characters who had been in the government at one time or another – not necessarily his administration but in earlier administrations – people like Dean Acheson, Jack McCloy and so on.[4] This had happened several times, and I had been present at these meetings several times and the same thing had always occurred. That is, everyone had been for going full speed ahead, except me.[5] But I'd made the same arguments there that I had made within the government, even though I was outside of it, but at this meeting something happened that was quite extraordinary. This was immediately after the Tet offensive and the group assembled in the evening before meeting the President. We heard two briefings, and they were very discouraging about the effect of the Tet offensive, and what it had done to set the whole cause back in Vietnam ... One was a military briefing and one was a civilian briefing. One was a briefing by [William] Colby [of the CIA]. They were very good. The next day, the group met. They were considering a request from Westmoreland for ... more troops or something of that sort. Secretary [of Defense] Clifford was there, and he was for limiting the response to a much smaller number, and he was beginning to develop grave doubts about the whole thing. So we had an argument in the morning, and again I repeated my usual arguments, and I found much more tendency to agree with me there than had happened up to then. So we decided that McGeorge Bundy [Johnson's special adviser on National Security] would be sort of the spokesman for the group.

The currently available verbatim accounts of the deliberations of the 'wise men' bear out Ball's recollections, and show former Secretary of State Dean Acheson to have been a decisive figure in the debate.

McGeorge Bundy: There is a very significant shift in our position. When we last met [in October 1967] we saw reasons for hope. We hoped then there would be slow but steady progress. Last night and today the picture is not so hopeful particularly in the countryside. Dean Acheson summed up the majority feeling when he said that we can no longer do the job we set out to do in the time we have left and we must begin to take steps to disengage.

That view was shared by: George Ball, Arthur Dean, Cy Vance, Douglas Dillon and myself ... There were three of us who took a dif ferent position: General Bradley, General Taylor, and Bob Murphy.[6]

The 'wise men' each responded to Bundy's summation

Ridgway: I agree with the summary as presented ...

Dean: I agree. All of us got the impression that there is no military conclusion in sight. We felt time is running out.

Acheson: Agree with Bundy's presentation. Neither the effort of the Government of [South] Vietnam or the effort of the U.S. government can succeed in the time we have left. Time is limited by reactions in this country. We cannot build an independent South Vietnam; there- fore, we should do something by no later than late summer to estab- lish something different.

Cabot Lodge: We should shift from search and destroy strategy to a strategy of using our military power as a shield to permit the South Vietnamese society to develop as well as North Vietnamese society has been able to ...

Dillon: We should change the emphasis. I agree with Acheson. The briefing last night led me to conclude that we cannot achieve military victory ... I would send only the troops necessary to support those there now.

Ball: I share Acheson's view. I have felt that way since 1961 – that our objectives are unobtainable ...

Vance: McGeorge Bundy stated my views. I agree with George Ball.

There were, as Ball suggested, some dissenters.

Bradley: People in this country are dissatisfied. We do need to stop the bombing if we can get the suggestion to come from the Pope or U Thant,[7] but let's not show them that we are in any way weakening.

We should send only support troops.

Murphy: I am shaken by the position of my associates. The interpretation given this action by Saigon would be bad. This is a 'giveaway' policy. I think it would weaken our position.

Taylor: I am dismayed. The picture I get is a very different one from that you have. Let's not concede the home front; let's do something about it.

Fortas:[8] The U.S. has never had in mind winning a military victory out there; we always have wanted to reach an agreement or settle for the status quo between North Vietnam and South Vietnam. I agree with General Taylor and Bob Murphy. This is not the time for an overture on our part. I do not think a cessation of the bombing would do any good at this time. I do not believe in drama for the sake of drama.

> An imperious intervention from Acheson then silenced the dissenters and established the consensus view that would be put to Johnson.

Acheson: The issue is not that stated by Fortas. The issue is can we do what we are trying to do in Vietnam. I do not think we can. Fortas said we are not trying to win a military victory. The issue is can we by military means keep the North Vietnamese off the South Vietnamese. I do not think we can. They can slip around and end-run them and crack them up.

> George Ball later recalled what happened next.

We then assembled in the Cabinet Room and the President wanted to hear our advice to him. ... And McGeorge Bundy led off saying that the group had met and that he had something he wanted to tell the President which he thought he would never say to him, that he now agreed with George Ball and this was the general sentiment of the group. And we went around, and it wasn't unanimous by any means; but there was strong advice to the President: 'Look, this thing is hopeless, you'd better begin to de-escalate and get out.' And this was the first time he'd ever heard anything of this kind, he could hardly believe his ears. I think he was very shocked. He was clearly disturbed and he kept asking probing questions. He really couldn't believe it ...

George Ball recollections in Michael Charlton and Anthony Moncrieff, *Many Reasons Why: American Involvement in Vietnam* (New York: Hill & Wang, 1989 edn), pp. 131–2; verbatim records of 'wise men' deliberations, 26 March 1968, in David M. Barrett (ed.), *Lyndon B. Johnson's Vietnam Papers: A Documentary Collection* (College Station: Texas A&M University Press, 1998), pp. 713–15.

### 5.14   The end of US escalation

The post-Tet review of US policy in Vietnam came to a decisive end on 31 March 1968 when President Johnson, accepting the majority verdict of the 'wise men', announced the end of escalation.

Good evening, my fellow Americans:

Tonight I want to speak to you of peace in Vietnam and Southeast Asia. No other question so preoccupies our people. No other dream so absorbs the 250 million human beings who live in that part of the world. No other goal so motivates American policy in Southeast Asia ... Tonight, I renew the offer I made last August – to stop the bombardment of North Vietnam. We ask that talks begin promptly, that they be serious talks on the substance of peace. We assume that during those talks Hanoi will not take advantage of our restraint.

We are prepared to move immediately toward peace through negotiations.

So, tonight, in the hope that this action will lead to early talks, I am taking the first step to deescalate the conflict. We are reducing – substantially reducing – the present level of hostilities.

And we are doing so unilaterally, and at once.

Tonight, I have ordered our aircraft and our naval vessels to make no attacks on North Vietnam, except in the area north of the demilitarized zone where the continuing enemy buildup directly threatens allied forward positions and where the movements of their troops and supplies are clearly related to that threat.

The area in which we are stopping our attacks includes almost 90 per cent of North Vietnam's population, and most of its territory ... Even this very limited bombing of the North could come to an early end – if our restraint is matched by restraint in Hanoi. But I cannot in good conscience stop all bombing so long as to do so would immediately and directly endanger the lives of our men and our allies. Whether a complete bombing halt becomes possible in the future will be determined by events.

> Johnson concluded his address with an unexpected announcement regarding his personal future. Vietnam, it seemed, had killed not just his dream of a Great Society, but his presidency as well.

... I have concluded that I should not permit the Presidency to become involved in the partisan divisions that are developing in this political year.

With America's sons in the fields far away, with America's future under challenge right here at home, with our hopes and the world's hopes for peace in the balance every day, I do not believe that I should devote an hour or a day of my time to any personal partisan causes or to any duties other than the awesome duties of this office – the Presidency of your country.

Accordingly, I shall not seek, and I will not accept, the nomination of my party for another term as your President.[9]

But let men everywhere know, however, that a strong, a confident and a vigilant America stands ready tonight to seek an honorable peace – and stands ready to defend an honored cause – whatever the price, whatever the burden, whatever the sacrifice that duty may require.

Thank you for listening.

Good night and God bless you all.

Johnson address to the nation, 31 March 1968, in *Public Papers of the Presidents: Lyndon B. Johnson, 1968–69* (Washington DC: Government Printing Office, 1970), pp. 469–76.

# 6

# Wars of peace, 1968–1975

As a result of the heavy losses inflicted on the Vietcong during the Tet offensive, North Vietnam's involvement in the campaign in the south increased at the expense of indigenous influence. For non-communists in the NLF, this was a matter of concern: despite assurances that communism would never be imposed on South Vietnam, many regarded Hanoi's burgeoning politico-military intervention as a worrying portent (6.3). For the moment, the war continued to rage, albeit in tandem with US–DRV diplomatic activity generated by Johnson's March 1968 initiative. Negotiations took place on two levels: an on–off public peace process based in Paris, and from early 1970 in secret dealings between high-level officials. The objective of the new Republican administration of Richard M. Nixon was 'peace with honor' – this meant, in effect, the continued existence of a separate South Vietnam after US military withdrawal. But with neither Hanoi nor the NLF–Vietcong willing to compromise on the question of future national unity, there was little progress on either the official or unofficial negotiating track (6.1, 6.2). The diplomatic impasse did not prevent the Nixon administration pressing forward with Vietnamisation – the withdrawal of US troops *pari passu* with the hand-over of defence responsibility to the Army of the Republic of Vietnam (ARVN) – both as an end in itself and as a means of drawing the sting of domestic anti-war protest (6.4). The policy succeeded in one sense: by 1972, the US troop presence was down to 24,000 from a high of 500,000. In other respects, the policy fared less well. To convince Hanoi that troop reductions did not betoken a lessening of its commitment to South Vietnam, the US government escalated in other directions, notably in Laos and Cambodia, actions that left the North Vietnamese unimpressed whilst widening the conflict to all of Indochina. On the home front, escalation in Cambodia in particular led to a recrudescence of anti-war activity (6.5).

By 1972, the Nixon administration had concluded that Viet-namisation was unlikely to permit total US withdrawal, such was the questionable martial quality of the ARVN. With Nixon anxious to achieve peace before the November 1972 presidential election, the hitherto stagnant diplomatic process began to assume new impor-tance. When efforts to secure the good offices of both the Soviet Union and Communist China through détente came to little – even if the inclination to pressure Hanoi into making concessions had been present in Beijing or Moscow, neither communist giant had as much leverage over the DRV as the Americans supposed – the Nixon admin-istration turned by default to direct negotiations with North Vietnam. For its part, the DRV was also keen on a settlement: the lesson of its failed spring offensive of 1972 was that the ARVN was only as strong as the US air power behind it, hence Hanoi's leaders were prepared to make whatever concessions necessary to effect full-scale American disengagement. This shared US–DRV desire for compromise pro-duced an interim agreement in October 1972, but it was quickly denounced by Nguyen Van Thieu, President of South Vietnam (6.6). The US government, conscious that any deal that appeared to betray Thieu was incompatible with 'peace with honor', asked the North Vietnamese to consider Saigon's objections. They refused, and the prospect of peace receded.

The United States, calculating that it might be easier to lever con-cessions from its enemy rather than its ally, thus embarked on the notorious Christmas bombing of December 1972. The tactic seemed to work: Hanoi returned to the negotiating table, and in Paris on 27 January 1973 a formal peace treaty was signed by the US and DRV governments, as well as the Saigon regime and the NLF (the latter now styling itself the Provisional Revolutionary Government of South Vietnam). However, because the final settlement bore an uncanny re-semblance to the US–DRV deal of October 1972, historians have of-ten speculated on why the Thieu government in particular approved that which it had so recently rejected. More than the Christmas bomb-ing prising concessions from Hanoi, it seems that personal assurances by Nixon that America would resume its air war against North Viet-nam if the peace was violated by the communists (a message conveyed to Hanoi as well), coupled with a threat that the US Congress would cut off aid to South Vietnam if peace were not now concluded, secured Thieu's final if grudging consent (6.7, 6.8). The term 'peace settle-

ment' is, of course, a misnomer: there was peace for America, but not
for Vietnam wherein all signatories to the agreement were guilty of
violating its terms (6.9). North Vietnam initially held back from
resuming full-scale hostilities out of concern about possible US retaliation, but in America, Congress passed legislation during 1973–74
that effectively ruled out that possibility, its actions justified on the
grounds that the conflict had all along been a presidential war waged
without the consent of the American people on behalf of a corrupt
dictatorship. Nixon would later argue that Congress actively undermined the deterrent quality of his warnings to North Vietnam about
the consequences of breaking the peace (6.10). In this, he may have
had a point, for Hanoi's timetable for reunification was certainly
brought forward in response to Washington's obvious reluctance to
honour its commitments to South Vietnam (6.11). This said, Nixon
perhaps knew that the settlement would not last, and that the best
America could hope for was a 'decent interval' between withdrawal
and the final communist victory. All that Congress did was speed the
inevitable. In the event, the interval was two years – hopelessly inadequate to disguise America's defeat alongside that of South Vietnam.
The Ho Chi Minh campaign, launched in the spring of 1975, swept
the North Vietnamese to victory (6.12). On 30 April 1975, what remained of the Saigon government surrendered (6.13). America looked
away as Vietnam emerged reunited, independent, and communist
after thirty years of war.

## 6.1  Negotiating positions, May 1969

Following President's Johnson's peace proposal of 31 March
1968, the North Vietnamese and US governments agreed to
meet to map out common negotiating ground. The Paris conference opened in May 1968, but made little headway: Hanoi
wanted the NLF fully represented at future peace talks, but
Washington, responding to the Saigon government's objections, would not agree. The NLF, meanwhile, anxious that its
viewpoint should not be ignored, made public its basic negotiating position.

The South Vietnam National Front for Liberation sets forth the principles and main content of an overall solution to the South Vietnam

problem to help restore peace in Vietnam as follows:

1. To respect the Vietnamese people's fundamental national rights i.e. independence, sovereignty, unity and territorial integrity, as recognized by the 1954 Geneva Agreements on Vietnam.

2. The U.S. Government must withdraw from South Vietnam all U.S. troops, military personnel, arms and war materiel, and all troops, military personnel, arms and war materiel of the other foreign countries of the U.S. camp without posing any condition whatsoever; liquidate all U.S. military bases in South Vietnam; renounce all encroachments on the sovereignty, territory and security of South Vietnam and the Democratic Republic of Vietnam.

3. The Vietnamese people's right to fight for the defense of their Fatherland is the sacred, inalienable right to self-defense of all peoples. The question of the Vietnamese armed forces in South Vietnam shall be resolved by the Vietnamese parties among themselves.

4. The people of South Vietnam settle themselves their own affairs without foreign interference. They decide themselves the political regime of South Vietnam through free and democratic general elections. Through free and democratic general elections, a Constituent Assembly will be set up, a Constitution worked out, and a coalition Government of South Vietnam installed, reflecting national concord and the broad union of all social strata.

5. During the period intervening between the restoration of peace and the holding of general elections, neither party shall impose its political regime on the people of South Vietnam. The political forces representing the various social strata and political tendencies in South Vietnam, that stand for peace, independence and neutrality ... will enter into talks to set up a provisional coalition government based on the principles of equality, democracy and mutual respect with a view to achieving a peaceful, independent, democratic and neutral Vietnam.

6. South Vietnam will carry out a foreign policy of peace and neutrality.

7. The reunification of Vietnam will be achieved step by step, by peaceful means through discussions and agreement between the two zones, without foreign interference.

Pending the peaceful reunification of Vietnam, the two zones reestablish normal relations in all fields on the basis of mutual respect.

The military demarcation line between the two zones at the 17th parallel, as provided for by the 1954 Geneva Agreements, is only of a provisional character and does not constitute in any way a political or territorial boundary ...

8. As provided for in the 1954 Geneva Agreements on Vietnam, pending the peaceful reunification of Vietnam, the two zones North and South of Vietnam undertake to refrain from joining any military alliance with foreign countries, not to allow any foreign country to maintain military bases, troops and military personnel on their respective soil, and not to recognize the protection of any country or military alliance or bloc.

9. To resolve the aftermath of the war:

(a) The parties will negotiate the release of armymen captured in war.

(b) The U.S. Government must bear full responsibility for the losses and devastation it has caused to the Vietnamese people in both zones.

10. The parties shall reach agreement on an international supervision about the withdrawal from South Vietnam of the troops, military personnel, arms and war materiel of the United States and the other foreign countries of the American camp.[1]

The principles and content of the overall solution expounded above form an integrated whole. On the basis of these principles and content, the parties shall reach understanding to the effect of concluding agreements on the above-mentioned questions with a view to ending the war in South Vietnam, and contributing to restore peace in Vietnam.

NLF statement, 8 May 1969, in Marvin E. Gettleman *et al.* (eds), *Vietnam and America: The Most Comprehensive Documented History of the Vietnam War* (New York: Grove Press, 1995), pp. 430–4.

## 6.2  Nixon responds

On 14 May 1969, President Nixon, in his first major public statement on Vietnam, articulated American negotiating objectives. The US and NLF–Vietcong/DRV positions were irreconcilable, and would remain so for the next two years, particularly on the issue of unilateral American (as opposed to mutual US–DRV) withdrawal from South Vietnam.

To make very concrete what I have said, I propose the following measures, which seem to me consistent with the principles of all parties.

These proposals are made on the basis of full consultation with President Thieu.

– As soon as agreement can be reached, all non-South Vietnamese forces would begin withdrawals from South Vietnam.[2]

– Over a period of 12 months, by agreed-upon stages, the major portions of all US, Allied and other non-South Vietnamese forces would be withdrawn. At the end of this 12-month period, the remaining US, Allied and other non-South Vietnamese forces would move into designated base areas and would not engage in combat operations.

– The remaining US and Allied forces would move to complete their withdrawals as the remaining North Vietnamese forces were withdrawn and returned to North Vietnam.

– An international supervisory body, acceptable to both sides, would be created for the purpose of verifying withdrawals, and for any other purposes agreed upon between the two sides.

– This international body would begin operating in accordance with an agreed timetable, and would participate in arranging supervised ceasefires.

– As soon as possible after the international body was functioning, elections would be held under agreed procedures and under the supervision of the international body.

– Arrangements would be made for the earliest possible release of prisoners of war on both sides.

– All parties would agree to observe the Geneva Accords of 1954 regarding Vietnam and Cambodia, and the Laos Accords of 1962 ...

We are willing to talk about anybody's program ... provided it can be made consistent with the few basic principles I have set forth here.

Nixon television address, 14 May 1969, in *Public Papers of the Presidents of the United States: Richard M. Nixon, 1969* (Washington DC: Government Printing Office, 1971), p. 373.

## 6.3   The NLF fragments

The NLF, though united in public, was beginning to fragment, with many non-communists uneasy at the increasingly overt politico-military domination of Front activities by the communists and, more especially, North Vietnam. The Tet offensive convinced a number of these disaffected patriots that the time had come to create a third force in South Vietnam, one that stood between the now communist-tainted NLF and the unpopular Saigon regime. One of the proponents of a third force was Truong Nhu Tang.

Over a period of time, North Vietnam had committed more and more of its resources to the war, until it had become, as Party leaders liked to phrase it, 'a giant rear area' supporting the front lines. As a result, the NLF had found itself ever more obviously dominated by the Party and by the Northern government.

It was now past time for a strong effort to reestablish the image of the South's revolution as a broad-based movement that included Southern nationalists of every stripe ... What was required was an organization structured along governmental lines, made up of the strongest nationalist figures in the South who had not joined the Front (and who consequently were not tainted, in the popular mind, by communist sympathies), an organization that could credibly maintain an aura of autonomy and independence. The fact that the Alliance would inevitably be branded by its enemies as a puppet of the NLF was not considered an overwhelming obstacle. At the very least the Alliance would add a substantial new counterweight to the Communist overbalance, and among the uncommitted it would help restore the NLF's eclipsed coalition-based orientation.

In March 1968, the first formal meeting of prospective Alliance members took place at the NLF's jungle headquarters.

Although these people ... had for years been in sympathy with many of the Front's goals, most had stopped short of associating themselves formally – for a variety of reasons. By and large these were Western-educated individuals with generally liberal and democratic (in the Western sense of the term) political principles. They tended to be sensitive to economic iniquities and social injustices, but not in a way that would move them to political action. They were decidedly not dogmatic people, and they had an instinctive distaste for those who were. On the other hand, their political open-mindedness was overlaid by a powerful sense of Vietnamese nationalism. As a consequence, their attitude toward the NLF was characteristically ambivalent. The Front's strong stand for independence and rejection of foreign domination appealed to them, but they were put off by the organization's deference to the Party and by the Communist ideologues who were playing key roles.

But as the conflict deepened, these people, along with the rest of the politically literate Southern population, were less and less able to maintain their preferred attitude of detachment. By 1968 the entire country was embroiled in a vicious all-out war, which had already ripped apart much of the fabric of society. A Northern army was operating in the countryside, the cities had swollen with homeless refugees, the Americans were subjecting their enemies (and anyone else who got in the way) to state-of-the-art methods of extermination. South Vietnam had been turned into a crucible of suffering – a nation that was finding out, in its flesh, what it means to be a pawn in a world of great powers. It was a situation that cried out for involvement.

> The founding conference of the Alliance took place in May 1968. Initially, the communists, both northern and southern, responded positively to the Alliance. However, such respect for the non-communist contribution to the struggle would not last much beyond the North Vietnamese triumph of April 1975 (see 7.6).

We prepared in advance its manifesto, program, and the various organizational details. In tone, the platform differed from that of the NLF by being somewhat more distinctively Southern and somewhat less revolutionary. 'At present,' it stated, 'our country has in fact two different political systems in the South and in the North. National reunification cannot be achieved overnight. Therefore, the South and the North should hold talks on the basis of equality and respect for the characteristics of each zone.'

... Setting up its own separate headquarters near the NLF [jungle] complex, the Alliance now joined COSVN[3] and the Front in coordinating strategy for the South. It was a period of frequent liaison meetings and open exchanges, symptomatic perhaps of the importance that Party leaders in Hanoi accorded the Southern resistance at this stage of the war. DRV attentiveness toward its allies was apparent in the receptivity COSVN showed toward proposals emanating from the Front and the Alliance, and by the general spirit of partnership that facilitated every sort of business.

Truong Nhu Tang (with David Chanoff and Doan Van Toai), *A Vietcong Memoir* (New York: Harcourt Brace Jovanovich, 1985), pp. 131–40.

## 6.4 Vietnamisation

> In November 1969, President Nixon announced publicly the
> beginning of Vietnamisation – the withdrawal of US forces
> from South Vietnam, and their replacement by South Vietnam-
> ese forces, trained and equipped for the task by the United
> States. Vietnamisation was an element in a larger process of US
> disengagement from global military commitments, that proc-
> ess being known as the Nixon Doctrine.

... Let me briefly explain what has been described as the Nixon Doctrine – a policy which not only will help end the war in Vietnam but
which is an essential element of our program to prevent future
Vietnams.

We Americans are a do-it-yourself people. We are an impatient
people. Instead of teaching someone else to do a job, we like to do it
ourselves. And this trait has been carried over into our foreign policy.

In Korea and again in Vietnam, the United States furnished most of
the money, most of the arms, and most of the men to help the people
of those countries defend their freedom against Communist aggression.

Before any American troops were committed to Vietnam, a leader
of another Asian country expressed this opinion to me ... He said:
'When you are trying to assist another nation defend its freedom, U.S.
policy should be to help them fight the war but not to fight the war for
them.'

Well, in accordance with this wise counsel, I laid down in Guam[4]
three principles as guidelines for future American policy toward Asia:

– First, the United States will keep all of its treaty commitments.

– Second, we shall provide a shield if a nuclear power threatens the
freedom of a nation allied with us or of a nation whose survival we
consider vital to our security.

– Third, in cases involving other types of aggression, we shall furnish military and economic assistance when requested in accordance
with our treaty commitment. But we shall look to the nation directly
threatened to assume the primary responsibility of providing the manpower for its defense.

After I announced this policy, I found that the leaders of the Philippines, Thailand, Vietnam, South Korea, and other nations which might be threatened by Communist aggression, welcomed this new direction in American foreign policy.

The defense of freedom is everybody's business – not just America's business. And it is particularly the responsibility of the people whose freedom is threatened. In the previous administration, we Americanized the war in Vietnam. In this administration, we are Vietnamizing the search for peace ... And now we have begun to see the results of this long overdue change in American policy in Vietnam. After five years of Americans going into Vietnam, we are finally bringing men home.

> Nixon added a swipe at anti-war protesters. The previous month had seen a series of massive marches and gatherings against the war. To Nixon's mind, these protesters were advocating peace at almost any price, whereas his government sought 'peace with honor'.

Let us be united for peace. Let us also be united against defeat. Because let us understand: North Vietnam cannot defeat or humiliate the United States. Only Americans can do that.

Nixon address to the Nation, 3 November 1969, in *Public Papers of the Presidents, 1969*, pp. 901–10.

## 6.5 America's non-invasion of Cambodia

In April 1970, American and South Vietnamese ground troops entered Cambodia. On the face of it, this appeared to mark an escalation of the war in Vietnam by an American government purportedly dedicated to its de-escalation. Nixon, conscious of the negative public reaction the move was likely to produce, sought to refute the notion of an 'invasion' by arguing that the action was integral to Vietnamisation and US troop withdrawals. Judging by the public reaction – a number of American student protesters would be shot dead by National Guardsmen while demonstrating against the action – Nixon failed to convince.

Ten days ago, in my report to the Nation on Vietnam, I announced a decision to withdraw an additional 150,000 Americans from Vietnam over the next year. I said then that I was making that decision despite our concern over increased enemy activity in Laos, in Cambodia, and in South Vietnam.

At that time, I warned that if I concluded that increased enemy activity in any of these areas endangered the lives of Americans remaining in Vietnam, I would not hesitate to take strong and effective measures to deal with that situation.

Despite that warning, North Vietnam has increased its military aggression in all these areas, and particularly in Cambodia.

After full consultation with the National Security Council, Ambassador Bunker,[5] General Abrams,[6] and my other advisers, I have concluded that the actions of the enemy in the last 10 days clearly endanger the lives of Americans who are in Vietnam now and would constitute an unacceptable risk to those who will be there after withdrawal of another 150,000.

To protect our men who are in Vietnam and to guarantee the continued success of our withdrawal and Vietnamization programs, I have concluded that the time has come for action …

Tonight, American and South Vietnamese units will attack the headquarters for the entire Communist military machine in South Vietnam. This key control center has been occupied by the North Vietnamese and Vietcong for 5 years in blatant violation of Cambodia's neutrality.

This is not an invasion of Cambodia. The areas in which these attacks will be launched are completely occupied and controlled by North Vietnamese forces. Our purpose is not to occupy the areas. Once enemy forces are driven out of these sanctuaries and once their military supplies are destroyed, we will withdraw … We take this action not for the purpose of expanding the war into Cambodia but for the purpose of ending the war in Vietnam and winning the just peace we all desire. We have made – we will continue to make every possible effort to end this war through negotiation at the conference table rather than through more fighting on the battlefield.

Nixon address to the Nation, 30 April 1970, in *Public Papers of the Presidents of the United States: Richard M. Nixon, 1970* (Washington DC: Government Printing Office, 1971), pp. 405–10.

## 6.6 Hanoi goes public on peace

In October 1972, North Vietnam and the United States finally agreed on the substance of a peace settlement. When, however, Washington sought to amend its terms to meet some of the Saigon government's objections, Hanoi revealed the draft settlement to the world – and revealed, in the process, the Nixon administration's back-sliding.

[B]y October 22, 1972, the formulation of the agreement was complete. The main issues of the agreement ... may be summarized as follows.

(1) The United States respects the independence, sovereignty, unity and territorial integrity of Vietnam as recognized by the 1954 Geneva agreements.

(2) Twenty-four hours after the signing of the agreement, *a cease-fire shall be observed throughout South Vietnam*. The United States will stop all its military activities, and end the bombing and mining in North Vietnam. Within 60 days, there will be a total withdrawal from South Vietnam of troops and military personnel of the United States and those of the foreign countries allied with the United States and the Republic of Vietnam. The two South Vietnamese parties shall not accept the introduction of troops, military advisors and military personnel, armaments, munitions, and war material into South Vietnam ... The United States will not continue its military involvement or intervene in the internal affairs of South Vietnam.

(3) The return of all captured personnel of the parties shall be carried out simultaneously with the US troops withdrawal.

(4) The principles for the exercise of the South Vietnamese people's right to self-determination are as follows:

a) the South Vietnamese people shall decide themselves the political future of South Vietnam through genuinely free and democratic elections under international supervision;

b) the United States is not committed to any political tendency or to any personality in South Vietnam, and it does not seek to impose a pro-American regime in Saigon;

c) national reconciliation and concord will be achieved, the democratic liberties of the people ensured;

d) an administrative structure called the National Council of Reconciliation and Concord of three equal segments will be set up to promote the implementation of the signed agreements by the Provisional Revolutionary Government of the Republic of South Vietnam[7] and the Government of the Republic of Vietnam and to organize the general elections;

e) the two South Vietnamese parties will consult about the formation of councils at lower levels;

f) the question of Vietnamese armed forces in South Vietnam shall be settled by the South Vietnamese parties in a spirit of national reconciliation and concord, equality and mutual respect, without foreign interference, in accordance with the post-war situation ...[8]

(5) The *reunification* of Vietnam shall be carried out step by step through peaceful means.

(6) There will be formed a four-party joint military commission, and a joint military commission of the two South Vietnamese parties. An international commission of control and supervision shall be established. An international guarantee conference on Vietnam will be convened within 30 days of the signing of this agreement.

(7) The Government of the Democratic Republic of Vietnam, the Provisional Revolutionary Government of the Republic of Vietnam, the Government of the United States of America, and the Government of the Republic of Vietnam shall strictly respect the Cambodian and Lao peoples' fundamental national rights ... [and] refrain from using the territory of Cambodia and the territory of Laos to encroach on the sovereignty and security of other countries. Foreign countries shall put an end to all military activities in Laos and Cambodia, totally withdraw from and refrain [from] reintroducing into these two countries troops, military advisers and military personnel, armaments, munitions and war material. The internal affairs of Cambodia and Laos shall be settled by the people of each of these countries without foreign interference.

The problems existing between the *three Indochinese countries* shall be settled by the Indochinese parties on the basis of respect for each other's independence, sovereignty, and territorial integrity, and non-interference in each other's internal affairs.

(8) The ending of the war, the restoration of peace in Vietnam will create conditions for establishing a new, equal, and mutually beneficial relationship between the Democratic Republic of Vietnam and the United States. The United States will contribute to healing the wounds of war and to post-war reconstruction in the Democratic Republic of Vietnam and throughout Indochina.

(9) This agreement shall come into force as of its signing. It will be strictly adhered to by all the parties concerned.

> As agreement with the United States neared, southern communists, recalling the lost peace of 1954, wondered if the peace of 1972 would be similarly compromised. The COSVN responded with a reassuring directive.

Today, in South Viet-Nam we have large liberated areas, a people's administration, and strong people's liberation armed forces, especially the main forces; we have a political force, a complete system of leadership from high to low levels and a time-tested infrastructure; we have the National Liberation Front for South Viet-Nam and the Provisional Revolutionary Government of the Republic of South Viet-Nam which enjoy a great prestige on the international scene; and we will occupy a position of equality in the administration of national concord ... Since the enemy's main support, which is the U.S. massive military strength and the war which is his key measure, will be limited, we will be in an advantageous position over the enemy. Especially our political superiority, which is our basic strength, will have the conditions to develop to the highest extent, opening new prospects.

DRV government statement via Radio Hanoi, 26 October 1972, in Gareth Porter (ed.), *Vietnam: The Definitive Documentation of Human Decisions*, 2 vols (London: Heyden, 1979), Vol. 2, pp. 575–6; COSVN directive, October 1972, cited in William J. Duiker, *Sacred War: Nationalism and Revolution in a Divided Vietnam* (New York: McGraw-Hill, 1995), pp. 239–40.

## 6.7   Nixon courts Thieu

Although the collapse of the agreement with Hanoi did not prevent Nixon's re-election as President in November 1972, he remained keen to terminate the war. Believing that the October deal was probably the best that the United States would get, and fearful that Congress, when it reconvened in January 1973, would act to end American involvement in Vietnam on any terms – thereby destroying his hopes for 'peace with honor' – Nixon sought to persuade President Thieu to drop his objections to the October deal. In doing so, Nixon employed classic carrot-and-stick methods. Thieu, for his part, was particularly exercised by Washington's readiness to tolerate the continued presence of the North Vietnamese army in South Vietnam.

I must explain in all frankness that while we will do our very best to secure the changes in the agreement which General Haig[9] discussed with you and those additional ones which Ambassador Bunker will bring you, we cannot expect to secure them all. For example, it is unrealistic to assume that we will be able to secure the absolute assurances which you would hope to have on the troop issue.

But far more important than what we say in the agreement on this issue is what we do in the event that the enemy renews its aggression. You have my absolute assurance that if Hanoi fails to abide by the terms of this agreement it is my intention to take swift and severe retaliatory action.

I believe the existing agreement to be an essentially sound one which should become even more so if we succeed in obtaining some of the changes we have discussed. Our best assurance of success is to move into this new situation with confidence and cooperation.

With this attitude and the inherent strength of your government and army on the ground in South Vietnam, I am confident this agreement will be a successful one.

If, on the other hand, we are unable to agree on the course that I have outlined, it is difficult for me to see how we will be able to continue our common effort towards securing a just and honorable peace. As General Haig told you, I would with great reluctance be forced to consider other alternatives. For this reason, it is essential that we have your agreement as we proceed into our next meeting with Hanoi's negotiators ... I cannot overemphasize the urgency of the task at hand nor my unalterable determination to proceed along the course which we have outlined.

... I repeat my personal assurances to you that the United States will react very strongly and rapidly to any violation of the agreement. But in order to do this effectively it is essential that I have public support and that your Government does not emerge as the obstacle to a peace which the American public now universally desires. It is for this reason that I am pressing for the acceptance of an agreement which I am convinced is honorable and fair and which can be made essentially secure by our joint determination.

Nixon letter to Thieu, 14 November 1972, in Porter (ed.), *Vietnam*, Vol. 2, pp. 581–3.


## 6.8 Nixon renews his promise

Having failed to move Thieu, and only too well aware of the political implications in America of concluding a 'separate' peace with North Vietnam, Nixon launched the 1972 Christmas bombing campaign in the hope of securing additional concessions from Hanoi. The bombing failed in this regard, although the peace talks began again in Paris in January 1973. On the eve of their resumption, Nixon felt compelled to renew his earlier promise to Thieu in order to secure his consent to the peace deal

With respect to the question of North Vietnamese troops, we will again present your views to the Communists as we have done vigorously at every other opportunity in the negotiations. The result is certain to be once more the rejection of our position. We have explained to you repeatedly why we believe the problem of North Vietnamese troops is manageable under the agreement, and I see no reason to repeat all the arguments.

> Nixon said that he expected both his government and that of the DRV to reach agreement in Paris.

The gravest consequences would then ensue if your government chose to reject the agreement and split off from the United States ... I am convinced that your refusal to join us would be an invitation to disaster – to the loss of all that we together have fought for over the past decade. It would be inexcusable above all because we will have lost a just and honorable alternative ...

I can only repeat what I have so often said: The best guarantee for the survival of South Vietnam is the unity of our two countries which would be gravely jeopardized if you persist in your present course. The actions of our Congress since its return have clearly borne out the many warnings we have made.[10]

Should you decide, as I trust you will, to go with us, you have my assurance of continued assistance in the post-settlement period and that we will respond with full force should the settlement be violated by North Vietnam. So once more I conclude with an appeal to you to close ranks with us.

Nixon letter to Thieu, 5 January 1973, in Porter (ed.), *Vietnam*, Vol. 2, p. 592.

### 6.9  Peace violations

Thieu was finally won over, and the Paris peace settlement ensued in January 1973. By March, all US military personnel had left South Vietnam. Yet, for the Vietnamese, there was no peace. War continued, albeit at a lower intensity, with both sides guilty of violating the provisions of the settlement. For President Nixon, however, it was communist violations that mattered, for a serious threat to the Saigon government's survival would raise the issue of re-opening US involvement.

In the case of these violations, we are concerned about them on two scores. One, because they occur, but two, we are concerned because of another violation that could lead to, we think, rather serious consequences. We do not believe it will. We hope that it will not. And that is the report that you ladies and gentlemen have been receiving from your colleagues in Vietnam with regard to infiltration.

You will note that there have been reports of infiltration by the North Vietnamese into South Vietnam of equipment exceeding the amounts that were agreed upon in the settlement.

Now, some equipment can come in. In other words, replacement equipment, but no new equipment, nothing which steps up the capacity of the North Vietnamese or the Vietcong to wage war in the South. No new equipment is allowed under the agreement.

Now, as far as that concern is concerned, particularly on the infiltration, that is the more important point, rather than the cease-fire violations which we think, over a period of time, will be reduced – but in terms of the infiltration, I am not going to say publicly what we have said.

I only suggest this: That we have informed the North Vietnamese of our concern about this infiltration and what we believe it to be, a violation of the cease-fire and the peace agreements. Our concern has also been expressed to other interested parties and I would only suggest that based on my actions over the past four years, that the North Vietnamese should not lightly disregard such expressions of concern, when they are made, with regard to violation. That is all I will say about it.

Nixon press conference, 15 March 1973, in Porter (ed.), *Vietnam,* Vol. 2, p. 631.

## 6.10 The congressional backlash

Nixon's threats to Hanoi, whether public and implied or private and explicit, were soon undermined by a raft of congressional legislation designed to prevent further US military action in Indochina. Nixon would later claim that Congress devalued the deterrent quality of his warnings to North Vietnam, encouraged communist aggression, and ultimately did much to aid the communist victory in 1975.

In short order [in 1973], two separate Senate committees voted to cut off funds for combat activities [in Indochina] ... The cutoff aid bill passed on June 25. I vetoed it, and in my veto statement I said, 'After more than ten arduous years of suffering and sacrifice ... it would be nothing short of tragic if this great accomplishment, bought with the blood of so many Asians and Americans, were to be undone now by congressional action.' The House of Representatives sustained my veto the same day, June 27, but it seemed clear that another cutoff bill would be proposed and that I could not win these battles forever. Therefore, we agreed to a compromise that set August 15, 1973, as the date for the termination of the U.S. bombing of Cambodia and required Congressional approval for the funding of U.S. military action in any part of Indochina. At least this gave us more time, but the invitation to aggression represented in any cutoff date remained unchanged.

The wording of Public Law 93-62, section 108, of 1 July 1973 – steered through Congress by Senators George Aiken and J. William Fulbright – was quite explicit.

SEC. 108. Notwithstanding any other provision of law, on or after August 15, 1973, no funds herein or heretofore appropriated may be obligated or expended to finance directly or indirectly combat activities by United States military forces in or over or from off the shores of North Vietnam, South Vietnam, Laos or Cambodia.

Nixon was unhappy, even incredulous.

I was determined that the historical record would mark Congress's responsibility for this reckless act, and on August 3, shortly before the scheduled mandatory cutoff, I wrote to House Speaker Carl Albert and Senate Majority Leader Mike Mansfield:

*... I can only hope that the North Vietnamese will not draw the erroneous conclusion from this Congressional action that they are free to launch a military offensive in other areas in Indochina. North Vietnam would be making a very dangerous error if it mistook the cessation of bombing in Cambodia for an invitation to fresh aggression or further violations of the Paris agreements. The American people would respond to such aggression with appropriate action.*

I knew that since Congress had removed the possibility of military action I had only words with which to threaten. The Communists knew it too. During this period [Secretary of State Henry] Kissinger held one of his regular luncheon meetings with [Anatoly] Dobrynin [Soviet Ambassador to Washington]. When Kissinger raised the question of the Communist violations of the cease-fire ... the Soviet ambassador scornfully asked what we had expected, now that we had no negotiating leverage because of the bombing cutoff imposed by Congress. Kissinger tried to be as menacing as he could, even though he knew that Dobrynin was right.

'There should be no illusion that we will forget who put us in this uncomfortable position,' he said.

'In that case,' Dobrynin replied, 'you should go after Senator Fulbright, not us.'

Richard Nixon, *RN: The Memoirs of Richard Nixon* (London: Sidgwick & Jackson, 1978), pp. 888–9; Porter (ed.), *Vietnam*, Vol. 2, p. 539.

## 6.11 ' ... if you offered them candy'

In December 1974, North Vietnam's leadership debated whether to launch an all-out push for victory in the south. The danger of American retaliation overhung the discussion, but Premier Pham Van Dong eventually put that possibility in perspective.

We are in a new phase. The United States has withdrawn its troops in accordance with the Paris Agreement, which it regards as a victory after suffering many defeats with no way out. Now, there is no way that they could intervene again by sending in troops. They may provide air and naval support, but that cannot decide victory or defeat. I'm kidding, but also telling the truth, when I say that the Americans would not come back even if you offered them candy.

Pham Van Dong to Politburo, 18 December 1974, cited in Duiker, *Sacred War*, p. 244.

## 6.12 The Ho Chi Minh campaign

On 31 March 1975, Hanoi instructed General Van Tien Dung to launch a general offensive – the Ho Chi Minh campaign – against Saigon with the object of achieving total victory in four weeks.

Strategically, militarily, we now possess overwhelmingly superior strength and the enemy is on the verge of disintegration. The United States appears virtually powerless, and even reinforcements cannot reverse the enemy's situation. The revolutionary war in the South has not only entered a stage of great leap forward but conditions are ripe for launching a general offensive and uprising in Saigon-Giadinh. From this moment, the final strategic decisive battle of our army and people has begun; its aim is to complete the people's national democratic revolution in the South and bring peace and the reunification of the Fatherland.

Van Tien Dung later recalled his reaction to Hanoi's exhortation.

In the past thirty years our people had witnessed and taken part in who knows how many operations for the independence and freedom of our Fatherland. There had not yet been a day when our people and our army had halted their operations. From South to North, from North to South, our fighters and people went the whole length of the land, going wherever the Fatherland needed them ... In the spring of 1975, in the formation of vehicles and artillery advancing to the Saigon front, just as in every village, on every dock, in every trench in the South, it was impossible to distinguish southerners from northerners. There were only Vietnamese, charging toward the final battle against U.S. imperialism and its lackeys, to win back complete independence, freedom, peace, and unity. The whole land was on the march at top speed. The whole land was going to the front. The spring of earth and heaven and the spring of our nation clung fast together in this historic April of 1975.

VWP Politburo directive, 31 March 1975, cited in William J. Duiker, *The Communist Road to Power in Vietnam* (Boulder: Westview Press, 1996 edn), p. 345; General Van Tien Dung, *Our Great Spring Victory* (New York: Monthly Review Press, 1977), p. 145.

### 6.13  Victory

On 30 April 1975, Saigon fell to the communists, the US Congress having refused to grant South Vietnam emergency military aid. On the spot, at the very centre of events, was Bui Tin, ex-colonel of the North Vietnamese army who was then reporting on the war for the Party newspaper, *Nhan Dan.*

Early on the morning of April 30, 1975 ... I was in Cu Chi and it was simply by chance that I ended up at Independence Palace in Saigon. When I arrived there I saw a tank commander who had been wounded. I was told there had been fighting near the An Quang and Xa Loi pagodas, which were the most militant in Saigon. Then Lt.-Col. Nguyen Van Han, the chief of security of the Fourth Army Corps with whom I had previously been closely associated, and Bui Van Tung, the political commissar of the 203rd Tank Regiment, informed me that Duong Van Minh – Big Minh as he was known – who had become president of South Vietnam two days earlier, was sitting inside the palace with all his cabinet, waiting. However there was nobody present of rank high enough to go and talk to him. In the People's Army of Vietnam, only officers of the rank of colonel or above were considered to have sufficient authority and seniority to make decisions. Lt.-Col. Han said he had been ordered to wait for such an officer to arrive before entering the building. He then asked me to go in and talk to the president because I held the rank of colonel. I replied that I was only a journalist now, but Lt.-Col. Han persisted. Eventually I agreed.

To reduce tension, I asked two young soldiers to leave their AK-47s outside. Then Lt.-Col. Han entered the room where Big Minh was waiting and announced that a high-ranking officer had arrived. Everybody stood up as I walked in with Lt.-Col. Nguyen Tran Thiet, another journalist from the army newspaper in Hanoi. As soon as we appeared Big Minh said 'We have been waiting for you all morning.'

By then it was mid-day and I did not know that much earlier that morning Minh had already announced a cease-fire over the radio, so I replied it was time to stop the war and avoid further sacrifice on both sides. At that time I believed our policy was to achieve reconciliation between all Vietnamese; at this point, seeing a lot of anxious and tense faces around me, I went on to say that all Vietnamese should consider this a happy day because our victory belonged to the whole people and only the American foreign invaders had been defeated.

Some of those present in the room, including Vu Van Mao the prime minister-designate, began to smile when suddenly there was a burst of gunfire outside which broke one of the window panes. Everybody ducked but I told them not to worry. Our soldiers were simply firing in the air to celebrate. One had raised the National Liberation Front flag over Independence Palace.

Once everybody had got up again, I tried to calm their nerves by asking Duong Van Minh whether he still played tennis. I then talked about his orchid collection. He was reputed to have over 600 species, some of which he had brought back from Thailand when returning from exile there. I also asked Vu Van Mau why his hair was so long, since he had vowed to wear it short for as long as Nguyen Van Thieu remained President. Thieu had resigned and left the country two weeks earlier. At this Big Minh laughed and said it was no wonder we had won the war because we knew everything.

Bui Tin, *Following Ho Chi Minh: The Memoirs of a North Vietnamese Colonel* (London: Hurst & Co., 1995), pp. 84–5.

# 7

# Assessments and reflections

## 7.1  Why America lost

In 1995, Robert S. McNamara, US Secretary of Defense under both Kennedy and Johnson, published a controversial memoir on the war. He concluded with a list of eleven reasons for American failure in Vietnam.

1. We misjudged then – as we have since – the geopolitical intentions of our adversaries (in this case, North Vietnam and the Vietcong, supported by China and the Soviet Union), and we exaggerated the dangers to the United States of their actions.

2. We viewed the people and leaders of South Vietnam in terms of our own experience. We saw in them a thirst for – and a determination to fight for – freedom and democracy. We totally misjudged the political forces within the country.

3. We underestimated the power of nationalism to motivate a people (in this case, the North Vietnamese and Vietcong) to fight and die for their beliefs and values – and we continue to do so today in many parts of the world.

4. Our misjudgments of friend and foe alike reflected our profound ignorance of the history, culture, and politics of the people of the area, and the personalities and habits of their leaders. We might have made similar misjudgments regarding the Soviets during our frequent confrontations – over Berlin, Cuba, the Middle East, for example – had we not had the advice of Tommy Thompson, Chip Bohlen, and George Kennan. These senior diplomats had spent decades studying the Soviet Union, its peoples and its leaders, why they behaved as they did, and how they would react to our actions. Their advice proved invaluable in shaping our judgments and decisions. No Southeast

Asian counterparts existed for senior officials to consult when making decisions on Vietnam.

5. We failed then – as we have since – to recognize the limitations of modern, high-technology military equipment, forces, and doctrine in confronting unconventional, highly motivated people's movements. We failed as well to adapt our military tactics to the task of winning the hearts and minds of people from a totally different culture.

6. We failed to draw Congress and the American people into a full and frank discussion and debate of the pros and cons of a large-scale U.S. military involvement in Southeast Asia before we initiated our action.

7. After the action got under way and unanticipated events forced us off our planned course, we failed to retain popular support in part because we did not explain fully what was happening and why we were doing what we did. We had not prepared the public to understand the complex events we faced and how to react constructively to the need for changes in course as the nation confronted uncharted seas and an alien environment. A nation's deepest strength lies not in its military prowess but, rather, in the unity of its people. We failed to maintain it.

8. We did not recognize that neither our people nor our leaders are omniscient. Where our own security is not directly at stake, our judgment of what is in another people's or country's best interest should be put to the test of open discussion in international forums. We do not have the God-given right to shape every nation in our own image or as we choose.

9. We did not hold to the principle that U.S. military action – other than in response to direct threats to our own security – should be carried out only in conjunction with multinational forces supported fully (and not merely cosmetically) by the international community.

10. We failed to recognize that in international affairs, as in other aspects of life, there may be problems for which there are no immediate solutions. For one whose life has been dedicated to the belief and practice of problem solving, this is particularly hard to admit. But, at times, we may have to live with an imperfect, untidy world.

11. Underlying many of these errors lay our failure to organize the top echelons of the executive branch to deal effectively with the extraordinarily complex range of political and military issues, involving the great risks and costs – including, above all else, loss of life – associated with the application of military force under substantial

constraints over a long period of time. Such organizational weakness would have been costly had this been the only task confronting the president and his advisers. It, of course, was not. It coexisted with the wide array of other domestic and international problems confronting us. We thus failed to analyze and debate our actions in Southeast Asia – our objectives, the risks and costs of alternative ways of dealing with them, and the necessity of changing course when failure was clear – with the intensity and thoroughness that characterized the debates of the Executive Committee during the Cuban Missile Crisis.

These were our major failures, in their essence. Though set forth separately, they are all in some way linked: failure in one area contributed to or compounded failure in another. Each became a turn in a terrible knot.

Robert S. McNamara, *In Retrospect: The Tragedy and Lessons of Vietnam* (New York: Time Books, 1995), pp. 321–4.

## 7.2 Challenging McNamara

Although McNamara's memoirs were praised in some quarters for their frankness and honesty, most commentators found them troubling and ultimately unsatisfactory. One of McNamara's fiercest critics is the historian Marilyn B. Young.

Why was the United States engaged in an effort to destroy a popular insurgency in South Vietnam? How can such an effort square with McNamara's conviction that he and his colleagues made an 'error not of values and intentions but of judgment and capabilities'?[1] What values does he continue to imagine reside in that purely criminal intention? McNamara claims to have made the decisions he made in Vietnam 'according to what we thought were the principles and traditions of this nation. We made our decisions in the light of those values. Yet we were wrong, terribly wrong.'[2] It would be possible to read the sentence as a confession that McNamara now understands that the 'principles and traditions of this nation' were 'wrong, terribly wrong.' Of course, this is not what McNamara means at all. For him, the wrongness was about practice, not principle.

Marilyn B. Young, 'The Closest of Hindsight', *Diplomatic History*, Vol. 20, No. 3 (1996), p. 442.

## 7.3 Why the communists won

McNamara, in seeking to explain why America lost in Vietnam, also ignored the reasons why the communists won. The historian William J. Duiker has offered a corrective to McNamara's analysis.

[T]he most significant thing about the conflict is not that the United States lost but that the Communists won. Since the end of the war in 1975, one of the main issues raised in the long debate over the 'lessons of Vietnam' has been whether that war could have been won at an acceptable risk and cost. Although few would deny that U.S. policymakers made a number of mistakes in the course of the country's long involvement in Vietnam ... it was not those errors but the actions taken by Washington's adversaries in Hanoi that were decisive in determining the outcome.

Over the years, a variety of factors have been advanced to explain the Communist victory in the Vietnam War. It has been popular to search for single causes. Some have ascribed it primarily to the party's superior organizational ability or to its selective use of terror to intimidate or eliminate opponents. Other have referred to the aura of legitimacy that the Communist Party acquired among the Vietnamese people by virtue of its generation of struggle against the French. Others still point to the extraordinary personality and capability of Ho Chi Minh and contend that, had France or the United States responded to his appeal for support in 1945, the outcome of the revolution might have been far different.

An analysis of the record shows that all of these factors played a role in the final outcome. The emphasis [in Duiker's work] has been placed primarily on the Communist Party's program and strategy. The genius of that program was that it was able to combine patriotic and economic themes in an artful way to win the allegiance of a broad spectrum of the Vietnamese population in the party's struggle against its adversaries. The political program of the Vietminh Front in 1941 linked the ICP with the most dynamic forces in Vietnamese society under French colonial rule, the desire for economic and social justice as well as the drive for the restoration of national independence. The alliance between those two forces enabled the Vietminh to mobilize a solid popular base for their struggle against the French. That alliance was revived during the war against the United States, when the NLF won widespread support from the rural and urban poor by its promises of social reform and national self-determination while at the same time allaying the fears of urban moderates and foreign observers alike that it would embark on a program of radical social change after the seizure of power in Saigon.

By contrast, rival nationalist parties were consistently unable to formulate a program that could appeal widely to the mass of the Vietnamese population. The ineffectiveness of the nationalist movement forced its political leaders from Bao Dai to Ngo Dinh Diem and Nguyen Van Thieu to rely on outside support for their survival. From the beginning, such individuals and their organizations were compromised in the minds of many Vietnamese by their lack of a coherent program for nation building and by their willingness to collaborate with the French or, later, with the United States. It is not too much to say that the ICP had won the political battle with its rivals by the mid-1940s and, despite massive efforts by the French and the Americans, was able to retain that advantage over the next generation.

A second major factor in Communist success lay in the domain of revolutionary strategy. Here the genius of the party's approach lay in its ability to make optimum use of a combination of political and military struggle. Those who claim that Hanoi's victory was primarily a military one miss the mark. The evidence shows that in the absence of foreign intervention, the party would have easily bested its nationalist rivals in the political arena. That had been the lesson of the August Revolution, and it was reaffirmed during the later struggles against the French and the United States. It was the political superiority of the Communists over their nationalist rivals that forced Paris, and then Washington, to turn to the military option and thus transform a civil conflict into a revolutionary war.

It was the introduction of outside armed force that compelled the Communists themselves to adopt a strategy of revolutionary violence. At first they seized on the Maoist model of people's war, which had worked so well in China. But they soon discovered that moving to the Maoist third stage of general offensive was not as easy against a powerful Western adversary as it had been for the CCP against Chiang Kai-shek. The result was the gradual adoption of a more flexible strategy that relied on a combination of political and military techniques in both urban and rural areas with a diplomatic and psychological offensive that undermined public support for the party's rivals, in France and the United States as well as in Vietnam itself. Once the conflict had escalated into a military conflict, Hanoi's ultimate strategic objective was not to win a total victory on the battlefield, but to bring about a psychological triumph over its adversaries, leading to a negotiated settlement under terms favorable to the revolution. Although, as many have pointed out, the final 1975 campaign was a conventional military assault by regular units of the North Vietnamese army, it was the strategy of combined political and military struggle, supplemented by diplomatic and psychological tactics to undermine the strength of the enemy, that had brought the war to that point and enabled the offensive to realize total success.

Because of his ability to grasp the underlying nature of the dynamic forces at work in modern Vietnam and to formulate a program and strategy appropriate to the circumstances, Ho Chi Minh is the central figure in the Vietnamese revolution. Although his compelling personality and his talent for reconciliation were trump cards in his contest with his adversaries, the ace in the hole lay in his ability to conceptualize the fundamental issues at stake in the Vietnamese revolution, and thus to give his movement an aura of legitimacy that was the underlying factor in its victory.

William J. Duiker, *Sacred War: Nationalism and Revolution in a Divided Vietnam* (New York: McGraw-Hill, 1995), pp. 251–3.

## 7.4  Ho Chi Minh's last testament

In his treatment of Ho Chi Minh in the previous extract, William Duiker omits to mention another important characteristic – Ho's refusal to take sides in the Sino-Soviet dispute that dominated international communism in the 1960s. Pragmatically, North Vietnam's interests were best served by playing the two communist giants off against one another, although there were times – particularly between 1950 and 1964 – when the Vietnamese communists were much closer to Beijing than Moscow. Yet, when the Soviet Union itself displayed greater interest in the Vietnamese revolution in 1964–65, Hanoi

moved to occupy the middle ground between its two benefac-
tors. Only after 1969 – and after Ho's death – did North
Vietnam shift very obviously into the Soviet camp. Ho's last
testament, written in May 1969 but only made public after his
death the following September, is a valuable historical source,
emphasising once more its author's ardent patriotism, but also
his communism – and, in his lament for the state of Sino-Soviet
relations, his *international* communism.

Tu Fu, the famous poet of the Tang period in China, wrote: 'In all
times, few are those who reach the age of seventy.' This year, being
seventy-nine, I can already count myself among those 'few' … But
who can say how much longer I shall be able to serve the revolution,
the Fatherland and the people?

I therefore leave these few lines in anticipation of the day when I
shall go and join Karl Marx, Lenin and other revolutionary elders;
this way, our people throughout the country, our comrades in the
Party, and our friends in the world will not be taken by surprise …

… Ours is a Party in power. Each Party member, each cadre must
be deeply imbued with *revolutionary morality*, and show industry,
thrift, integrity, uprightness, total dedication to the public interest and
complete selflessness. Our Party should preserve absolute purity and
prove worthy of its role as the leader and very loyal servant of the
people … The Party must work out effective *plans* for economic and
cultural development so as constantly to *improve the life of our
people*.

*The war of resistance against US aggression* may drag on. Our people may have to face new sacrifices of life and property. Whatever
happens, we must keep firm our resolve to fight the US aggressors till
total victory.

> *Our mountains will always be, our rivers will always be,*
>   *our people will always be;*
> *The American invaders defeated, we will rebuild our land*
>   *ten times more beautiful*

No matter what difficulties and hardship lie ahead, our people are
sure of total victory. The US imperialists will certainly have to quit.
Our Fatherland will certainly be reunified. Our fellow-countrymen in
the South and in the North will certainly be re-united under the same
roof. We, a small nation, will have earned the signal honour of defeat-

ing, through heroic struggle, two big imperialisms – the French and the American – and of making a worthy contribution to the world national liberation movement.

*About the world communist movement*: Being a man who has devoted his whole life to the revolution, the more proud I am of the growth of the international communist and workers' movement, the more pained I am by the current discord among the fraternal allies.

I hope that our Party will do its best to contribute effectively to the restoration of unity among the fraternal parties on the basis of Marxism-Leninism and proletarian internationalism, in a way which conforms to both reason and sentiment.

I am firmly confident that the fraternal parties and countries will have to unite again.

*About personal matters*: All my life, I have served the Fatherland, the revolution and the people with all my heart and strength. If I should now depart from this world, I would have nothing to regret, except not being able to serve longer and more.

When I am gone, a grand funeral should be avoided in order not to waste the people's time and money ... My ultimate wish is that our entire Party and people, closely joining their efforts, will build a peaceful, reunified, independent, democratic and prosperous Viet Nam, and make a worthy contribution to the world revolution.

Ho Chi Minh, *Selected Writings, 1920–1969* (Hanoi: Foreign Languages Publishing House, 1973), pp. 358–62.

## 7.5  Chinese and Soviet aid for North Vietnam

It is a commonplace observation of Sino-Soviet aid to North Vietnam that China supplied the quantity and the Soviets the quality. Using newly available evidence, the historian Qiang Zhai has confirmed the quantity argument, particularly in regard to the 1954–63 period when Beijing was Hanoi's principal prop of support.

Although before 1962 Beijing policy makers were not eager to see a rapid intensification of the revolutionary war in South Vietnam, neither did they discourage their comrades in Hanoi from increasing military operations there. Between 1956 and 1963, China provided the DRV with 270,000 guns, over 10,000 pieces of artillery, nearly 200 million bullets, 2.02 million artillery shells, 15,000 wire transmitters, 5,000 radio transmitters, over 1,000 trucks, 15 aircraft, 28 war ships, and 1.18 million sets of uniforms. The total value of China's assistance to Hanoi during this period amounted to 320 million yuan.

> It was only in 1964 that the Soviet Union became a major supplier of North Vietnam – partly to win over a potential ally in its increasingly bitter dispute with China, and partly to prove that Moscow, not just Beijing, could be relied upon to support wars of national liberation in the Third World. Given the traditional Vietnamese mistrust of all things Chinese, the emergence of the Soviet Union as a meaningful ally was no doubt welcomed in Hanoi. However, as Ilya Gaiduk has discovered from documents released in Moscow, the Soviet government had additional motives in offering aid.

Military factors constituted one major positive incentive favoring a more active Soviet involvement, according to archival documents. There were two principal, interconnected perceived opportunities: Vietnam offered a live battlefield testing ground for Soviet military hardware ... and also a chance to obtain a windfall of hard information about up-to-date U.S. weaponry, by inspecting the war booty captured or obtained by the DRV forces. The North Vietnamese air defense was fully equipped with modern Soviet hardware ... [and] the North Vietnamese used the Soviet-made Grad artillery shelling systems, which were highly effective in attacks on U.S. bases, airfields, ammunition depots, etc., as well as MiG-21 jets.

The Soviet military also relished the opportunity to pore over the latest U.S. military hardware. In accordance with a Soviet–North Vietnamese agreement signed in the spring of 1965, the Vietnamese undertook to transfer to the USSR models of captured U.S. military hardware for inspection. All difficulties notwithstanding ... a total of 700 models were delivered to the USSR between May 1965 and January 1967 ... However, apart from the obvious assets the USSR gained in the course of the Vietnam war, its expenditures were likewise enormous, primarily in the sphere of ever increasing material assistance to Vietnam. In 1966–1968 the Soviet Union undertook to render to the DRV economic assistance to the tune of 121.6 million rubles, but in fact the assistance was far greater in view of Hanoi's incessant requests for additional supplies. In 1968 Soviet assistance to the DRV totalled 524 million rubles, with 361 million rubles transferred as a gift.

> Another historian who has used newly available communist sources is Chen Jian. It may be – as Gaiduk suggests – that the Soviets did supply 'quality' items like MiG fighters, but this should not diminish the importance of Chinese aid. Indeed, in the form of thousands of engineers and anti-aircraft personnel, it was PRC assistance that allowed North Vietnam the scope to keep sending manpower to South Vietnam. Chen Jian also notes that China's supplies to the DRV increased in 1965, as Sino-Soviet competition intensified to the ultimate benefit of North Vietnam.

Compared with 1964, the supply of guns [in 1965] increased 1.8 times, from 80,500 to 220,767; gun bullets increased almost 5 times, from 25.2 million to 114 million; pieces of different types of artillery increased by over 3 times, from 1,205 to 4,439; and artillery shells increased nearly 6 times, from 335,000 to 1.8 million. The amount of China's military supply fluctuated between 1965 and 1968, although the total value of material supplies remained at roughly the same level ...

To summarize, although Beijing's decision to support Vietnam had its own logic and considerations, China's aid to Vietnam during 1965–69 was substantial. Beijing provided the Vietnamese with large amounts of military and other material assistance. Over 320,000 Chinese engineering and anti-aircraft artillery forces (the peak year was 1967, when 170,000 Chinese troops were present in Vietnam) were directly engaged in the construction, maintenance and defence of North Vietnam's transport system and strategically important targets ... Such support allowed Hanoi to use its own manpower for more essential tasks, such as participating in battles in the South, and maintaining the transport and communication lines between the North and the South ... It is therefore fair to say that, although Beijing's support may have been short of Hanoi's expectations, without the support, the history, even the outcome, of the Vietnam War might have been different.

Qiang Zhai, 'Beijing and the Vietnam Conflict, 1964–1965: New Chinese Evidence', and Ilya V. Gaiduk, 'The Vietnam War and Soviet–American

Relations, 1964–1973: New Russian Evidence', in *The Cold War International History Project Bulletin* 6–7 (Winter 1995/96), pp. 235, 253; Chen Jian, 'China's Involvement in the Vietnam War, 1964–69', *China Quarterly*, Vol. 142 (June 1995), pp. 377–8.

## 7.6   The Vietnamese revolution betrayed?

Thanks in part, then, to Soviet and Chinese aid, the Vietnamese communists won the 'total victory' predicted by Ho Chi Minh in his last testament (7.4), but did they go on to win the peace? For many non-communists in the NLF, the elation of victory in April 1975 quickly gave way to fear and foreboding. The hope that Hanoi would not impose communism on the south in the post-war period – and the related belief that a pluralistic government, responsive to the particularist needs of the south, would be permitted – were soon proved false. For some, like Truong Nhu Tang of the Justice Ministry of the Provisional Revolutionary Government (PRG) in Saigon in 1975, the sense of betrayal was acute.

[A]s the weeks slid by, it became impossible to shut our eyes to the emerging arrogance and disdain of our [Communist] Party staff cadres. In the Justice Ministry, my administrators began claiming that they had to carry out orders from their superiors in the Northern government, rather than the directives they received from us ... As the cadres' demands became more and more heated, I remained adamant, continuing to operate on the theory that authority would have to be grasped. Eventually, my obstinacy brought results – visitors from the North. I received word that the chiefs of the High Tribunal, the Censorate, and the Juridical Committee would meet with me to resolve the impasse that had developed. In an afternoon of discussion, my guests succeeded in conveying to me the fundamentality of the North's resolve to control the Provisional Government.

As we talked, the true outlines of power revealed themselves with painful clarity. Suddenly all the creeping fear that, until now, I had succeeded in holding down were released ... By the time this diplomatic encounter was over, I had no illusions about what was happening, and I knew that neither I nor my colleagues would be in office for long ...

It was a time of unalloyed cynicism on the part of the Workers'

Party and stunned revulsion for those of us who had been their brothers-in-arms for so long. About this period the Northern Party historian Nguyen Khac-Vien comments, 'The Provisional Revolutionary Government was always simply a group emanating from the DRV. If we (the DRV) had pretended otherwise for such a long period, it was only because during the war we were not obliged to unveil our cards.' Now, with total power in their hands, they began to show their cards in the most brutal fashion. They made it understood that the Vietnam of the future would be a single monolithic block, collectivist and totalitarian, in which all the traditions and culture of the South would be ground and molded by the political machine of the conquerors. These, meanwhile, proceeded to install themselves with no further regard for the niceties of appearance.

The PRG and the National Liberation Front, whose programs had embodied the desire of so many South Vietnamese to achieve a political solution to their troubles and reconciliation among a people devastated by three decades of civil war – this movement the Northern Party had considered all along as simply the last linkup it needed to achieve its own imperialistic revolution. After the 1975 victory, the Front and the PRG not only had no further role to play; they became a positive obstacle to the rapid consolidation of power.

This obstacle had to be removed. As Truong Chinh, spokesman for the Politburo, put it, 'The strategic mission for our revolution in this new phase is to accelerate the unification of the country and lead the nation to a rapid, powerful advance toward socialism.' Chinh's phrases were not simple rhetoric. They conveyed policy decisions that were to change the fabric of the South's political, social, and economic life. No longer would South Vietnam be regarded as 'a separate case' whose economy and government would have the opportunity to evolve independently, prior to negotiating a union with the DRV. All of the NLF and PRG emphasis on civil rights, land reform, and social welfare was 'no longer operative.' The program now was to strip away as fast as possible the apparent respect for pluralistic government, neutrality, and national concord and reconciliation in the South that the DRV had maintained with such breathtaking pretence for twenty-one years. We had entered, in Chinh's words, 'a new phase.'

Truong Nhu Tang (with David Chanoff and Doan Van Toai), *A Vietcong Memoir* (New York: Harcourt Brace Jovanovich, 1985), pp. 266–9.

## 7.7 'We were drunk with victory'

It was not only non-communist southerners like Truong Nhu Tang who felt betrayed in the immediate post-war period. Northern communists, too, were uneasy. Peace was meant to lead to national reconciliation and concord. Former supporters of the old Saigon regime were not to be punished, merely re-educated and then re-integrated into the new Vietnam. Special camps were set up for the purpose, but they soon metamorphosed into concentration camps. The re-education occurred, but seldom the re-integration.

In early 1975 I was nearly fifty years old and had spent the major part of my life serving the Revolution. I had fought against the French and the Americans in various different capacities. On several occasions I had fallen ill and thought I would die. Like so many other soldiers, I had suffered from persistent dysentery and malaria, and I bore the scars of blisters and boils. I had also been wounded three times by mortar shells and artillery. So the first days of May that year [1975] were overflowing with the elation of victory. Then I began to ponder and became uneasy.

Various questions troubled my mind as I tried to comprehend the fate of my compatriots. It was strange. During our hard struggle, life had seemed so simple and easy, but now there was much that was difficult to understand. The war had wasted so many Vietnamese lives on both sides and they were all our blood relatives. And for what? We were told it was to liberate the country.

At first there were many people who did not realise the implications of our victory. They saw it simply as the end of a long war and believed that immediately thereafter we would rebuild the country for the next generation. What they did not realise is that fighting a war is easy compared with reconstruction. They thought that with continuing help from our international friends, our towns and cities would soon become beautiful. Only gradually did they come to realise that coping with an economy in times of peace is far more difficult than waging a war. Besides, Communist propaganda is good at painting a one-sided picture. It never depicts the real problems, and in 1975 we were much too shortsighted to look at the rest of the world objectively and learn from others. We were drunk with victory.

That attitude was disastrous. We were arrogant in our ignorance.

The Party claimed to be the servant of the people but it did not listen to them at all. Just like during the land reform campaign in the 1950s, policy was handed down from above. National reconciliation, which had been one of the cornerstones of our policy before our victory, soon turned into recrimination ...

> In the first post-war months, Bui Tin interviewed a number of high-ranking officials and military figures from the former South Vietnamese regime.

At first our discussions were amicable. They had been led to believe they were being sent for courses of re-education lasting several days. Then it became several months and the period was progressively prolonged. What had happened was that the Defence Ministry initially assumed responsibility for dealing with its former opponents, but within a short time the Ministry of the Interior took over the task. It already had a network of detention camps in the North under the administration of General Le Phu Qua, and soon a similar system was established in the South. As a result, men who had been regarded as prisoners of war became transformed into political criminals, needing to be punished.

In my capacity as a newspaper correspondent, I went to visit re-education camps at Thu Duc, Long Thank, Quang Trung, Bo Ria and Tay Ninh. I also saw camps in the North in the Tuyen Quang region. All this worried me. There seemed to be no explanation. Communists generally consider themselves to be compassionate. So why pursue a policy of such harshness towards hundreds of thousands of people?

... I never did find out from whom or from where the idea of re-education had originated or whether it had been properly discussed, and its pros and cons weighed up. It was after all a national policy affecting the lives and psychology of tens of thousands of people and families as well as millions of their friends and relatives – in fact the whole society of the South. People were sent to what were called re-education camps, which in reality were prisons ... Previously I have maintained that if only Chairman Ho Chi Minh had lived until 1975, the epidemic of arrogance which spread with our victory would soon have been stopped because he always reminded us not to be discouraged in defeat or proud in victory. He also said that if we did win we would have to guard against acquiring the spoils of war to an excessive degree, as this could only lead to corruption. Also, the harsh and extensive measures taken against those detained in what were called re-education camps would probably not have occurred because Ho Chi Minh was compassionate and had a deep sense of human values. He was also very decisive and capable of overturning existing policy. However, in this case we cannot use the word 'if'. It is not possible, nor is it scientific. Ho Chi Minh had died more than five years previously.

Bui Tin, *Following Ho Chi Minh: The Memoirs of a North Vietnamese Colonel* (London: Hurst & Co., 1995), pp. 88–93.

## 7.8  Explaining My Lai

The My Lai massacre of March 1968, in which more than 200 civilians were murdered by US troops, is perhaps the most notorious atrocity of the war. Such butchery was not, of course, confined to the American side – the communists, too, could be just as brutal – but it has come in for closer scrutiny. Philip Caputo, who fought in South Vietnam in 1965, later attempted an explanation of what motivated American soldiers to commit what many critics denounced as war crimes.

There is [an] aspect of the Vietnam War that distinguished it from other American conflicts – its absolute savagery. I mean the savagery that prompted so many American fighting men – the good, solid kids from Iowa farms – to kill civilians and prisoners ...

There has been a good deal of exaggeration about U.S. atrocities in Vietnam, exaggeration not about their extent but about their causes. The two most popularly held explanations for outrages like My Lai have been the racist theory, which proposes that the American soldier found it easy to slaughter Asians because he did not regard them as human beings, and the frontier-heritage theory, which claims he was inherently violent and needed only the excuse of war to vent his homicidal instincts.

Like all generalizations, each contains an element of truth; yet both ignore the barbarous treatment the Viet Cong and ARVN often inflicted on their own people, and neither confront the crimes committed by the Korean division,[3] probably the most bloody-minded in

Vietnam, and by the French during the first Indochina war.

The evil was inherent not in the men – except in the sense that a devil dwells in us all – but in the circumstances under which they had to live and fight. The conflict in Vietnam combined the two most bitter forms of warfare, civil war and revolution, to which was added the ferocity of jungle war. Twenty years of terrorism and fratricide had obliterated most reference points from the country's moral map long before we arrived. Communists and government forces alike considered ruthlessness a necessity if not a virtue. Whether committed in the name of principles or out of vengeance, atrocities were as common to the Vietnamese battlefields as shell craters and barbed wire. The marines in our brigade were not innately cruel, but on landing at Danang [in March 1965] they learned rather quickly that Vietnam was not a place where a man could expect much mercy if, say, he was taken prisoner. And men who do not expect to receive mercy eventually lose their inclination to grant it.

At times, the comradeship that was the war's only redeeming quality caused some of its worst crimes – acts of retribution for friends who had been killed. Some men could not withstand the stress of guerrilla-fighting: the hair-trigger alertness constantly demanded of them, the feeling that the enemy was everywhere, the inability to distinguish civilians from combatants created emotional pressures which built to such a point that a trivial provocation could make these men explode with the blind destructiveness of a mortar shell.

Others were made pitiless by an overpowering greed for survival. Self-preservation, that most basic and tyrannical of all instincts, can turn a man into a coward or, as was more often the case in Vietnam, into a creature who destroys without hesitation or remorse whatever poses even a potential threat to his life. A sergeant in my platoon, ordinarily a pleasant young man, told me once, 'Lieutenant, I've got a wife and two kids at home and I'm going to see 'em again and don't care who I've got to kill or how many of 'em to do it.'

General Westmoreland's strategy of attrition also had an important effect on our behavior. Our mission was not to win terrain or seize positions, but simply to kill: to kill Communists and to kill as many of them as possible. Stack 'em like cordwood. Victory was a high body-count, defeat a low kill-ratio, war a matter of arithmetic. The pressure on unit commanders to produce enemy corpses was intense, and they in turn communicated it to their troops. This led to such practices as counting civilians as Viet Cong. 'If it's dead and Vietnamese, it's VC,' was a rule of thumb in the bush. It is not surprising, therefore, that some men acquired a contempt for human life and a predilection for taking it.

Finally, there were the conditions imposed by the climate and country. For weeks we had to live like primitive men on remote outposts rimmed by alien seas of rice paddies and rain forests. Malaria, black-water fever, and dysentery, though not the killers they had been in past wars, took their toll. The sun scorched us in the dry season, and in the monsoon season we were pounded numb by ceaseless rain. Our days were spent hacking through mountainous jungles whose immensity reduced us to an antlike pettiness. At night we squatted in muddy holes, picked off the leaches that sucked on our veins, and waited for an attack to come rushing at us from the blackness beyond the perimeter wire.

The air-conditioned headquarters of Saigon and Danang seemed thousands of miles away. As for the United States, we did not call it 'the World' for nothing; it might as well have been on another planet. There was nothing familiar out there where we were, no churches, no police, no laws, no newspapers, or any of the restraining influences without which the earth's population of virtuous people would be reduced by ninety-five percent. It was the dawn of creation in the Indochina bush, an ethical as well as a geographical wilderness. Out there, lacking restraints, sanctioned to kill, confronted by a hostile country and a relentless enemy, we sank into a brutish state. The descent could be checked only by the net of a man's inner moral values, the attribute that is called character. There were a few – and I suspect Lieutenant Calley[4] was one – who had no net and plunged all the way down, discovering in their bottommost depths a capacity for malice they probably never suspected was there.

Most American soldiers in Vietnam – at least the ones I knew – could not be divided into good men and bad. Each possessed roughly equal measures of both qualities. I saw men who behaved with great compassion toward the Vietnamese one day and then burned down a village the next. They were, as Kipling wrote of Tommy Atkins, neither saints 'nor blackguards too/But single men in barracks most remarkable like you.' That may be why Americans reacted with such horror to the disclosures of U.S. atrocities while ignoring those of the other side: the American soldier was a reflection of themselves.

Philip Caputo, *A Rumor of War* (London: Macmillan, 1977), pp. xvi–xix.

## 7.9 '... someone else to pull the trigger'

Whatever motivated ordinary young Americans to fight in
Vietnam, as veterans they continue to suffer. Appreciating this
consequence of the war is not to deny the sufferings of the peoples of Indochina, only to acknowledge the democracy of suffering that the conflict generated. Here, the historian Marilyn
B. Young, herself a critic of American policy (see 7.2), makes a
moving plea for understanding, not condemnation, of those
Americans who survived their tour of duty in Vietnam.

Over 26 million American men came of draft age during the Vietnam
war; 2.15 million of them went to Vietnam, 1.6 million were in combat. Those who fought the war and died in it were disproportionately
poor, badly educated, and black ... It was also a teen-aged army – over
60 percent of those who died in Vietnam were between the ages of
seventeen and twenty-one, and the average age of those who served
was nineteen, five to seven years younger than in other American wars
...

Each young man who went to war had an individual tour of duty,
365 days, and then home, on his own, with no effort on anyone's part
to prepare for the shock of return, to help make the transition from
war to peace, from the privileging of violence to its prohibition, from
the sharp edge death brings to the life of a solider to the ordinary daily
life of a civilian, which denies death altogether. They had spoken always of coming back 'to the world', counting each day 'in country'
which brought them closer to the end of their tour. But the homecom-
ing was harder than any of them had expected. Later, many veterans
would tell stories of having been spat upon by anti-war protesters, or
having heard of veterans who were spat on. It doesn't matter how
often this happened or whether it happened at all. Veterans *felt* spat
upon, stigmatized, contaminated. In television dramas, veterans were
not heroes welcomed back into the bosom of loving families, admiring
neighborhoods, and the arms of girls who loved uniforms; they were
psychotic killers, crazies with automatic weapons. It was as if the
country had assumed that anyone coming back from Vietnam would,
even should, feel a murderous rage against the society that had sent
him there. The actual veteran – tired, confused, jet-propelled from
combat to domestic airport – disappeared. Or rather, he became a
kind of living hologram, an image projected by conflicting interpreta-

tions of the war: a victim or an executioner, a soldier who had lost a war, a killer who should never have fought it at all.

Of course there were also just the daily bread-and-butter problems of finding work in an economy far less open than it had been when the war was young. Today [the early 1990s], from one quarter to one third of the homeless (between one quarter and three quarters of a million men) are Vietnam-era veterans. Without training or skills, without any public sense that the country owed them anything at all, many Vietnam veterans found themselves not only unrewarded but even disadvantaged by their service records. The war had begun to unravel even as it was being fought, so that by 1971 dissent and disobedience within the armed forces were endemic. The result was a tremendous increase in the number of less than honorable discharges – 'bad paper' – which have followed the 500,000 to 750,000 men who received them ever since, making it difficult for them to get and keep jobs, and depriving them of educational and even medical benefits.

The lack of skills, the bad service records, the war wounds, have been only part of the difficulty many veterans face. At first, the widespread appearance of psychological problems was named 'postwar trauma' and assimilated to the literature on the problems of veterans of other wars. It soon became clear, however, that Vietnam veterans were not like veterans of other wars ... Even the Veterans Administration, obviously reluctant to single out Vietnam veterans as having any particular difficulties (especially in the light of the meager benefits accorded them), reported a 'greater distrust of institutions' and a 'bitterness, disgust and suspicion of those in positions of authority and responsibility.'

More disturbing was the persistence – or sudden onset ten or even fifteen years after the war – of symptoms of acute distress, accompanied by flashbacks, severe sleep problems, depression, and rage. 'Postwar trauma' was renamed 'post-traumatic stress disorder' and assimilated not to battle fatigue or shell shock but to what people experience as survivors of floods or earthquakes. A [Veterans Administration] doctor estimates that as many as 700,000 veterans suffer from some form of 'post-traumatic stress disorder'.

... 'The war is never over,' one homeless man explained to a reporter in 1987. 'You drink one too many beers and it pops up ... Sometimes, I hope to settle down somewhere where I won't be reminded of what I've seen. But I really don't see a future for myself.' Being unable to imagine a future precludes having one. More veterans have committed suicide since the war than died in it – at least sixty thousand. Nor is the connection between their war experience and their death at all obscure ...

In May 1971, Medal of Honor winner Dwight W. Johnson was shot dead by the owner of a store he was attempting to rob. In Vietnam, Johnson killed 'five to 20 enemy soldiers, nobody knows for sure,' when the tank crew he was trying to rescue blew up in front of his eyes. 'When he ran out of ammunition,' his obituary continues, 'he killed one with the stock of his machine gun.' Unskilled and jobless in Detroit, Skip Johnson's fortunes turned when he was awarded the Medal of Honor for his heroism that day. Civic notables showered him with gifts and the Army persuaded him to return to the service as a recruiter in Detroit's predominantly black high schools. But his wife noticed some changes in him, as she had in other veterans she knew: 'They get quiet. It's like they don't have too much to say about what it was like over there. Maybe it's because they've killed people and they don't really know why they've killed them.'

Eventually Skip Johnson went AWOL from his recruiter's job and ended up in Valley Forge VA Hospital, where the head psychiatrist reached a preliminary diagnosis: 'Depression caused by post-Vietnam adjustment problem.' Later, the doctor observed Johnson's guilt over having survived the tank ambush and over 'winning a high honor for the one time in his life he had lost complete control of himself. He asked: "what would happen if I lost control of myself in Detroit and behaved like I did in Vietnam?" The prospect of such an event apparently was deeply disturbing to him.' The psychiatrist refrained from answering Johnson's question; but a store manager in the western end of Detroit was more forthcoming: '"I first hit him with two bullets," the manager said later. "But he just stood there, with the gun in his hand, and said, 'I'm going to kill you ...' . I kept pulling the trigger until my gun was empty."'

Johnson's mother, thinking about her son's life and death after he was buried at Arlington National Cemetery with full military honors, wondered whether he had simply 'tired of life and needed someone else to pull the trigger.'

Marilyn B. Young, *The Vietnam Wars, 1945–1990* (New York: HarperCollins, 1991), pp. 319–24.

## 7.10 'If I recall correctly ...'

The US Vietnam veterans were, in some ways, victims of President Gerald Ford's injunction to the American people in 1975 to put the Vietnam experience behind them – an appeal, in Stephen Ambrose's words, for 'amnesia, not analysis' of what happened to America in Vietnam.[5] A later President, Ronald Reagan, evidently took this advice to heart: at a press conference in April 1982, Reagan offered a very singular version of history. Dare it be suggested that if the following appeared in an undergraduate essay, that essay would be deemed a fail?

If I recall correctly, when France gave up Indochina as a colony, the leading nations of the world met in Geneva in regard to helping those colonies become independent nations. And since North and South Vietnam had been previous to colonization two separate countries, provisions were made that these two countries could by a vote of all their people together decide whether they wanted to be one country or not ... And there wasn't anything surreptitious about it, but when Ho Chi Minh refused to participate in such an election and there was provision that the peoples of both countries could cross the border and live in the other country if they wanted to, and when they began leaving by the thousands and thousands from North Vietnam to live in South Vietnam, Ho Chi Minh closed the border and again violated that part of the agreement ... And openly, our country sent military advisers there to help a country which had been a colony have such things as a national security force, an army if you might say, or a military, to defend itself. And they were doing this, I recall correctly, also in civilian clothes, no weapons, until they began being blown up where they lived, in walking down the streets by people riding by on bicycles and throwing pipe bombs at them, and then they were permitted to carry side arms or wear uniforms ... But it was [not] totally a program until John F. Kennedy, when these attacks and forays became so great, that John F. Kennedy authorized the sending in of a division of marines, that was the first move toward combat moves in Vietnam.

Reagan press conference, April 1982, in *Public Papers of the Presidents of the United States: Ronald Reagan, 1982* (Washington DC: Government Printing Office, 1983), pp. 184–5.

## 7.11 'The circus is back in town'

Twenty-five years on from reunification, Vietnam – the Social-ist Republic of Vietnam – appears to be more at peace with itself. It is also more at peace with the United States: in 1995, the Clinton administration set in train the process that would lead to full and formal diplomatic relations between the two countries. However, if the war was fought on the Vietnamese side in order (in part at least) to prevent American domination, recent events suggest that the United States may have won a kind of victory after all. This, at any rate, is the verdict of journalist John Pilger, who visited Vietnam in 1995.

After 1975 the US imposed a punishing embargo [on Vietnam], cover-ing trade and humanitarian aid ... The blockade ended any hope of the Hanoi government lessening the dependence on the Soviet Union. For ordinary people, bitter years of austerity and repression followed. Former soldiers and servants of the old regime were sent to re-educa-tion camps, Vietnam's gulag, and liberty was often measured by your standing in the Communist Party; and thousands took to the sea ... Asked for humanitarian aid, President Carter made the extraordinary statement: 'We owe them nothing. The damage was mutual.' When I was in Hanoi 10 days after the end of the war it looked as I had imag-ined the East End of London in Victorian times, even though visible poverty was controlled.

That began to change dramatically after 1986 when the govern-ment declared a policy of Doi Moi, which means 'renovation' or loosely 'our way'. The 'free market' was embraced as a means of breaking down the embargo; and within two years the World Bank had arrived, followed by the Japanese and Europeans. Last year, Presi-dent Clinton finally lifted the American embargo and appeared to put to rest the specious 'MIA [Missing In Action] issue'. (No president ever mentioned the 200,000 Vietnamese MIAs).

Today, Vietnam is an open marketplace, and foreign 'investors' en-couraged by a privileged coterie in the government are achieving what years of bombs and Napalm failed to. As one American banker put it, 'The circus is back in town.' It is both a strange and very familiar circus. In the bar of the Hoa Binh hotel in Hanoi, Joe, a former Ameri-can helicopter pilot, says he now runs a fleet of corporate jets flying in American businessmen, many of them from companies that profited from the war. Next door are the new offices of the Bank of America, a pillar of the American war ...

Peter Purcell is building the Hanoi Club, where membership fees range from $6,500 to $15,000 and which 'will only work if it's exclusive'. With an initial capital of $14 million, he has probably already made $50 million, and he still has a vacant lot. He told me the story of a senior [Vietnamese] government official who asked him, on the quiet, to explain to him what a share was. 'Is this a country being ripped off?' I asked. 'Yes,' he said. 'It's part of the education programme of converting into this wonderful world of capitalism.'

> Pilger spoke to Nguyen Xuan Oanh, a former senior economic adviser to the Vietnamese Prime Minister, Vo Van Kiet.

What is interesting about this man is that not only is he the architect of Vietnam's 'market socialism', as he calls it, but he was deputy prime minister in the old Saigon regime. I said South Vietnam is remembered as having an economy based on a black market, drugs, prostitution and war profiteering.

'We had a bad administration,' he replied.

'But you were number two in that administration.'

'I tried very hard to help, but not successfully.'

I said that an American businessman here told me that Vietnam would soon be capitalist.

'I hope so,' he replied.

John Pilger, 'Nam Now', *Guardian Weekend*, 22 April 1995, pp. 19–20.

# Notes

## Introduction

1 James Cable, *The Geneva Conference of 1954 on Indochina* (London: Macmillan, 1986), p. 1.

2 George C. Herring, *America's Longest War: The United States and Vietnam, 1950–1975*, 2nd edn (New York: McGraw-Hill, 1986), p. xii.

3 See Gary R. Hess's excellent historiographical article, 'The Unending Debate: Historians and the Vietnam War', *Diplomatic History*, Vol. 18, No. 2 (1994), pp. 239–64.

4 Robert A. Divine, 'Vietnam Reconsidered', *Diplomatic History*, Vol. 12, No. 1 (1988), p. 81.

5 US Department of Defense, *The Pentagon Papers: The Defense Department History of United States Decision-making on Vietnam*, Senator Gravel edn, 5 vols (Boston: Beacon Press, 1971).

6 Divine, 'Vietnam Reconsidered', pp. 81–2.

7 R. B. Smith, *An International History of the Vietnam War*, 3 vols (London: Macmillan, 1983–91).

8 On the Soviet side, the work of Ilya Gaiduk stands out, notably *The Soviet Union and the Vietnam War* (Chicago: Ivan R. Dee, 1996), and also Gaiduk's 'Soviet Policy towards US Participation in the Vietnam War', *History*, Vol. 81, No. 261 (1996). For a Chinese perspective, see the work of Qiang Zhai, particularly *The Dragon, the Lion and the Eagle: Chinese–British–American Relations, 1949–58* (Kent, OH: Kent State University Press, 1996), and *China and the Vietnam Wars, 1950–1975* (Chapel Hill: University of North Carolina Press, 2000); also of importance is the work of Chen Jian, such as 'China and the First Indo-China War', *China Quarterly*, Vol. 133 (1993), and 'China's Involvement in the Vietnam War, 1964–69',

*China Quarterly*, Vol. 142 (1995). On British involvement, particularly during the Franco-Vietminh war, see Cable, *Geneva Conference*; Geoffrey Warner, 'Britain and the Crisis over Dienbienphu, April 1954: The Failure of United Action', and 'From Geneva to Manila: British Policy toward Indochina and SEATO, May–September 1954', in Lawrence S. Kaplan *et al.* (eds), *Dien Bien Phu and the Crisis of Franco-American Relations, 1954–1955* (Wilmington: Scholarly Resources Press, 1989); Kevin Ruane, 'Anthony Eden, British Diplomacy and the Origins of the Geneva Conference of 1954', *Historical Journal*, Vol. 31, No. 1 (1994), and 'Refusing to Pay the Price: British Foreign Policy and the Pursuit of Victory in Vietnam, 1952–54', *English Historical Review*, Vol. CX, No. 435 (1995).

9 *The Foreign Relations of the United States 1961–1963*, Vols I–III, and *1964–68*, Vols I–IV covering 1964–66 (Washington DC: Government Printing Office, 1988–98); Michael R. Beschloss (ed.), *Taking Charge: The Johnson White House Tapes, 1963–1964* (New York: Touchstone, 1997).

10 The role of President Johnson in the escalation of American involvement in Vietnam is a good example of the continuing vigour of the historiographical debate on the American side of the war. See for example George C. Herring, *LBJ and Vietnam: A Different Kind of War* (College Station: University of Texas Press, 1996); Irving Bernstein, *Guns or Butter?: The Presidency of Lyndon Johnson* (Oxford: Oxford University Press, 1996); Michael H. Hunt, *Lyndon Johnson's War: America's Cold War Crusade in Vietnam, 1945–1968* (New York: Hill & Wang, 1996); Brian VanDeMark, *Into the Quagmire: Lyndon Johnson and the Escalation of the Vietnam War* (Oxford: Oxford University Press, 1991); Lloyd C. Gardner, *Pay Any Price: Lyndon Johnson and the Wars for Vietnam* (Chicago: Ivan R. Dee, 1995); Robert Dallek, *Flawed Giant: Lyndon B. Johnson, 1960–1973* (Oxford: Oxford University Press, 1998).

11 Frederik Logevall, *Choosing War: The Lost Chance of Peace and the Escalation of War in Vietnam* (Berkeley: University of California Press, 1999).

12 For valuable historiographical surveys, see Divine, 'Vietnam Reconsidered' and Hess, 'The Unending Debate'. The historian Edwin E. Moise, author of *Land Reform in China and North Vietnam: Consolidating the Revolution at the Village Level* (Chapel Hill:

University of North Carolina Press, 1983), has constructed the most comprehensive bibliography of the Vietnam wars to date. Constantly updated, it can be accessed via the World Wide Web at http://hubcap.clemson.edu/~eemoise/bibliography.html. See also the scholarly debate generated by Logevall's *Choosing War* and archived at the H-Diplo WWW-site at http://www2.h-net.msu.edu/~diplo/.

13 Jean Lacouture, *Ho Chi Minh* (London: Allen Lane, 1968), p. 4.

14 Smith, *International History*, Vols 1–3; William J. Duiker, *The Communist Road to Power in Vietnam*, 2nd edn (Boulder: Westview Press, 1996); also Duiker, *Sacred War: Nationalism and Revolution in a Divided Vietnam* (New York: McGraw-Hill, 1995); Gabriel Kolko, *Anatomy of a War: Vietnam, the United States and the Modern Historical Experience* (New York: Pantheon, 1985); Carlyle Thayer, *War by Other Means: National Liberation and Revolution in Vietnam, 1954–60* (Sydney: Allen & Unwin, 1989); James W. Trullinger, *Village at War: An Account of War in Vietnam* (Stanford: Stanford University Press, 1994); Eric Bergerud, *The Dynamics of Defeat: The Vietnam War in Hau Nghia Province* (Boulder: Westview Press, 1991).

15 Duiker, *Communist Road to Power*, p. 3.

16 Amongst the most important memoirs to emerge in recent years are: General Van Tien Dung, *Our Great Spring Victory* (New York: Monthly Review Press, 1977); Truong Nhu Tang (with David Chanoff and Doan Van Toai), *A Vietcong Memoir* (New York: Harcourt Brace Jovanovich, 1985); Hoang Van Hoan, *A Drop in the Ocean: Hoang Van Hoan's Revolutionary Reminiscences* (Beijing: Foreign Languages Publishing House, 1988); Le Ly Hayslip (with Jay Wurts), *When Heaven and Earth Changed Places: A Vietnamese Woman's Journey from War to Peace* (New York: Doubleday, 1989); Bui Tin, *Following Ho Chi Minh: The Memoirs of a North Vietnamese Colonel* (London: Hurst & Co., 1995).

17 See note 8 above.

18 The contact address is: Cold War International History Project, Woodrow Wilson International Center for Scholars, 1 Woodrow Wilson Plaza, 1300 Pennsylvania Avenue NW, Washington DC 20523.

19 The Project's WWW address is: http://cwihp.si.edu. The *CWIHP Bulletin* 6–7 (1995–96) was devoted to 'The Cold War in Asia', and

included articles by Chen Jan on 'Beijing and the Vietnam Conflict, 1964–1965' and by Ilya V. Gaiduk on 'The Vietnam War and Soviet–American Relations, 1964–73'. CWIHP Working Papers with a Vietnam theme include: No. 7 (1993) Mark Bradley and Robert K. Brigham, 'Vietnamese Archives and Scholarship on the Cold War Period: Two Reports'; No. 18 (1997) Qiang Zhai, 'Beijing and the Vietnam Peace Talks, 1965–68: New Evidence from Chinese Sources'; No. 22 (1998) Odd Arne Westad, Chen Jian, Stein Tonnesson, Nguyen Vu Tung and James G. Hershberg, '77 Conversations between Chinese and Foreign Leaders on the Wars in Indochina, 1964–77'; No. 25 (1999) Stephen J. Morris, 'The Soviet–Chinese–Vietnamese Triangle in the 1970s: The View from Moscow'.

20  Ang Cheng Guan, *Vietnamese Communists' Relations with China and the Second Indochina Conflict* (Jefferson, NC: McFarland & Co., 1998); Robert K. Brigham, *Guerrilla Diplomacy: The NLF's Foreign Relations and the Viet Nam War* (Ithaca: Cornell University Press, 1999).

21  CWIHP Working Paper No. 7, p. 25.

22  Marilyn B. Young, *The Vietnam Wars, 1945–1990* (New York: HarperCollins, 1991); Justin Wintle, *The Viet Nam Wars* (London: Weidenfeld & Nicolson, 1991).

23  I am particularly indebted to the following: Bernard B. Fall (ed.), *Ho Chi Minh on Revolution: Selected Writings, 1920–66* (New York: Praegar, 1967); Allan W. Cameron (ed.), *Vietnam Crisis: A Documentary History*, 2 vols (Ithaca: Cornell University Press, 1971); Ho Chi Minh, *Selected Writings, 1920–1969* (Hanoi: Foreign Languages Publishing House, 1973); John Clark Pratt (ed.), *Vietnam Voices: Perspectives on the War Years, 1941–1982* (New York: Penguin, 1984); Gareth Porter (ed.), *Vietnam: The Definitive Documentation of Human Decisions*, 2 vols (London: Heyden, 1979); George Katsiaficas (ed.), *Vietnam Documents: American and Vietnamese Views of the War* (New York: M. E. Sharpe, 1992); James W. Mooney and Thomas R. West (eds), *Vietnam: A History and Anthology* (New York: Brandywine Press, 1994); Marvin E. Gettleman, Jane Franklin, Marilyn B. Young and H. Bruce Franklin (eds), *Vietnam and America: The Most Comprehensive Documented History of the Vietnam War* (New York: Grove Press, 1995).

## Notes

### Chapter 1

1 The Communist International – Comintern.
2 The Japanese were in effective occupation of much of Vietnam by 1941, using the French colonial regime – isolated since the fall of metropolitan France in June 1940 – to administer the colony on their behalf.
3 The Japanese incarceration of the French colonial administration.
4 The Emperor of Annam and head of the 'independent' native Vietnamese government established by the Japanese in the wake of the coup against the French administration in March 1945.
5 The Big Three conference at Teheran of November–December 1943, and the founding conference of the United Nations at San Franciso of April–June 1945, at which the principle of national self-determination was repeatedly asserted.
6 Vo Nguyen Giap, a leading member of the ICP and the Vietminh's military commander.
7 The Chinese section, or suburb, of Saigon.
8 This referred to the traditional-historical geographical division of Vietnam into Tonkin (north), Annam (centre), and Cochinchina (south). A referendum would be held in Cochinchina, then under direct French control, to decide whether or not it should be reunited with Tonkin and Annam.

### Chapter 2

1 Ho quite deliberately linked peace in Indochina with the 'European Defence Pact', or European Defence Community (EDC) project, the scheme by which West Germany was to be rearmed as an accretion of strength to the North Atlantic Treaty Organisation (NATO). The EDC was very unpopular in France – for obvious reasons – and Ho played on this fact in arguing that peace in Indochina would allow French forces to return to Europe thereby reducing the need for German troops in NATO.
2 Vietnam, Laos and Cambodia – whose freedom the French acknowledged *within* the French Union.
3 Winston S. Churchill, *The Second World War: Volume II, Their Finest Hour* (London: Cassell, 1949).
4 A collective defence pact for the Pacific and Southeast Asia; the

Americans wanted to move forward with a pact while the Geneva conference was in session, but the British feared that such a move would damage the chances of an agreement at Geneva since the Chinese in particular were bound to feel that the pact, in spite of its professed defensive nature, was directed against them.

5 The International Supervisory Commission would comprise representatives from the Western bloc (Canada), the Eastern bloc (Poland), and the neutral or non-aligned bloc (India).

6 The Berlin foreign ministers conference of January–February 1954 ended in an agreement to convene another East–West conference in April devoted to Asian issues – the Geneva conference.

7 A prominent figure in the Vietnam Workers' Party in 1954, Le Duan succeeded Ho Chi Minh as Party leader in 1969.

## Chapter 3

1 The 'republican regime' refers to the Republic of Vietnam and its government, established in 1955 with Diem as its President.

2 Diem had faced, and overcome, a number of non-communist threats to his rule from dissident army officers, the Binh Xuyen (the Saigon mafia), and two popular religious sects that possessed their own armed forces, the Cao Dai and Hoa Hao.

3 Promulgated in May 1959, Law 10/59 gave the Diem regime wide powers of arrest and provided a legal underpinning to its repressive campaign against all forms of political opposition.

4 A precursor to the notorious Strategic Hamlets, the so-called 'agroville' programme began in 1958–59. It was designed, according to George Herring, 'to relocate the peasantry in areas where the army could protect them from Vietcong terror and propaganda, and the [Saigon] government sought to make it attractive by providing the new communities with schools, medical facilities, and electricity. But the peasants deeply resented being forcibly removed from their homes and from the lands which contained the sacred tombs of their ancestors ... The agroville programme was eventually abandoned, but only after it had spawned tremendous rural discontent with the government.' See Herring, *America's Longest War: The United States and Vietnam, 1950–1975* (New York: McGraw-Hill, 1986 edn), pp. 68–9.

5 The Bandung conference of April 1955 – a gathering of 'developing'

nations – collectively espoused anti-colonialism, a foreign policy of non-alignment in the Cold War, and the principle of peaceful co-existence between nations of differing political ideologies.

## Chapter 4

1 Henceforth 'Vietcong', as the most common usage in the documents, will be used to describe the PLAF.
2 A small village near Danang, central Vietnam, now called Xa Hoa Qui.
3 General Paul S. Harkins, commander, US Military Assistance Command, Vietnam.
4 The statement, issued on the back of the McNamara–Taylor report, expressed the hope that the US military's task in Vietnam could be completed by the end of 1965.
5 A military government – the Military Revolutionary Council – had succeeded the Diem regime in November 1963 under the leadership of General Duong Van Minh.
6 A critical reference to the South East Asia Treaty Organisation (SEATO), a collective defence grouping formed in September 1954 by the United States, Britain, France, Australia, New Zealand, Thailand, Pakistan and the Philippines.
7 The French President, Charles de Gaulle, publicly championed a political solution, and a reconvened Geneva conference; the US government opposed this course, and relations with France became strained.
8 The general offensive/general uprising was the ultimate aim of DRV–Vietcong revolutionary warfare methodology, just as it had been the Vietminh's overriding objective.
9 South Vietnam was one such 'protocol state'. Although not a member of SEATO, the territory of South Vietnam, as well as Laos and Cambodia, came within the Organisation's geographical purview thanks to a special protocol to the Manila Treaty of September 1954.

## Chapter 5

1 In 1950, Communist China sought to bring Tibet under its authority, employing brutal methods to suppress subsequent eruptions of

Tibetan nationalism; in 1962, Chinese forces briefly entered Indian territory near to the Indo-Tibetan border; and in January 1951, the United States had promoted a United Nations resolution condemning Beijing's aggression in intervening in the Korean war in November 1950.

2 A prominent feature of Johnson's Great Society programme.

3 It seems unlikely that the communists would have been fully aware in 1967–68 of the doubts of some in Washington about the wisdom of continued escalation – doubts that would prompt McNamara's eventual resignation as Secretary of Defense.

4 Dean Acheson, US Secretary of State 1949–53, and John J. McCloy, former Ambassador to the Federal Republic of Germany. In addition to Ball himself, other 'wise men' included Douglas Dillon (former Treasury Secretary), Cyrus Vance (former Under-Secretary of Defense), Generals Omar Bradley and Maxwell Taylor (former chairmen of the Joint Chiefs of Staff), General Matthew Ridgway (NATO Supreme Commander, 1952–53), and Henry Cabot Lodge (ex-Ambassador to Saigon).

5 George Ball, as Under-Secretary of State between 1961 and 1966, often counselled disengagement rather than escalation.

6 Robert D. Murphy, an ex-diplomat of great experience and high standing.

7 Burmese statesman and UN Secretary General.

8 Abe Fortas, Washington lawyer, Supreme Court Justice (1965–69) and a close Johnson associate.

9 A presidential election was to be held in 1968, and Johnson was expected to run for a second full term in office.

## Chapter 6

1 Both the NLF–Vietcong and Hanoi regime, refuting the notion of 'two' Vietnams, regarded the US troops as the only *foreign* forces in South Vietnam; hence, although the US would have to withdraw, the North Vietnamese army, being indigenous not foreign, should be allowed to remain in position in the south.

2 Here Nixon means a North Vietnamese withdrawal alongside US disengagement.

3 Central Office for South Vietnam, the communist military headquarters.

4 A reference to Nixon's press conference at Guam on 25 July 1969, during which the Nixon (or Guam) Doctrine was first formulated.

5 Ellsworth Bunker, US Ambassador to Saigon, 1967–73.

6 General Creighton Abrams, US Commander in South Vietnam.

7 The new name for the National Liberation Front of South Vietnam.

8 Crucially, under this agreement, North Vietnamese armed forces would be allowed to remain in South Vietnam while American forces would be obliged to leave. This was an extraordinary concession by the United States – given to an enemy on behalf of an ally – and testifies to the Nixon administration's intense desire to be rid of the burden of Vietnam once and for all. The post-war status of North Vietnamese troops would be worked out between the various native factions in South Vietnam.

9 General Alexander Haig, US government intermediary to the South Vietnamese government.

10 US legislators were mobilising to reduce military assistance to South Vietnam.

## Chapter 7

1 Robert S. McNamara, *In Retrospect: The Tragedy and Lessons of Vietnam* (New York: Time Books, 1995), p. xvi.

2 McNamara, *In Retrospect*, p. xvi.

3 The South Korean government was one of the few to respond to the Johnson administration's 'more flags' campaign – the search for like-minded allies to share the burden of the war.

4 Lieutenant William Calley was adjudged to have been primarily responsible for the My Lai massacre, and was tried and found guilty in 1969.

5 Stephen E. Ambrose and Douglas G. Brinkley, *Rise to Globalism: American Foreign Policy since 1938* (London: Penguin, 1997 edn), p. 251.

# Guide to further reading

In order to avoid too great an overlap with the historiographical discussion and recommendations contained in the Introduction to this book, the following texts are all 'general' or 'overview' in nature. For recommendations on more specific aspects of the Vietnam wars, the reader should return to the Introduction.

William J. Duiker has produced a masterly yet succinct account of the Vietnam wars (one that focuses on communist decision-making whilst relating that process to the international situation) in *Sacred War: Nationalism and Revolution in a Divided Vietnam* (New York: McGraw-Hill, 1995). Duiker's more detailed treatment of the communist side of the war is contained in *The Communist Road to Power in Vietnam* (Boulder: Westview Press, 1996 edn). Another exhaustive treatment of Vietnamese communism within the international context is R. B. Smith's *An International History of the Vietnam War*, 3 vols (London: Macmillan, 1983–91), although, as yet, the series does not cover the conflict beyond 1966. Two further excellent overviews are Gary R. Hess, *Vietnam and the United States: Origins and Legacy of War* (Boston: Twayne, 1990), and William Turley, *The Second Indochina War: A Short Military and Political History* (Boulder: Westview, 1986). Stanley Karnow's *Vietnam: A History* (London: Century Hutchinson, 1983) is an excellent read, not least for the 'human dimension', although undergraduates sometimes find its size – more than 700 pages – difficult to navigate. Other important general histories include: Marilyn B. Young, *The Vietnam Wars 1945–1990* (New York: HarperCollins, 1991), in which US policy is given over to sustained criticism; Justin Wintle, *The Viet Nam Wars* (London: Weidenfeld & Nicolson, 1991), a much underrated study; and Anthony Short, *The Origins of the Vietnam War* (London: Longman, 1989), which takes a long-term view of causal factors, but ends its analysis with the US decisions of 1965 on the bombing of North Vietnam and the despatch of ground troops to South Vietnam. For an edited collection incorporating a number of perspectives on the conflict, see Peter Lowe (ed.), *The Vietnam War* (New York: St Martin's Press, 1999). My own short study is useful for undergraduate students – Kevin Ruane, *War and Revolution in Vietnam, 1930–1975* (London: UCL Press, 1985) – as is Robert J. McMahon (ed.), *Major Problems in the History of the Vietnam War: Documents and Essays* (Lexington: Heath & Co., 1995).

General texts on American involvement are predictably profuse. One that stands the test of time is George C. Herring, *America's Longest War: The United States and Vietnam, 1950–1975* (New York: McGraw-Hill, 1986 edn). More recent valuable additions to the literature are Robert D. Schulzinger, *A Time for War: The United States and the Vietnam War 1941–1975* (Oxford: Oxford University Press, 1997); Gerard J. De Groot, *A Noble Cause: America and the Vietnam War* (London: Longman, 1999). The following are also well worth reading: David L. Anderson, *Shadow on the White House: Presidents and the Vietnam War, 1945–1975* (Kansas: University of Kansas Press, 1993), an edited collection of essays; Michael Charlton and Anthony Moncrieff, *Many Reasons Why: American Involvement in Vietnam* (New York: Hill & Wang, 1989 edn), a selection of oral testimony; William J. Duiker, *US Containment Policy and the Conflict in Indochina* (Stanford: Stanford University Press, 1994); and Gabriel Kolko, *Anatomy of a War: Vietnam, the United States and the Modern Historical Experience* (New York: Pantheon, 1985), which provides a critique of US policy alongside an exposition of Vietnamese communist decision-making. Finally, two edited collections that straddle both the American and the wider international and Vietnamese perspectives are Jayne Werner and Luu Doan Huynh (eds), *The Vietnam War: Vietnamese and American Perspectives* (New York: M. E. Sharpe, 1993), and Elizabeth Errington and Brian McKercher (eds), *The Vietnam War as History* (New York: Praegar, 1990).

The last word in any bibliographic or historiographical discussion must go to Edwin Moise and his WWW-site on the Vietnam wars – mentioned in the Introduction, but worth repeating here as an exemplar of the value of the Internet to historians and students as well as a testament to Moise's own high scholarship and industry. The site is: http://hubcap.clemson.edu/~eemoise/bibliography.html.

# Index

Note: 'n' after a page reference indicates a note on that page.

Abrams, General Creighton 137
Acheson, Dean 37, 101, 122–4
agroville programme 177n
Aiken, George 144
Albert, Carl 145
Ambrose, Stephen 169
Ang Chen Guan 6
Associated State of Vietnam 38, 43
August Revolution (1945) 10, 21–2, 25, 29, 153
Australia 97

Ball, George 122–3, 124
Bandung conference (1955) 177n
Bao Dai, Emperor 23, 153
Bergerud, Eric 5
Berlin 107, 149
Berlin conference (1954) 51, 177n
Bidault, Georges 28
Binh Xuyen 177n
Bodard, Lucien 54
*Bolshevik* 17
Bonnet, Henri 28
Bradley, General Omar 123
Briere, Marie 26
Brigham, Robert K. 6
Britain 47
    and Franco-Vietminh War 26–7, 34, 42–6

British Commonwealth 43
Buddhists 84
Bui Tin 26, 147, 162
Bui Van Tung 147
Bundy, McGeorge 99, 101–2, 122–3
Bunker, Ellsworth 137, 141
Burma 41, 47, 97

Cable, James 1
Calley, Lieutenant William 165, 180n
Cambodia 7, 38, 49, 51, 97, 105, 116, 127, 132, 137, 139, 144–5
Cao Dai 177n
Caputo, Philip 114, 163
Caravelle manifesto (1960) 70–2
Carter, Jimmy 170
Central Office for South Vietnam (COSVN) 58, 134, 140, 179n
Chamberlain, Neville 100
Chen Jian 158
China 10, 20, 83, 101
    Communist *see* People's Republic of China (PRC)
    Nationalist 10, 29, 30, 54
Chinese Communist Party (CCP) 54, 153

Chinese Military Advisory Group (CMAG) 53–4
Christmas bombing (1972) 128, 142
Churchill, Winston S. 42, 43, 45
  administration (1951–55) 42
Clifford, Clark 122
Clinton, William J. 170
Colby, William 122
Cold War 2, 7, 28, 33, 34, 36, 37, 56, 99, 177n
Cold War International History Project 5
colonialism 9, 12–14, 36, 75
Communist International (Comintern) 9, 12–15, 17–18
containment strategy 2
COSVN *see* Central Office for South Vietnam
'counter-insurgency' 81
Cronkite, Walter 89
Cuba 149
Cuban missile crisis (1962) 151

de Gaulle, Charles 178n
Dean, Arthur 123
'decent interval' 129
Democratic Republic of Vietnam (DRV) 10, 22–4, 37–8, 56–8, 91, 82, 86–7, 101–2, 103–4, 108–10, 115–16, 117, 120–1, 127–9, 130–2, 133–5, 137, 141, 142, 149, 152–4, 156–8, 159–60, 179n
  attitude to national reunification (1954–65) 57–8, 62–4, 67–70, 72, 74–5, 108, 127, 130, 139, 146, 155–6
  land reform programme (1954–56) 56, 65–7
  negotiations with United States 103–4, 108–9, 127–9,
  138–40
  relations with PRC 5, 33, 35, 37–8, 51–5, 56, 57, 64, 66–7, 128, 154–8
  relations with Soviet Union 38, 51–2, 56, 57, 64, 128, 154–8
  strategy in South Vietnam (1965–75) 82, 93–6, 103–4, 106, 109–11, 115–16, 127–9, 133–5, 141, 153–5
  US bombing of (1965–72) 82–3, 105, 116–17
détente 128
Dienbienphu, battle of (1954) 34, 41, 45–7, 53–4
Dillon, Douglas C. 123
Divine, Robert A. 3
Dobrynin, Anatoly 145
Doi Moi 170
domino theory 44–5, 56, 88, 96–7, 103, 107
  antecedents 38–9, 40–1
Ducoux, Jospeh 24
Duiker, William J. 4–5, 12, 151, 154
Dulles, John Foster 41–2, 46
Duong Van Minh 147–8, 178n

Easter Offensive *see* Spring Offensive
Eden, Anthony 46
Eisenhower, Dwight D. 43–4
  administration (1953–61) 34, 42, 44, 57, 58, 81
European Defence Community (EDC) 40, 176n

First World War 11
Ford, Gerald R. 169
*Foreign Relations of the United States* 4
Formosa *see* Taiwan
Fortas, Abe 124

France 9, 28–31, 34, 39–40,
42–3, 47, 48, 53, 54–5, 58,
68, 71, 84, 94, 152–4, 161,
164, 169, 176
colonial rule in Vietnam 9–12,
21, 23, 27, 28, 30, 33, 38,
40, 84, 152, 176n
Franco-Vietminh War (1946–54)
1, 7, 11, 31–2, 33–55, 84,
152–3, 164, 169
French Communist Party 13
French Socialist Party 11–13
French Union 29, 176n
Fulbright, J. William 144, 145

Gaiduk, Ilya 157
Geneva conference (1954) 34–5,
42, 44–7, 48, 53, 56, 58,
169, 176n, 178n
Final Declaration/Accords 34,
49–50, 52, 58, 61, 62, 69,
71, 84, 86, 108–9, 130–1,
132, 138, 140
Germany 40
Gracey, Major-General Douglas
27
Great Society 83, 99–101,
117–18, 126
Gulf of Tonkin incident/resolution
(1964) 97–8

Haig, Alexander 141
Haiphong, shelling of (1946) 11,
31
Hanoi, battle of (1946) 11, 31
Harkins, General Paul 90
Harriman, Averell 99
Herring, George C. 2
Hirohito, Emperor 44
Hitler, Adolf 44
Ho Chi Minh 4, 9–21, 22–6,
28–32, 33–4, 36–9, 47–8,
50–1, 52, 54, 56, 62–3,
65–7, 74–5, 84, 100, 111,

152, 154–6, 159, 152–3,
169
Ho Chi Minh Campaign (1975)
129, 146–7
Ho Chi Minh Trail 103–4
Hoa Hao 177n
Hoang Van Hoan 53
Hong Kong 41, 43
Ho–Sainteny agreement (1946)
29–30
hydrogen bomb 45

ICP *see* Indochinese Communist
Party
India 40–1, 97, 107
Indochina 13, 27, 34, 40–1, 43,
46, 47, 119, 127, 139, 143,
145, 166
Indochinese Communist Party
(ICP) 9–10, 17–19, 29–30,
37, 152–3
Indochinese Federation 29
Indonesia 41, 97
International Supervisory Com-
mission 50, 177n

Japan 9–10, 19–20, 22–3, 41,
175n, 176n
Johnson, Harold K. 112
Johnson, Lyndon B. 3, 4, 82–3,
90, 92–3, 96–101, 103–5,
107, 111–13, 119, 122,
124–6, 127, 129, 149
administration 2, 4, 96, 97–8,
99, 103–5, 107, 111–12,
180n
and bombing of North Vietnam 82, 96, 98, 101–2,
105, 124–6
and Great Society 83, 99–101,
126
and war in South Vietnam 82,
92, 98, 103–5, 107–8,
111–13

Kennan, George F. 149
Kennedy, John F. 3, 4, 81, 90,
    91–2, 106, 149, 169
    administration (1961–63) 81,
    86–7, 88
    and alleged withdrawal plans
    82, 88–93
Khrushchev, Nikita 64
Kim Hanh 26
King Jr, Martin Luther 117
Kissinger, Henry 145
Kolko, Gabriel 5
Korea 47, 54, 107, 112, 135–6,
    163, 178n

Lacouture, Jean 4
Lansdale, Colonel Edward 59
Laos 7, 49, 51, 61, 97, 105, 106,
    127, 132, 137, 139, 145
Le Duan 52, 62, 111, 177n
Le Phu Qua 162
Lenin, Vladimir I. 11–15, 155
Lodge Jr, Henry Cabot 123
Logevall, Frederik 4

MacArthur, General Douglas 99
MacDonald, Admiral David L.
    112
McCarthy, Joseph 101
McCloy, John J. 121
McNamara, Robert S. 88, 90, 93,
    99, 111–12, 119, 149–51,
    179n
Malaya 41, 46
Malaysia 97
Mansfield, Mike 145
Mao Zedong 33, 67
Marxism-Leninism 13, 15, 155–5
Mendès-France, Pierre 47
Middle East 41, 149
Military Revolutionary Council
    178n
Murphy, Robert D. 123–4
Mussolini, Benito 44

My Lai massacre (1968) 163–4

National Liberation Front of
    South Vietnam (NLF) 6, 58,
    72–80 *passim*, 81, 83–6
    *passim*, 108–9, 117, 127–8,
    129–35, 140, 153, 159,
    160, 179n
National Security Council 40, 89,
    122, 137
New Zealand 43, 97
Ngo Dinh Diem 35, 56–61, 63–4,
    69–80 *passim*, 81, 82, 84,
    86, 91, 93, 106, 153, 177n
Nguyen Ai Quoc 9, 17–18, 25
    *see also* Ho Chi Minh
Nguyen Khac Vien 160
Nguyen Manh Ha 25
Nguyen Ngoc Tho 91
Nguyen Tran Thiet 148
Nguyen Van Hau 147–8
Nguyen Van Thieu 128, 132,
    140–1, 142, 148, 153
Nguyen Xuan Oanh 171
*Nhan Dan* 147
Nixon, Richard M. 4, 127–8,
    131–2, 135–7, 140–5
    administration 127–9, 138,
    180n
    'doctrine' 135
NLF *see* National Liberation
    Front of South Vietnam
North Atlantic Treaty (1949) 38
North Vietnam 6, 7, 56–8, 68, 71,
    81–2, 84, 86, 96, 98, 101,
    198, 116, 119, 124, 128,
    132, 145
    *see also* Democratic Republic
    of Vietnam

October Revolution (1917) 11

Pakistan 41
Paris Peace agreement (1973)

128, 143, 145, 146
Pathet Lao 61
*Pentagon Papers, The* 3
People's Liberation Armed Forces
    (PLAF) *see* Vietcong
People's Republic of China (PRC)
    5, 33, 34, 38, 41–2, 43–4,
    45, 46, 52, 54, 83, 99, 101,
    107, 112, 117, 128, 149,
    153, 154, 178n
  military support for DRV 33,
    53–5, 112, 156–8, 159
  relations with DRV 5, 35,
    47–8, 51–5, 56, 64, 66–7,
    128, 153, 154–6
People's War 33, 35–6, 150, 153
Pham Van Dong 146
Philippines 43, 97, 136
Pleiku incident (1965) 101–2
Potsdam conference (1945) 10
Provisional Revolutionary
    Government (PRG) 128,
    139, 140, 159–60

Qiang Zhai 156
quagmire theory 3

Radford, Admiral Arthur W. 45,
    46
Reagan, Ronald 169
Republic of Vietnam (RVN) 6,
    56–8, 61, 67, 70–2, 81–3,
    84–6, 91, 92, 94, 103–4,
    119, 127–9, 136, 138–45,
    147–8, 161, 177n
  communist-led insurgency
    against (1959–65) 58–9,
    67–70, 81–2, 91
  relations with United States
    57–60, 86–8, 89, 91–3,
    140–3
  as theatre of war (1965–75)
    84–6, 103–4, 113–15,
    133–4, 147–8, 163–4

Ridgway, General Matthew 123
'Rolling Thunder' 101–2, 103,
    107, 109
Roosevelt, Franklin D. 28
Rusk, Dean 99
Russell, Richard 98
RVN *see* Republic of Vietnam

Sainteny, Jean 29
San Francisco conference (1945)
    23, 28, 176n
Second World War 7, 9, 20, 28,
    100, 114
Siam *see* Thailand
Sino-Soviet tensions 7, 154–6
Sino-Soviet treaty (1950) 45
Smith, R. B. 4, 52–3
South Vietnam 56–7, 58, 62,
    68, 71, 81, 82, 84, 86–8,
    92–3, 94, 96, 100, 101–2,
    103–4, 107–8, 111, 114,
    119, 122–4, 127, 128, 130,
    132, 137, 143, 145, 149,
    156
  *see also* Republic of Vietnam
Southeast Asia 34, 39, 40, 42, 43,
    56, 70, 73, 80, 88, 94,
    97–9, 108, 118, 125,
    149–50
Southeast Asia Treaty Organisa-
    tion (SEATO) 93–5, 98, 99,
    178n
Soviet Union 5, 10, 28, 34, 36,
    41, 42, 83, 110, 116, 117,
    128, 149, 154
  aid to DRV 38, 110, 156–8,
    159
  relations with DRV 47–8,
    51–2, 56, 64, 128, 154–6
Spring Offensive (1972) 128
Stalin, Joseph 39, 67
Stettinius, Edward 28
Strategic Hamlet Programme 81,
    91, 93

Taiwan 54

Taylor, General Maxwell D. 90, 123–4

Teheran conference (1943) 23, 176n

Tet Offensive 119–21, 122, 125, 127, 132–3

Thailand 41, 43, 46, 97, 107, 112, 136

Thayer, Carlyle 5

*Their Finest Hour* 44

Third International *see* Communist International

Tibet 178n

Tran Huy Lieu 25

Tran Van Tra 119

Trullinger, William 5

Truman, Harry S. 3, 28, 101
administration 28

Truong Chinh 160

Truong Nhu Tang 72, 73, 75, 116, 159–60, 161

*Tuoi Tre* 26

Turkey 41

U Thant 123

United Action (1954) 34, 41–5

United Nations 28, 97–8, 178n

United States 2, 10, 20, 22, 28, 36, 38, 40, 43, 45, 47, 48, 53, 62, 64, 69, 75, 81–3, 84, 88, 90–3, 105, 110, 119, 122, 127–9, 135, 141, 144–5, 149–51, 152–5 *passim*, 161, 163–4
bombing of North Vietnam (1965–72) 82–3, 96–7, 98, 101–2, 103–4, 107–8, 116–17, 121–6, 128
and defeat in Vietnam 3, 129, 144–7
domestic anti-war discontent 2–3, 8, 99, 104, 109, 117–18, 119, 127–8, 129, 136–7
and Franco-Vietminh War 36–9, 40–6, 84
military assistance to France 33, 43
military assistance to the Republic of Vietnam 56–9, 81, 87, 128
negotiations with DRV 103–4, 107–8, 122, 125, 127–9, 131–2, 140–3
relations with Republic of Vietnam 56–60, 86–8, 89, 91–3, 127, 140–3
war in South Vietnam (1965–73) 2–3, 7, 82–3, 92–3, 95–7, 102, 103–5, 107–9, 111–15, 119, 121–5, 135–6, 136–7, 144–6

United States Congress 97–8, 100, 128–9, 140, 142, 144–5, 146, 150

Van Tien Dung, General 146

Vance, Cyrus 99, 123

Vietcong (People's Liberation Armed Forces, PLAF) 6, 58, 81, 83–6 *passim*, 91, 93, 101–2, 103, 105, 114–15, 116, 119–20, 127, 131, 143, 146, 149, 163–5, 177n, 178n, 179n
strategy for war in South Vietnam 104–5, 119–20

Vietminh (Vietnamese Independence League) 10–11, 18–22, 27, 30–2, 33–6, 39–41, 43, 46–8, 50–5, 57, 61, 73, 152
armed forces 31, 35–6, 38, 54–5
negotiations with France (1946) 29–31
strategy in Franco-Vietminh War 33, 35–6, 48–9, 152–3

Vietnam 1, 4, 34, 37, 39, 44,
    49–50, 54, 62, 83–4, 86,
    96, 97, 101–5, 112, 115,
    117–18, 125, 128–30,
    135–6, 150, 166
  projected nationwide elections
    (1956) 35, 49–50, 56, 61–2
Vietnam, Socialist Republic of
    170
Vietnam veterans (US) 166–8
Vietnam wars
  casualties during 1, 46
  historians on 1–6, 82–3, 90,
    98, 99–100, 119, 128, 151
Vietnam Workers' Party (VWP)
    48, 58, 62, 63–4, 65–7,
    68–70, 74–5, 93–6,
    109–11, 119–21, 133–5,
    146, 152, 155–6, 159–60,
    161–2, 170
Vietnamese Communist Party 6,
    16–17
  see also Indochinese Commu-
    nist Party; Vietnam Work-
    ers' Party

Vietnamese nationalism 9–10, 16,
    19, 31, 56, 57, 133
Vietnamese peasantry 15–16, 18,
    56, 65–7, 77, 83–6 *passim*
Vietnamese revolution 9–10,
    12–13, 15–16, 18–19, 23,
    31–2, 35, 68–70, 95–6,
    110–11, 120, 129, 146,
    153–4, 159–63
Vietnamisation 127–8, 135–6,
    137
Vo Nguyen Giap 25, 35–6, 54,
    176n
Vu Van Mao 148

Wei Guoqing, General 53, 54
Westmoreland, William C. 103–5,
    113, 121–2, 164
Wheeler, General Earle 111
Wintle, Justin 7
'Wise Men' 104, 121–5

Young, Marilyn B. 7, 151, 166

Zhou Enlai 44, 52